PRINCIPLED LABOR LAW

Principled Labor Law

U.S. LABOR LAW THROUGH A LATIN AMERICAN METHOD

Sergio Gamonal C.
and César F. Rosado Marzán

OXFORD
UNIVERSITY PRESS

OXFORD
UNIVERSITY PRESS

Oxford University Press is a department of the University of Oxford. It furthers the University's objective of excellence in research, scholarship, and education by publishing worldwide. Oxford is a registered trademark of Oxford University Press in the UK and certain other countries.

Published in the United States of America by Oxford University Press
198 Madison Avenue, New York, NY 10016, United States of America.

Library of Congress Cataloging-in-Publication Data

Names: Gamonal Contreras, Sergio, 1966– author. | Rosado Marzan, Cesar F., 1975–, author,
Title: Principled labor law : U.S. labor law through a Latin American method /
Sergio Gamonal C. & Cesar F. Rosado Marzan.
Description: New York : Oxford University Press, 2019. | Includes bibliographical references and index.
Identifiers: LCCN 2018051610 | ISBN 9780190052669 ((hardback) : alk. paper)
Subjects: LCSH: Labor laws and legislation—United States. | Labor laws and legislation—Latin America. | Comparative law.
Classification: LCC KF3319 .G36 2019 | DDC 344.7301—dc23
LC record available at https://lccn.loc.gov/2018051610

9 8 7 6 5 4 3 2

Printed by Sheridan Books, Inc., United States of America

Note to Readers
This publication is designed to provide accurate and authoritative information in regard to the subject matter covered. It is based upon sources believed to be accurate and reliable and is intended to be current as of the time it was written. It is sold with the understanding that the publisher is not engaged in rendering legal, accounting, or other professional services. If legal advice or other expert assistance is required, the services of a competent professional person should be sought. Also, to confirm that the information has not been affected or changed by recent developments, traditional legal research techniques should be used, including checking primary sources where appropriate.

(Based on the Declaration of Principles jointly adopted by a Committee of the American Bar Association and a Committee of Publishers and Associations.)

To my parents and my daughter, María José (S.G.C.)
To Marina, Juan Francisco, and Salvador (C.F.R.M.)

Contents

Acknowledgments

THIS BOOK IS the result of years of collaboration between the authors, with the support of many colleagues and friends. We must first thank María Ester Feres, former Director of the Chilean *Dirección del Trabajo*, for planting the seed of the need for an English-language book on Latin American labor law principles. In 2007, Rosado Marzán interviewed Feres on labor inspection reforms. In the interview, Feres constantly referred to the "principles of labor law," and particularly the principle of "primacy of reality" and "nonwaiver." She assumed that Rosado Marzán, a law professor, knew perfectly what she was talking about, despite the fact that Rosado Marzán was a U.S-trained lawyer working and teaching in the United States. Frankly, Rosado Marzán had no idea what Feres was talking about, so he asked her for some reading materials to get caught up on what appeared to be commonly understood labor law principles in Chile, and perhaps elsewhere in Latin America.

About two years later, Rosado Marzán met Sergio Gamonal C. when Gamonal C. was giving a class to Chilean labor judges on the principles of labor law. A friendship ensued, and Gamonal C. suggested to Rosado Marzán that they work on a joint venture that would result in an English-language publication. Given the scarcity of English-language legal scholarship detailing the basic principles of labor law used in Latin America, we decided to focus on said principles.

Once the project started, this book benefited from comments made to early drafts of one or more chapters presented in Stockholm University's Institute for Social Private Law (Nov. 2012), the Law and Society Annual Meetings (2012–2017), the

Labor Law Research Network's First and Second Meetings (2013 and 2015), the Annual Colloquium on Scholarship in Employment and Labor Law (2013 and 2018), the LatCrit Annual Meetings (2013), the faculty workshop of the University of Minnesota Law School (2013), two Chicago-Kent faculty workshops (2017 and 2018), and a workshop at the Law Faculty of the Universidad Adolfo Ibáñez (2014).

We are particularly grateful to the following individuals who read earlier parts of the book and provided comments: Pablo Arellano, Bruno Debenedetti, Caterina Guidi, Adelle Blackett, Niklas Bruun, Carol L. Chomsky, Paola Díaz, Ruth Dukes, Howard Eglit, Judy Fudge, Mario Garmendia, Henrique Hinz, Marc Linder, Martin H. Malin, Jonathan Miller, Juan Pablo Mugnolo, Ann Numhauser-Henning, Silvana Sciarra, Patricia Spiwak, Joan Steinman, and José Luis Ugarte.

The following individuals gave us specific comments either in conferences or informal conversation, which we found particularly useful: Stephen F. Befort, Magdalena Nogueira, James Pope, Carolyn Shapiro, Marley Weiss, Barbara Welke, and Rebecca E. Zietlow.

The authors also thank Sarah Bahn, Laura Caringella, Patrick Ferrell, Miranda Huber, Sharon Wyatt-Jordan, Meron Kebede, Mandy Lee, Tobias Rodriguez, Daniela Rossi, Philip Vieira, and Clare Willis for editorial and/or research assistance throughout the life stages of this project.

The authors also thank the Series Editors—Alan Bogg, Keith Ewing, and Mark Freedland—and one anonymous reviewer for comments made to parts of this book's manuscript.

A book like this one requires time for its authors to research, ponder, write, and rewrite, as well as travel resources for the authors to meet, discuss, and collaborate more closely. While both authors put significant personal resources into the book, Gamonal C. must thank Rodrigo Correa and Ramiro Mendoza, former Dean and current Dean of the Faculty of Law of the Universidad Adolfo Ibáñez, respectively, for the facilities and resources they provided to him to work and collaborate in this endeavor. Rosado Marzán thanks Stockholm University and the Regulating Markets and Labour Research Program, the Swedish Council for Working Life and Social Research, the Chicago-Kent Handelsman Fund, the Chicago-Kent Freehling Fellowship, and the Universidad Nacional Autónoma de Madrid's Visiting Scholars program. They all provided Rosado Marzán with resources to write, research, travel, and/or bring scholars together for this project.

Because this has been a project eight years in the making, we likely omitted some colleagues and friends. Apologies and a great "thank you" to those individuals are in order.

Finally, the authors thank their families for the time and patience given to us throughout the process of writing this book. Gamonal C. thanks his family for their permanent support of his projects. Rosado Marzán thanks his wife, Marina Del Rios, and his two sons, Juan Francisco and Salvador, for their tremendous understanding and unconditional love.

Our hope is that the time and effort put into this book by so many individuals, not just the authors, results in fairer and more just treatment of the workers of the world. We dare not shy away from such idealism.

Chicago and Santiago, September 2018

"Would you tell me, please, which way
I ought to go from here?"
"That depends a good deal on where you
want to get to," said the Cat.
"I don't much care where—" said Alice.
"Then it doesn't matter which
way you go," said the Cat.[1]

1

INTRODUCTION

A Principled Method, Even for the United States

IMAGINE THE FOLLOWING scenario: In the City of Gotham, somewhere in the United States, hundreds of ride-sharing drivers of Gotham Share, a ride-sharing company, drive their vehicles into busy city blocks. However, rather than taking passengers, they park on the right lanes of the streets, log out of the app, and make themselves unavailable to prospective riders. The drivers tweet to @GothamShare, the Twitter account of their company, stating, "Strike!" Hundreds of riders, noticing that Gotham Share drivers do not appear in their app, and learning through social media that Gotham Share drivers are on strike, begin to hail regular cabs or other ride-share drivers using a different app. The strike costs Gotham Share money while profiting its competition. Gotham Share texts its drivers a message that states, "Please desist from striking against the company. Your strike violates antitrust laws. Courts can stop you and find that you are liable for very large sums of money if you persist in striking."

The Gotham Share drivers are striking to protest that Gotham Share is not paying them the mandatory minimum wage. They also allege that the company keeps part of the tips left by customers, which is against minimum wage laws. Gotham Share rejects the drivers' claims. It claims that the drivers are not its legal employees, but are "independent contractors" and, as such, Gotham Share does not have to pay them

[1] LEWIS CARROLL, ALICE'S ADVENTURES IN WONDERLAND 78 (Dover Publications 2012) (1865).

Principled Labor Law. Sergio Gamonal C. and César F. Rosado Marzán.

under wage and hour laws. Additionally, since they are independent contractors, according to the employer, they may be liable under antitrust laws.[2] Moreover, it alleges that the drivers could not sue as a class, which they have done in this hypothetical case, because they signed waivers stating that if the drivers had any contractual claim against the company, they must file an individual, private arbitration grievance. In other words, Gotham Share insists that the drivers have no substantive legal claims to make, have no collective, procedural channel in which to bring claims to court or arbitration, and even lack the right to strike against the firm.

Generally, whether the drivers have the right to receive the legal minimum wage and tips, sue collectively in court, or strike against the company hinges on the rights afforded to them by labor and employment laws,[3] referred to in this book simply as "labor law," as in most of the world. They must be generally considered statutorily protected employees and not independent contractors, as the employer sustained. In the United States, the jurisdiction this book uses as a test case, important labor laws—namely, the National Labor Relations Act (NLRA) and the Fair Labor Standards Act (FLSA)—were mostly crafted by the U.S. Congress in the 1930s and 1940s, when the idea of hailing cabs with an app was either inconceivable or a science fiction dream. Hence, one could argue that the law is probably silent, or at best unclear, as to whether ride-sharing drivers are protected employees. Moreover, even if drivers are protected employees, they may need to prove to an administrative agency or a court that their class waiver is unenforceable as a matter of law to sue collectively in a class or collective action suit.[4] Otherwise, each driver might have to sue in individual arbitration. As detailed further in chapter 4 of this book, given the way individual, private arbitration is controlled by employers, at least to date, individual arbitration in the United States is a forum where employment rights go to die.

The scenario painted here in our imaginary city of Gotham is not entirely fictional. There are countless drivers working for ride-sharing companies such as Uber and Lyft who are embroiled in similar disputes with their companies.[5] Meanwhile,

---

[2] *See* Sanjukta Paul, *The Enduring Ambiguities of Antitrust Liability for Worker Collective Action*, 47 LOY. U. CHI. L.J. 969 (2016) (describing antitrust liability against any nonemployee in the United States who engages in concerted activity to improve her economic circumstances).

[3] For the federal labor law providing most private sector employees' right to strike in the United States, *see* National Labor Relations Act (NLRA), 29 U.S.C. § 163 (2012). *But see* NLRB v. Mackay Radio, 304 U.S. 333 (1938) (stating in *dicta* that employees may be permanently replaced under the NLRA). For the federal wage and hour law covering most private sector employees, *see* Fair Labor Standards Act (FLSA), 29 U.S.C. 201 *et seq.* (2012).

[4] Epic Systems Corp. v. Lewis, 138 S. Ct. 1612 (2018) (declaring class action waivers enforceable under the Federal Arbitration Act and not in violation of the National Labor Relations Act).

[5] Professor Veena Dubal noted that in 2017 there were at least seventeen lawsuits in the United States filed by ride-sharing drivers against their companies, all making employment claims. V. B. Dubal, *Wage Slave or Entrepreneur?: Contesting the Dualism of Legal Worker Identities*, 105 CAL. L. REV. 65, 68 n.6 (2017).

the companies argue not only that the drivers are not employees under the law—and hence do not have to be paid under wage and hour laws—but also that they cannot file class action suits because the drivers have often waived their right to sue as a class, or to go to court at all.[6] In those cases, the companies argue that drivers must file individual, private arbitration claims.[7]

Ride-sharing drivers do not have a long history of strikes over their pay and classification issues—mostly because Uber, Lyft, and other similar apps have only been available since about 2012.[8] However, taxi drivers do have a long history of strikes and other concerted activities against their superiors and government regulators in the United States, sometimes leading to violent confrontations.[9] Historically, the main sources of contention between taxi or chauffeur drivers and their companies has been how much taxi drivers could make per fare,[10] and how they ought to be classified—as independent contractors or employees—which then determines their access to legal benefits that only come with classification as an employee.[11] Ride-sharing drivers' disputes, when considered "chauffeur drivers" of some sort, are thus part of decades, if not a century, of industrial conflict in the United States.[12] As such, perhaps our "old" laws still have something to say about these disputes. In fact, as this book will argue, they still do.

In the last decade, many articles and books have been written on nonstandard employment or precarious employment, and how these forms of employment challenge existing labor law.[13] The rise of the so-called gig economy, Uber, and others have added to that rich literature on the future of labor law.[14] This literature links the

---

[6] *Id.* at 68–69.

[7] *Id.*

[8] *Id.* at 101.

[9] *Id.* at 84; Graham Russell Gao Hodges, Taxi! A Social History of the New York City Cabdriver 135–37, 140–41, 150 (2007).

[10] Katrina Miriam Wyman, *Problematic Private Property: The Case of New York Taxicab Medallions*, 30 Yale J. on Reg. 125, 168 (2013); Gao Hodges, *supra* note 9, at 135–37, 140–41, 150.

[11] Dubal, *supra* note 5, at 69, 95 (describing the history of taxi and Uber drivers in San Francisco and the contentious history over "employee" classification).

[12] *Id.* at 121 n.199.

[13] *See, e.g.*, Rethinking Workplace Regulation: Beyond the Standard Contract of Employment (Katherine Stone & Harry Arthurs eds., 2013); Arne Kalleberg et al., *Bad Jobs in America: Standard and Nonstandard Employment Relations and Job Quality in the United States*, 65 Am. Soc. Rev. 256 (2000). *But see* Julia Tomassetti, *Who Is a Worker? Partisanship, the National Labor Relations Board, and the Social Content of Employment*, 37 Law & Soc. Inquiry 815 (2012) (describing the ideological and partisan underpinnings of employee status).

[14] *See, e.g.*, Jeremias Prassl, Humans as a Service: The Promise and Perils of Work in the Gig Economy (2018); Guy Davidov, *The Status of Uber Drivers: A Purposive Approach*, 6 Spanish Lab. L. & Emp. Rel. J. 6, 10–13 (2016) (arguing that under a purposive lens aiming to protect subordinated and dependent work, Uber drivers are "employees"); Brishen Rogers, *Employment Rights in the Platform Economy: Getting Back to Basics*, 10 Harv. L. & Pol'y Rev. 479, 483 (2016) (explaining that even though Uber drivers may not fall neatly into the employee categories under existing law, they are subordinated, and under the "anti-domination" principle, they should be found to be employees); Orly Lobel, *The Law of the Platform*, 101

increase in nonstandard employment[15] (in which we could also fit the so-called gig economy) to changes in the organization of capitalist productive relations (including "fissuring," i.e., contracting, global supply chain management, and franchising[16]), in a general context of increasing global economic integration, or "globalization," as it is commonly referred to in the popular media.[17] In addition to changing work relationships, globalization has made re-regulating work relationships harder than in past decades because global market actors have overpowered national state institutions and hence drowned the states' regulatory capacities, including those related to work.[18] Therefore, labor law is said to be in a state of crisis, as it can no longer cope with the realities of contemporary capitalism.[19] Notably, Professor Cynthia Estlund, after looking at the sea of changes in the empirical realities surrounding labor law, has prognosticated labor law's "death"[20] after its "ossification."[21] Canadian Professor Harry Arthurs even argues for the need to rethink labor law after the end of "labor."[22] For Arthurs, labor is a sociological category with a history—a beginning and an end—that appears to have run its course, requiring legal minds to search for a new legal subject that better encompasses relations of economic subordination. As

Minn. L. Rev. 87, 136 (2016) (describing how there are some scholars who call for the recognition of a third category of employment for those workers dependent on one particular employer without necessarily being "controlled" under traditional common law views used to understand employment or independent contractor status).

[15] *See, e.g.*, Stone & Arthurs, *supra* note 13.

[16] *See, e.g.*, David Weil, The Fissured Workplace: Why Work Became So Bad for So Many and What Can Be Done to Improve It 189–90 (2014) (arguing that the diminished quality of jobs in the United States has mostly occurred from corporate strategies requiring lead firms to contract out, manage productive chains, and franchise).

[17] Michel Coutu et al., *Broken Paradigms: Labor Law in the Wake of Globalization and the Economic Crisis*, 34 Comp. Lab. L. & Pol'y J. 565, 566–68 (noting the economic determinants of labor law's crisis).

[18] Charles Tilly, *Globalization Threatens Labor's Rights*, 47 Int'l Lab. & Working-Class Hist. 1 (1995).

[19] Coutu et al., *supra* note 17, at 565–66; Michel Coutu, *With Hugo Sinzheimer and Max Weber in Mind: The Current Crisis and the Future of Labor Law*, 34 Comp. Lab. L. & Pol'y J 605 (2013) (explaining how labor's fate is intricately tied to the state of the economy and the labor market); *See also* Guy Davidov, A Purposive Approach to Labour Law 1 (2016) (explaining how labor law is perpetually in crisis given that it has to adapt to incessant capitalist transformations).

[20] Cynthia Estlund, *The Death of Labor Law*, 2 Ann. Rev. L. & Soc. Sci. 105 (2006) (explaining how collective labor law in the United States is in decline but could be salvaged through "new governance," or a strategy that is fundamentally contractual in nature).

[21] Cynthia Estlund, *The Ossification of American Labor Law*, 102 Colum. L. Rev. 1527, 1530 (2002) (U.S. labor law has been rendered ineffective because it has been isolated from "democratic revision and renewal and from local experimentation and innovation.").

[22] Harry Arthurs, *Labour Law after Labour*, *in* The Idea of Labor Law 13 (Guy Davidov & Brian Langille eds., 2011).

a result, some labor law scholars are calling for the reconceptualization of labor law.[23] The path forward appears difficult for labor law as we know it.

THE UNLIKELIEST CASE

But different from scholars who argue for labor law's reconceptualization, this book argues that the basic principles of labor law, which stem from an understanding of subordinated and dependent work, and which are enshrined in international labor standards, remain as relevant as ever. In Latin America, courts and other adjudicative bodies, as well as legislators and policymakers, use these principles to interpret law, and to make new law, despite changes in capitalist organization, and even after periods of brutal dictatorships that smashed labor unions to enact neoliberal reforms. We thus offer a Latin American, "principled" method, based on labor law's traditional precepts, as a tool to defend and reconstruct labor law in the United States and elsewhere where labor law jurisprudence appears to be in tatters.

We offer the principled method by focusing on the least likely, contemporary case of labor protection in the industrialized world, the United States of America. The United States is among the most liberal market societies in the world, with some of the lowest levels of union representation and coverage in the private sector, lacking basic dismissal protections for workers, and enabling employers to permanently replace employees who strike for economic reasons, while banning secondary activities; it fails to abide with basic international labor standards.[24] Yet, we use the United States as a least likely case to show how, even there, a principled method can provide for more coherent, labor-protective jurisprudence.

Hence, our goals here are twofold. First, we aim to provide U.S. lawyers, policymakers, legislators, and others with a tool to robustly and more systematically protect U.S. workers, bringing the United States more in line with international

[23] *See, e.g.*, DAVIDOV, *supra* note 19, at 1–4; RUTH DUKES, THE LABOUR CONSTITUTION: THE ENDURING IDEA OF LABOUR LAW 1–3 (2014); Guy Davidov & Brian Langille, *Introduction*, *in* THE IDEA OF LABOUR LAW 1–2 (Guy Davidov & Brian Langille eds., 2011).

[24] *See, e.g.*, LANCE COMPA, UNFAIR ADVANTAGE: WORKERS' FREEDOM OF ASSOCIATION IN THE UNITED STATES UNDER INTERNATIONAL HUMAN RIGHTS STANDARDS (ILR Press 2000) (U.S. labor law fails to guarantee basic freedom of association rights); Kate Andrias, *The New Labor Law*, 126 YALE L.J. 2 (2016) (U.S. labor law is broken, and the United States needs an entirely new system of collective bargaining based on sectoral bargaining, rather than plant-level bargaining); Clyde W. Summers, *Individual Protection against Unjust Dismissal: Time for a Statute*, 62 VA. L. REV. 481 (1976) (workers in the United States lack basic dismissal protections, and federal law needs to regulate employment termination based on established norms set up by unions and employers in their collective bargaining agreements).

labor standards. Second, we want to use the U.S. case to show the rest of the world the utility of principled labor law.

A RIPE TIME FOR PRINCIPLED LABOR LAW

Some might argue that our proposal for a principled labor law seems out of touch with the times, where market fundamentalism appears to reign supreme. We disagree. Principled labor law cannot come at a riper time. Not only has capitalist reorganization confused many labor law scholars about the relevance of labor law, but there is also a widespread unease with socioeconomic conditions, income inequality, and democratic governance in industrial democracies. Evidence of this unease exists, on one hand, in the vast amounts of publications on economic inequality coming out these days, the popularity of left-leaning socialists Bernie Sanders and Alexandria Ocasio-Cortez in the United States, and Jeremy Corbyn in the United Kingdom. On the other hand, a much darker, sinister, and much less palatable alternative to this social unease is also opening the way for demagogues such as Donald Trump, leaders of Italy's Five Star Movement, the Polish Law and Justice Party, and so many other groups playing fascist. The time to reinvigorate labor law is now.

CAN LATIN AMERICA TEACH US ANYTHING?

Some readers may feel an urge to resist condescension when they read that we propose Latin America—the region of "magic realism"—as a model for global labor law, be it for the United States or elsewhere. Isn't the region poor and underdeveloped? Isn't the region mired in perpetual problems with the "rule of law" and weak institutions? Doesn't Latin America skirt labor regulations, contributing to a larger than life informal sector?

Yes. The answer to all of those questions is mostly "yes." The region suffers from weak institutions and rule of law problems. Many workers' rights remain aspirational and ineffective. Latin American informality is widespread.[25] Some countries may have overly rigid rules covering the employment relationship and other areas of economic regulation.[26] However, the best social science research on the informal

[25] *See, e.g.*, Shelley Marshal & Colin Fenwick, *Labour Law and Development: Characteristics and Challenges*, *in* LABOUR REGULATION AND DEVELOPMENT: SOCIO-LEGAL PERSPECTIVES 1 (Shelley Marshal & Colin Fenwick eds., 2016) (describing the challenges of informality in the developing world, including Latin America).

[26] *See* Alejandro Portes & Richard Schauffler, *Competing Perspectives on the Latin American Informal Sector*, 19 POPULATION & DEV. REV. 33, 56 (1993).

sector has shown that effective law and informality are complex issues related to policy development and implementation that are not reducible to the substantive content of laws.[27] Protective labor jurisprudence can hardly be scapegoated for the region's institutional deficiencies. Moreover, protective labor jurisprudence—i.e., judicial and administrative adjudication— provides ample space for policymakers, legislators, and public administrators to put in place the policies and rules that make the most sense in their regulatory areas. All legal principles do is help solve legal questions where legislators have provided unclear rules or, simply, where gaps remain in the law. It is a method that has retained its coherence and legitimacy in Latin America even though the region suffers from institutional problems, and even after many years of neoliberal reforms.[28] This book proffers this durable and institutionalized method for the idea of labor law.

We must also underscore that Latin jurisdictions, including Latin America, have played a historical role in developing global labor law.[29] Throughout the twentieth century, international labor and socialist networks, the International Labor Organization (ILO), and social Catholicism generated a conversation between European, U.S., Australasian, Latin American, and other jurists that gave shape

---

[27] *Id.* ("Complete absorption of the labor force into the formal sector is desirable, but it will not occur without relaxation of rigid labor rules. Transformation of subsistence activities into dynamic autonomous small firms is equally desirable, but it will not occur through simple removal of state controls without sustained programs in support of this aim.") *But see* HERNANDO DE SOTO, THE OTHER PATH: THE ECONOMIC ANSWER TO TERRORISM (2002) (arguing that informality in Latin America has exclusive roots in overzealous regulation and the lack of protection of property rights).

[28] Adrian Goldin, *Global Conceptualizations and Local Constructions of the Idea of Labour Law, in* THE IDEA OF LABOR LAW 69 (Guy Davidov & Brian Langille eds., 2011); *see also* Graciela Bensusán, *Legislation and Labor Policy in Latin America: Crisis, Renovation, or Restoration?*, 34 COMP. LAB. L. & POL'Y J. 655, 656 (describing how after the 2008 crisis many Latin American countries, "especially those where the old instruments of state intervention remained intact and where parties or coalitions of the center-left held political power, there was a return to using labor institutions to favor workers and a revitalization of social policies, particularly by expanding protection to sectors excluded from formal employment."); César F. Rosado Marzán, *No More Solitude? Workers' Conditions and Rights in Latin America During the Great Recession*, 17 EMP. RTS. & EMP. POL'Y J. 291, 293 (2013) (explaining how the Latin American region generally experienced better social and economic indicators and improved substantive labor protections after the 2008 crisis).

[29] *See* LABOR JUSTICE ACROSS THE AMERICAS (Leon Fink & Juan Manuel Palacio eds., 2018); Diego López-Medina, *El nacimiento del derecho comparado moderno como espacio geográfico y como disciplina: instrucciones básicas para su comprensión y uso desde América Latina*, 26 INT'L L.: REV. COLOMBIANA DE DER. INTERNACIONAL 117 (2015); Diego López-Medina, *La teoria impura del diritto: La trasformazione della cultura giuridica latino americana*, 29 RIVISTA DI DIRITTO PRIVATO 195 (2011) (It.); HECTOR HUGO BARBAGELATA, CURSO SOBRE LA EVOLUCIÓN DEL PENSAMIENTO JUSLABORALISTA 71–74 (2009), *citing* Emilio Frugoni, *Discurso Inaugural de la Cátedra de la Facultad de Derecho de Montevideo* (Uruguayan scholar commenting in 1926 about English factory legislation); ALFREDO GAETE BERRÍOS, PRINCIPALES MODIFICACIONES QUE HA INTRODUCIDO EL DERECHO SOCIAL AL DERECHO CIVIL EN MATERIA DE CONTRATOS Y OBLIGACIONES (1936) (describing the European historical process that created labor law); MOISÉS POBLETE TRONCOSO, EVOLUCIÓN DEL DERECHO SOCIAL EN AMÉRICA (1942) (providing a Latin American perspective on the development of labor law).

to labor law as a global legal discipline.[30] Latin American labor law has also been closely related to European labor law; the work of European labor law scholars such as Ludovico Barassi, Francesco Carnelutti, Leon Duguit, Philippe Lotmar, Paul Pic, Gustavo Radbruch, George Scelle, Hugo Sinzheimer, among others, was intensely debated during the formative years of labor law in Latin America.[31] We should also not lose sight of the fact that when the Weimar constitution of 1919 was drafted, with its thick protection of workers' rights inspiring the founders of labor law, the Mexican constitution of 1917, even richer in social rights, was already two years old.[32] It was used as an inspirational document for the founding of the ILO in 1919.[33] Finally, we cannot forget that Latin America has been an important source for norm diffusion in the field of economic development and human rights, two key areas closely related to labor law.[34] Because Latin America has been an important source of labor law and related disciplines, this book fills a contemporary gap in the future of labor law and its "idea."

LEGAL PRINCIPLES: WHAT ARE THEY, AND WHAT ARE THEY GOOD FOR?

By "principle" this book will mean—following Uruguayan Professor Américo Plá Rodríguez's seminal work on labor law principles—a guideline, directive, or parameter that helps judges and other adjudicators to interpret and apply the law.[35] Thus,

---

[30] Juan Manuel Palacio, *From Social Legislation to Labor Justice*, *in* LABOR JUSTICE ACROSS THE AMERICAS 18–19, 22 (Leon Fink & Juan Manuel Palacio eds., 2018).

[31] *See* BARBAGELATA, *supra* note 29, at 75–150. Moreover, one of Mexico's and Latin America's greatest labor law scholars, Mario de la Cueva, was in the 1930s commenting on German labor law, including about the changes made to the Weimer-era system by the Nazis. ANA LUISA IZQUIERDO Y DE LA CUEVA, EL HUMANISMO JURÍDICO DE MARIO DE LA CUEVA 54–68 (1994). *See also* WILLIAM J. SUAREZ-POTTS, THE MAKING OF LAW: THE SUPREME COURT AND LABOR LEGISLATION IN MEXICO, 1875–931, at 104–07 (2012) (describing the early debates between Mexican and European labor law scholars).

[32] PALACIO, *supra* note 30, at 24.

[33] *Id.*

[34] *See, e.g.*, RAUL PREBISCH, THE ECONOMIC DEVELOPMENT OF LATIN AMERICA AND ITS PRINCIPAL PROBLEMS (1950) (developing the theory of import substitution industrialization); KATHRYN SIKKINK, EVIDENCE FOR HOPE: MAKING HUMAN RIGHTS WORK IN THE 21ST CENTURY (2017) (describing Latin American contributions to international human rights).

[35] AMÉRICO PLÁ RODRÍGUEZ, LOS PRINCIPIOS DEL DERECHO DEL TRABAJO 14 (3rd ed. 1998). Our conception of principles differs from those used by other influential authors, such as Ronald Dworkin and Robert Alexy. For Professor Dworkin, principles serve as standards that must be observed due to pressing justice concerns or because some other moral imperative. He counterpoised principles to rules; rules can be applicable disjunctively. RONALD DWORKIN, TAKING RIGHTS SERIOUSLY (1975). For Professor Alexy, principles are optimization mandates that can be complied with in different degrees. Rules, which he differentiates from principles, can be complied with or not. Therefore, for Alexy, adjudicators may resolve conflict of rules by

for example, in contract law, contractual autonomy is paramount.[36] In criminal law, jurists make reference to the principle of "presumption of innocence," i.e., of the presumed innocence of the accused until proven otherwise.[37]

Under the above-stated view of general legal principles, Professor Plá Rodríguez defined *labor* law principles as: "Guidelines that inform some norms and directly or indirectly inspire a series of solutions [to cases], so that they promote and channel the adoption of new norms, guide the interpretation of existing ones, and resolve unforeseen cases and controversies."[38] In this light, labor law principles are treated as interpretative tools. They help us understand existing law and develop it, and its jurisprudence.[39]

So, what are the principles of Latin American labor law? While Latin American authors differ in the exact taxonomy of labor law principles, those principles that scholars mostly refer to are the following:

- Protection (over individual freedom of contract);
- Primacy of reality (or primacy of fact);
- Nonwaiver (or nonrenounceability) of rights; and
- Continuity of the employment relationship (over precarious employment).[40]

---

introducing an "exception clause." If the adjudicator cannot establish an exception to the rules, then he should apply the rule highest in hierarchy (a superior law will prevail over the inferior one), the most recent one (applying the temporality principle), or the most specific one (applying the specialty principle, where a special law prevails over a general law). However, a collision of principles demands weighting or balancing the principles in the specific case to determine which of the principles must yield to the other, and how much. ROBERT ALEXY, A THEORY OF CONSTITUTIONAL RIGHTS 44–68 (Julian Rivers trans., 2010).

[36] *See, e.g.*, CHARLES FRIED, CONTRACT AS PROMISE: A THEORY OF CONTRACTUAL OBLIGATION 16–17 (1981).

[37] *See* François Quintard-Morénas, *The Presumption of Innocence in the French and Anglo-American Legal Traditions*, 58 AM. J. COMP. L. 107, 109 (2010) (describing how the principle of the presumption of innocence has existed in France and in common law jurisdictions, albeit at certain times the principle was also understood as an evidentiary rule, affording less protections to the accused).

[38] PLÁ RODRÍGUEZ, *supra* note 35, at 14. We should underscore that principles could matter beyond mere interpretation of the law. In Latin America, scholars have argued that legislators consider, or should consider, principles as "preexisting realities" when they attempt to amend existing labor laws. Hence, Latin American scholars speak about "informing principles" that inspire legislators. *Id.* at 22.

[39] The notion of principles as "guidelines, parameters, line matrixes, or guides" that serve the judge to apply the law and which guide legislators in making new law, is not our own or merely of Latin America. This view of interpretation principles also exists in Spain, Portugal, France, and Italy. *See, e.g.*, LOS PRINCIPIOS DEL DERECHO DEL TRABAJO (Luis Enrique de la Villa Gil & Lourdes López Cumbre eds., 2003) (discussing the *pro operario* principle, minimum and most favorable norms, most beneficial condition, employment stability, among others in Spain). *See also* A. L. MONTEIRO FERNANDES, DIREITO DO TRABALHO 114 (11th ed., 1999) (describing principles in Portugal); J. JAVILLIER, DERECHO DEL TRABAJO 64 (1982) (detailing principles in France); GIORGIO GHEZZI & UMBERTO ROMAGNOLI, IL RAPPORTO DI LAVORO 330 (2nd ed., 1987) (describing nonwaiver principles in Italy); RICCARDO GUASTINI, DISTINGUIENDO: ESTUDIOS DE TEORÍA Y METATEORÍA DEL DERECHO 152–53 (1999).

[40] Latin American scholars have recognized various labor law principles, sometimes up to ten of them. *See* ALBERTO J. RUPRECHT, LOS PRINCIPIOS FORMATIVOS LABORALES Y SU PROYECCIÓN EN LA

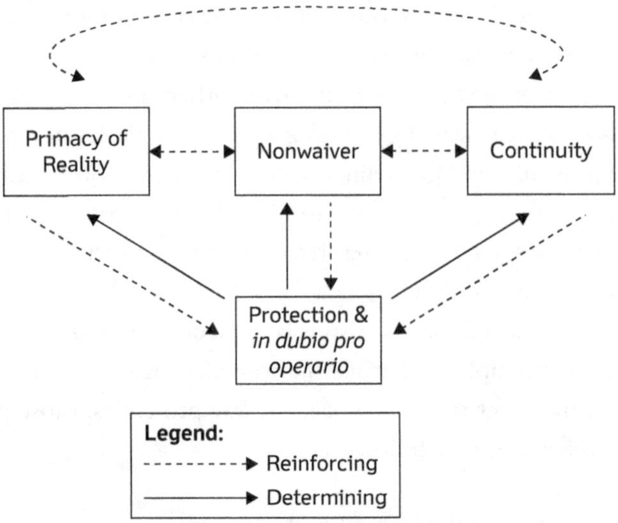

FIGURE 1.1 Relationships Between the Principles of Labor Law.

Here we argue that these four principles are interrelated: protection logically requires primacy of reality, nonwaiver, and continuity. Moreover, all four principles reinforce each other (see Figure 1.1).

The principle of protection, or the protective principle, is, under a Latin American view, the raison d'être of labor law.[41] Essentially, Latin American labor law presumes that subordinated and dependent work requires special protections.[42] If society leaves subordinated and dependent workers subject to individual freedom of contract and the market, employers can treat workers as commodities, compromising workers' humanity and society's moral interests.[43] Therefore, moral concerns require that law temper the power imbalance between subordinated and dependent workers and their employers.[44] In this fashion, notions of subordination and dependency, also discussed in comparative labor law as "inequality of bargaining power," and the moral dangers of capitalist treatment of labor as a commodity, inform Latin American labor law at its core.[45]

LEGISLACIÓN 7 (1994). Even though scholars have not agreed on the total number and types of principles, there is significant consensus regarding the four principles enumerated in this book. *See* PLÁ RODRÍGUEZ, *supra* note 35, at 13; SERGIO GAMONAL C., FUNDAMENTOS DE DERECHO LABORAL 104–15 (2008); SERGIO GAMONAL C., INTRODUCCIÓN AL DERECHO DEL TRABAJO 132–48 (1998).

[41] Óscar Ermida Uriarte, *Protección, Igualdad, Dignidad, Libertad y No Discriminación*, 15 CADERNOS DE AMATRA IV 11 (2011) (Braz.).

[42] *See* chapter 2.

[43] Ermida Uriarte, *supra* note 41.

[44] *Id.*

[45] Judy Fudge, *Labour as a "Fictive Commodity": Radically Reconceptualizing Labour Law*, *in* THE IDEA OF LABOUR LAW 120, 122 (Guy Davidov & Brian Langille eds., 2011).

The protective principle has also led to the development of an important rule in Latin American jurisprudence, *in dubio pro operario*.[46] In our view, *in dubio pro operario* is what makes Latin American labor law particularly relevant and unique to our discussion of the idea and future of labor law. In essence, the rule states that the judge or any other adjudicator should decide a labor law case or controversy in favor of workers when rules are ambiguous or vague, when there is a gap in the law, or when any other application appears inequitable.[47] We will see that *in dubio pro operario* plays a central role in Latin American jurisprudence, guiding and limiting—in effect channeling—adjudicative discretion in cases where there are several interpretations of the law, particularly in the so-called hard cases.[48] *In dubio pro operario* provides an opportunity for labor law jurisprudence to remain normatively coherent and "empirically valid"—that is, capable of shaping the behavior of the intended legal subjects,[49] despite vague law and gaps, but always channeled in a pro-worker direction. Such broad reading of labor law statutes follows the traditional common law's statutory construction canon, as developed by William Blackstone, calling for a liberal, or broad, reading of those statutes that derogate the common law.[50]

In chapter 2 we argue that U.S. law from two key historical times when antisubordination ideas reigned strong, Reconstruction and the New Deal, most solidly contains the protective principle. This law includes the Thirteenth Amendment banning involuntary servitude, a product of Reconstruction, and the NLRA and the FLSA, products of the New Deal. The Thirteenth Amendment directs Congress to protect free labor, while the policy statements prefacing the NLRA and the FLSA, and many of their operative clauses, provide for explicit worker protection. The NLRA and the FLSA assert that there is inequality in bargaining power between "employers" and "employees," requiring and justifying legal protections for employees. Those concrete protections include employees' rights to form unions, bargain collectively, and otherwise act in concert for their "mutual aid and protection," and enjoy a minimum wage while also being afforded some protections against overly demanding hours. The FLSA also forbids certain forms of child labor. Hence,

---

[46] *See* PLÁ RODRÍGUEZ, *supra* note 35, at 40.

[47] *Id.*

[48] Ronald Dworkin defines hard cases as those when "a particular lawsuit cannot be brought under a clear rule of law, laid down by some institution in advance" and the judge may thus decide the case either way. DWORKIN, *supra* note 35, at 81.

[49] Coutu, *supra* note 19, at 612–14 (describing how labor law should retain normative coherence, empirical validity, and legitimacy to remain effective as "law").

[50] ANTONIN SCALIA & BRYAN A. GARNER, READING LAW: THE INTERPRETATION OF TEXTS 365 (2012) (*citing* WILLIAM BLACKSTONE, COMMENTARIES ON THE LAWS OF ENGLAND 86 (4th ed. 1770)).

we argue that U.S. positive federal labor law recognizes the protective principle. U.S. jurisprudence also recognized something similar to *in dubio pro operario* in the FLSA's "humanitarian" and "remedial" character. A lot of that labor-protective jurisprudence has been lost after decades of pro-employer domination in the United States, but it can be brought back.

In chapter 3, we move into the principle of primacy of reality, or fact. It posits that if we accept that workers in capitalist employment relationships are subordinated and dependent on the employer, thus requiring special legal protections, then it necessarily follows that employers cannot simply get out of their obligations toward workers by characterizing what appear to be employment relationships as something else, such as an independent contractor relationship, a franchising agreement, or a pedagogical relationship (such as the case of graduate student assistants and research assistants seeking unionization in the United States) that lies outside of labor law. Employers may attempt to siphon off all employees from their businesses by hiring contractors or contracting with franchisees, for example, but courts and other adjudicators must take a hard look at the facts and not defer to employers' characterization of the relationship before ruling that the presumed employer has no employees, only contractors, franchisees, students, or anything else they might call the workers. Primacy of reality thus posits that facts must be given preference over what is contained in legal texts, documents, or agreements.[51]

Primacy of reality becomes increasingly relevant in employee classification issues, such as the issue the Gotham drivers faced in the earlier hypothetical. When employers claim that people who work for them are independent contractors and not statutory employees, for example, courts have to interrogate the facts to determine whether the relationship is truly one of an employer and employee. It also becomes relevant when patterns and practices contradict what is stated in the employment contract, or what the parties may have otherwise agreed outside a written document. For example, if the employer pays, in fact, a wage that exceeds what is stated in the contract, primacy of reality would dictate that the prevailing wage in that relationship should be the one established by those facts and not the one in the agreement.[52]

We argue that the principle of primacy of reality exists in U.S. labor law. Most legal tests to determine employee status in the United States require either a common law "control test" or, if the FLSA applies, the use of an "economic realities test." These tests require that adjudicators look at the facts of cases and not simply at formal agreements between the parties.

---

[51] *See* chapter 3.

[52] This is true unless the employer is paying below what is stated in the contract, in which case the contractual term would be binding. PLÁ RODRÍGUEZ, *supra* note 35, at 388–89. The *pro operario* criterion would operate.

However, we also recognize that many cases implicating employee or independent contractor status have been wrongly decided despite the fact that adjudicators have interrogated the facts. Factor tests, such as the control tests, require weighing multiple, nondeterminative factors that may lead to contradictory results. Rules may not be clear as to who should be classified as a covered "employee." In those instances, and if adjudicators find that the putative employee reasonably meets the employment tests, it makes sense to refer to the protective principle and *in dubio pro operario* to rule in favor of employee status. U.S. adjudicators can summon a rule such as *in dubio pro operario* by referencing Blackstone's canon of statutory interpretation calling for broad construction of laws that derogate the common law, the NLRA's goals to equalize bargaining relationships between employers and employees, and the FLSA's "humanitarian and remedial" purposes.

If we accept the importance of the protective principle, then we must also accept that the employer and worker may not agree to waive labor rights through a private agreement or contract. This brings us to the principle of nonwaiver, which we describe in chapter 4. Nonwaiver generally posits that rights provided to weaker parties in employment relations are simply not waivable. Latin American doctrine posits that the nonwaiver principle is the "traveling companion" of the principle of protection, as protection would dissipate if workers could waive their rights through a private agreement with the employer, a stronger bargaining agent.[53] Waiver of statutory workers' rights would undo what the legislature mandated. The nonwaiver principle guarantees the continued validity of worker protection[54] and constitutes a necessary part of workers' rights.[55]

We argue that the nonwaiver principle exists in the United States through its ban of the so-called yellow dog contract, where workers agree not to join unions as a condition of employment. It also exists under the FLSA, its rules, and its jurisprudence. However, the U.S. Supreme Court has recently decided that employers can demand that employees waive their rights to seek judicial redress of their employment claims, even when these are collective claims arguably protected by the NLRA, and file, instead, a claim in individual, private arbitration.[56] Despite the U.S. Supreme Court's recent ruling,[57] we argue, as others before us, that such waivers constitute violations

---

[53] *See* Luis Roa, *Irrenunciabilidad de derechos: itinerarios de un principio general*, *in* ESTUDIOS DE TEORÍA CRÍTICA DE DERECHO DEL TRABAJO 241 (Guillermo Gianibelli & Oscar Zas eds., 2006).

[54] Olga Castillejo de Arias, *Teoría General del derecho del Trabajo*, *in* DERECHO DEL TRABAJO 117 (Carlos A. Livellara ed., 2004). *See also* DE LA VILLA GIL & LÓPEZ CUMBRE, *supra* note 39; MANUEL MONSALVO, CURSO DE DERECHO DEL TRABAJO Y DE LA SEGURIDAD SOCIAL 116 (2009).

[55] MAURICIO GODINHO DELGADO, PRINCÍPIOS DE DIREITO INDIVIDUAL E COLETIVO DO TRABALHO 89 (2nd ed. 2004).

[56] Epic Systems Corp. v. Lewis, 138 S. Ct. 1612 (2018).

[57] *Id.*

of labor laws and deprive workers of the protections given to them by Congress. A better understanding of the importance of the protective principle and its necessary, derivative principle of nonwaiver could help reverse this rather alarming jurisprudential tendency to favor individual, private arbitration that jeopardizes the core of labor law.

Ultimately, if we accept the protective principle, then we must also acknowledge, as we explain in chapter 5, that an employer cannot simply escape his or her obligations toward his or her workers by terminating the employment contract, or by threatening workers with dismissal. This brings us to the principle of continuity, also referred to as the principle of employment stability. The principle of continuity presumes that the employment contract is of indefinite duration.[58] This is why, in most countries, employers must generally show cause to terminate the employment contract.

As we discuss in this book, continuity is the principle least present in the United States given the continued relevance of employment at will in that country. However, continuity exists in U.S. collective bargaining agreements and in the public sector, where the employer can only sever employment relationships if he or she shows cause. Moreover, under most U.S. labor laws, if employees show that an employer illegally discriminated against workers because of their race, sex, union support, and other reasons, or if employers took some sort of retaliatory action against workers, including termination, because the workers were attempting to assert a right under the labor laws (such as requesting a job, a promotion, or filing claims of discrimination), the law will require the employer to provide contrary evidence to avoid liability. In such cases, if the employer fails to prove a legitimate reason for its actions against employees, the court may order reinstatement, back pay, and other remedies.[59]

Finally, courts have further curtailed employment at will through the law of wrongful dismissal, which posits that termination of the employment relationship cannot go against specific laws or public policy.[60] Wrongful dismissal doctrine initially puts the burden of proof on the employee, not the employer; the employee must prove that the termination was against the law or some public policy. However, once employees assert the negative employer action and the plausibility that the action was against the law or public policy, the employer must provide evidence to

---

[58] *See* PLÁ RODRÍGUEZ, *supra* note 35, at 157.

[59] For example, the NLRA states than employer must show cause when the NLRB's general counsel has established that the employer may have discriminated against an employee engaging in protected activity under the NLRA. 29 U.S.C. § 160(c) (2012). The FLSA similarly states that employers cannot discriminate against an employee who has filed an action against an employer under that law, or who has participated in a procedure where the employer was accused of violating the law. 29 U.S.C. § 215(a)(3) (2012).

[60] Cynthia Estlund, *Wrongful Discharge Protections in an At-Will World*, 74 TEX. L. REV. 1655, 1662 (1996).

the contrary.[61] If the employer is unpersuasive, the court will fashion a remedy for the aggrieved employees. In this fashion, a spotty and weaker version of continuity exists in the United States.

We argue in chapter 5 that generous unemployment compensation benefits, lifetime training, and strong job creation would fully extend the principle of continuity in United States.[62] These "flexicurity" programs, if structured effectively (and very few have been around the world) could meet the requirements of continuity without prescribing statutory "just-cause" termination. However, the United States would likely better extend the principle of continuity by legislating for "just-cause" termination. Flexicurity policies are complex and expensive, and require a level of economic coordination absent in the U.S. liberal market economy.[63] Therefore, we argue that statutory dismissal protections—which are simpler to legislate, administer, and enforce—remain preferable for the United States.

PRINCIPLES IN ACTION: A TEASER

So, exactly how can principles reinvigorate labor law? Let's take the Gotham Share hypothetical to explain it: assuming that U.S., Anystate, or Gotham laws have no clear rules on the employee status of ride-share drivers, and assuming that the facts suggest that the drivers could reasonably be employees or independent contractors,[64] an adjudicator guided and limited by principles should rule that the drivers are employees

[61] *See, e.g.*, Phipps v. Clark Oil, 396 N.W.2d 588, 592 (Minn. Ct. App. 1987) ("Once the employee has demonstrated that the discharge may have been motivated by reasons that contravene a clear mandate of public policy, the burden then shifts to the employer to prove that the dismissal was for reasons other than those alleged by the employee."); Thompson v. St. Regis Paper Co., 102 Wash.2d 219, 232–33 (1984) (". . . once the employee has demonstrated that his discharge may have been motivated by reasons that contravene a clear mandate of public policy, the burden shifts to the employer to prove that the dismissal was for reasons other than those alleged by the employee.").

[62] *See* Thomas Bredgaard, *Flexibility and Security in Employment Regulation: Learning from Denmark*, *in* Rethinking Workplace Regulation: Beyond the Standard Contract of Employment 213 (Katherine V. W. Stone & Harry Arthurs eds., 2013) (explaining the Danish system of flexicurity).

[63] *See, e.g.*, Kathleen Thelen, Varieties of Liberalization and the New Politics of Social Solidarity (2014) (coordinated market economies, such as those in northern Europe, are better adapted to implement these flexicurity schemes than liberal market economies where the market, rather than institutional labor market actors—such as labor unions, employers, and the state—have a tradition of setting and implementing labor market policies).

[64] While employers and their attorneys have argued that ride-share drivers are independent contractors and not employees, some scholars have argued that drivers are "employees" under U.S. law. *See, e.g.*, Rogers, *supra* note 14 (explaining that even though Uber drivers may not fall neatly into the employee category under existing law, they are subordinated, and under that principle should be considered employees). Other scholars may support the idea that ride-sharing drivers fall into some sort of intermediate category that should be legally recognized to provide at least some partial protections. *See* Lobel, *supra* note 14 (discussing authors who call

covered by labor law. It would not matter what the employer calls the drivers. The principle of primacy of reality would guide the adjudicator to search the facts to determine employee status. Even if the law is unclear about employee status—as it might be given the meandering factor tests used to determine such statuses—the protective principle and *in dubio pro operario* would mandate the adjudicator to hold in favor of employee status. Once the workers are considered statutory employees and hence protected, wage and hour laws would cover them. If the workers can prove that the employer failed to pay them their wages under the law, the employer would then be liable for those payments. The workers would also have the protected right to strike and would not be liable under antitrust laws.

Moreover, because the workers would be protected employees, principled labor law would lead us to determine that employers cannot compel workers to waive their statutory rights to form class or collective actions. The legislature provided workers with the right to file claims in court individually or collectively to make the wage and hour laws effective. Collective claims are especially important in the United States because individual claims are uneconomical, given the high costs of litigation in comparison with the recovered funds an individual worker making a wage claim can collect.[65] As such, if workers could waive their rights to join a class or collective action, their wage claims would never be litigated and employers could get away with violating substantive worker rights. Under principled labor law, courts would invalidate litigation and class action waivers to safeguard the basic rights of workers to be paid under the law and to act in concert for their mutual aid and protection.

However, as we explain further in chapter 4, individual, private arbitration has a statutory basis in the Federal Arbitration Act (FAA), which the U.S. Supreme Court esteemed crucial in enabling class action waivers. Therefore, legislators should not only amend the FAA to clearly exclude all workers under the regulatory power of the U.S. Congress but also constitutionalize the NLRA under the Thirteenth Amendment to send a clear signal to U.S. courts of the great importance labor law and workers' freedom have in its legal and constitutional system. Labor law should, thus, not be seen merely as another piece of economic regulation, on par with

---

for the recognition of a third category of employment for those workers dependent on one particular employer without necessarily being "controlled" under traditional common law views used to understand employment or independent contractor status).

[65] *See* Jean Sternlight, *Disarming Employees: How American Employers Are Using Mandatory Arbitration to Deprive Workers of Legal Protection*, 80 BROOK. L. REV. 1309, 1334–36 (2015) (detailing how individual employment claims are simply uneconomical for most plaintiff lawyers in the United States, leaving independent plaintiffs without access to justice or a way to enforce their rights).

the arbitration of commercial disputes, but as one that stems from a fundamental right: workers' freedom.

We should, however, underscore that pro-worker or *pro operario* worker principles do not mean that workers always win. If the adjudicator determines that the positive law in the hypothetical case above was clear as to employee status, right to minimum wages, and waiver of class actions, principles would not determine the case—the rules would. In this way, principles exist only to aid the adjudicator when he or she confronts an interpretation quandary.

SUPPLEMENTING THE LABOR CONSTITUTION

While this book proposes principled labor law to defend and rebuild labor law, it does not necessarily argue that legal interpretation alone will do the job. Labor unions and collective bargaining are an essential element for labor law renewal, even if we do not expressly focus on union renewal or freedom of association rights in these pages. We find agreement between what we argue here, for example, and the work of Professor Ruth Dukes.[66] Dukes argues that traditional labor law ideas are still useful for workers, especially those stemming from the German legal scholar Hugo Sinzheimer and his pupil, Otto Kahn-Freund, who based their scholarship on the premise that labor law arises from a pressing need to protect dependent and subordinated work.

In her work, Dukes advances an ambitious goal, that of reasserting a "labor constitution," a goal of Hugo Sinzheimer, to make workers participants not only in workplace decisions that impact their terms and conditions of employment but also in the more encompassing political economy of capitalism.[67] Her book reasserts the idea of real (rather than formal) citizenship for workers, underscoring the role of politics over the economy. For that reassertion of citizenship, social democracy is needed, or democratic politics, widely conceived, where worker organizations, collective bargaining, and full freedom of association permeate in the political economy.[68] We can't help but agree with her positions and others who make similar points. We just would emphasize that a labor-protective jurisprudence is also a necessary part of the mix. Labor law renewal is multipronged.

---

[66] DUKES, *supra* note 23, at 1, 14–17.

[67] *Id.* at 212–21.

[68] *Id.* at 213. Dukes also mentions the important work of Sidney and Beatrice Webb, *Industrial Democracy*, published in 1897, as foundational for the work of Sinzheimer and his view of the labor constitution. *Id.* at 212 and n.99. Moreover, while Otto Kahn-Freund, Sinzheimer's pupil who wrote from Oxford where he was exiled, is most famously known for his advocacy of "collective *laissez faire*," that idea was also subjected to the general principle of balancing power asymmetries between workers and capitalists. *Id.* at 212 (internal citations omitted).

A SIMPLER AND MORE COHERENT ALTERNATIVE TO DAVIDOV'S "PURPOSIVISM"

This book also shares some commonalities with the so-called purposive perspective of labor law.[69] Guy Davidov wrote the most recent monograph (and perhaps most complete, as far as labor law goes) on this subject.[70] In his book, he argues that labor law is always in "crisis" given the steady state of capitalist changes. Because legislatures are slow to amend positive law, legislative purpose can help fill gaps in the law left when capitalism changes. Hence, purpose, for Davidov, takes a similar role to the one we assign to principle. Moreover, Davidov underscores that labor law must remedy power asymmetries between employers and workers, as Latin American doctrine generally posits.[71] Throughout this book we use legislative purpose to find legal principles. Hence, principled labor law is purposive.

However, Professor Davidov recognizes other purposes in labor law than that of remedying structural inequalities, which contrasts with principled labor law. According to Davidov, these purposes include redistributing resources, power, and risks; promoting human rights and human dignity; promoting social inclusion or citizenship; providing stability and security; promoting efficiency; maximizing human freedoms and capabilities; emancipating individuals; promoting social equality; and perhaps other goals.[72] Courts should engage in means-goals (rules-purposes) matching when lacunas exist in the law.[73]

Purpose plurality, coupled with judicial discretion, makes Davidov's purposivism markedly different from Latin America's more rulified and principled labor law. Under principled labor law, the protective principle and *in dubio pro operario* order the judge to rule in favor of the worker when there are doubts about the law. The Latin American method narrows judicial discretion in the hard case, while Davidov's amplifies it.

---

[69] DAVIDOV, *supra* note 19.

[70] *Id.*

[71] *Id.* at 52–54, 118–19. While agreeing that labor law attempts to remedy "inequality in bargaining power," he argues that there never is true equality in any bargaining relationship, which makes that traditional phrase vague and overinclusive. Davidov prefers to more directly shift the analysis to remedying "democratic deficits" as traditionally understood, and "dependency," which can be economic as well as social and psychological. *Id.* at 119.

[72] *Id.* at 54–68.

[73] *Id.* at 16, 198, 218.

Moreover, Davidov recognizes that purposes may not always align one with the other, but somehow live "side by side."[74] But it is clear to us that these purposes may actually conflict and may even lead to indeterminate legal conclusions, some of which may be detrimental to workers.[75] For example, we can see how Davidov's purposive approach differs from principled labor law on the issue of whether tips should be counted toward an employer's duty to pay a minimum wage.[76] In his book, Davidov details how an Israeli court, following a purposive approach, determined in *dicta* that an employer could count an employee's earned tips toward the satisfaction of the minimum wage.[77] According to Davidov, the Israeli law does not provide clear rules as to whether the minimum wage has to be paid directly by the employer in full, or whether it can be satisfied through payments received by the worker from patrons and clients through tips.[78] Because in the particular case decided by the Israeli court the employer did not pay the worker at all—the worker received all her pay through tips—and the employer did not make any legally required deductions (taxes, social security, etc.), the court determined that the employer failed to pay the worker appropriately under the wage and hour laws.[79] However, the court also stated, in *dicta*, that if the facts had shown that the employer was making all the legal deductions and the employee made wages above the minimum wage, the tips could be counted against any wage payments directly from the employer. Davidov agreed with the court's *dicta*, given that the purposes of the Israeli law were to redistribute wealth and protect the human dignity of those workers in particularly low-paid, vulnerable situations. As he argued, "This [was] not a situation of low wage that should be seen as an assault to dignity or a need to redistribute in his favor. . . . The goals of the minimum wage law do not justify the application of this law on people whose income is much higher than the minimum wage."[80]

The Latin American principled method would differ. Absent clear rules, tips would not count toward the minimum wage. As we will see in this book, the protective principle, and its correlative rule *in dubio pro operario*, would command the judge to rule in the manner most favorable to the worker absent clear law. This

---

[74] *Id.* at 55. Davidov, however, also argues that universally applicable goals should be subsidiary to "selective" goals, or those more traditionally found in labor law, particularly those dealing with ameliorating democratic deficits or worker vulnerabilities. *Id.* at 70–71.

[75] *See also* Joe Atkinson, *Book Review: A Purposive Approach to Labour Law*, 46 INDUS. L.J. 303, 305–06 (2017) (noting that Davidov's goals of labor law may conflict and offers no principled method to select among the various goals).

[76] DAVIDOV, *supra* note 19, at 198.

[77] *Id.* at 198–99, *citing* DGMB Eilat Restaurants, Ltd. v. Malka (2005) 40 PDA 769 (Isr. Nat'l Lab. Ct.).

[78] *Id.*

[79] *Id.*

[80] *Id.*

would mean that the employer would have to pay the worker a minimum wage, and the worker would retain all tips. While Davidov would seek clarity in the law to exclude tips from the minimum wage if the tip income exceeds the minimum wage amount, a Latin American "principled" methodology would require clarity only to count the tips as part of the employer's obligations.[81]

There are sound policy reasons to protect the worker even if he or she makes above the legal minimum wage. First, the minimum wage may simply be inadequate, as it is in many countries of the world.[82] Second, employers may abuse their control over workers' time when they pay nothing to the employee. What if the employer asks that all waiting staff stay after hours to clean the restaurant, when the workers cannot collect any tips? Put differently, how much work, and of what sort, can the employer demand from a waiter who earns money only when patrons are paying tips? Third, a rule where the employer pays the employee nothing may spread too much risk to a dependent and subordinated worker, given that the employer makes all business decisions of the firm. An employee working only for tips might feel denigrated even if he or she receives compensation nominally commensurate with the minimum wage. The employer might just control too much of the workers' time and capacity to earn tips to make the bargain a dignified one. But since circumstance might not give the worker an alternative source of income, the worker might have to accept that unfair, undignified bargain, not wholly in accordance with his or her will, nor with that of the law.

Principled labor law would thus protect all workers, the low-paid and those that are more middle-class. If the legislature believes that tips should count toward the employer's obligation to pay a minimum wage, the legislature, not the court, should provide for a rule that explicitly provides that tips count toward the minimum wage. Put simply, principled labor law has a built-in presumption in favor of the worker from which adjudicators may not deviate, absent clear rules.

Whether Davidov's particular purposive method—a pluralist one—or the principled, more singular method is superior is a question that requires assessing and balancing policy goals. Scholars have noted certain benefits of vague law ("standards") over clear law ("rules"), including that vague law is less rigid and can better deal

---

[81] As Davidov states, "My point is that absent such a determination in legislation, it is not required by purposive interpretation, quite the contrary." *Id.* at 199.

[82] In Mexico, for example, the minimum wage "lost seventy-five percent of its buying power between 1982 and 2014, and it falls below the poverty line," despite being among the most productive economies in Latin America. Graciela Bensusán, *Organizing Workers in Argentina, Brazil, Chile and Mexico: The Authoritarian-Corporatist Legacy and Old Institutional Designs in a New Context*, 17 Theoretical Inquiries L. 131, 145 (2016). In the United States, federal minimum wages have lost significant purchasing power, compelling local governments and states to establish higher levels. Andrias, *supra* note 24, at 51–52.

with changing circumstances or unexpected cases. Clear law tends to be over- and underinclusive, as the old adage goes. It may also become ossified and irrelevant given changing circumstances. In the labor law field, obsolete law may throw workers back to the unregulated market, exacerbating worker subordination and dependence.[83]

However, scholars have also noted that vague law leads to less consistent results, creating serious problems for law as a rational system. And as we noted earlier, Davidov's labor law goals may not always agree with one another. Sometimes "human rights" may be opposed by "social inclusion." Take the case of Friedrich Hayek, for example, who may have opposed freedom of association and collective bargaining—considered human rights—because these human rights lead groups of "insiders" who necessarily keep "outsiders" (i.e., the poor and the unemployed) beyond the mainstream sociolegal space.[84] In this sense, human rights and social inclusion may conflict. If judges have to balance these two goals, which goal do they give preference to? Or take the U.S. case, where the concept of "agency fees"—in which employees must pay union service fees when the union must represent the worker under the U.S. rule of exclusive representation—is counterpoised by democratic values, particularly those democratic values regarding free speech.[85] In those cases, the free rider's free speech rights may be protected to the detriment of those workers who want to have effective unions. Which goals should the judges choose? And of course, property rights are sacred and inviolable human rights in the United States.[86] When property rights conflict with freedom of association, courts almost always rule in favor of the side alleging property rights violations, the employer. In other words, the goals of labor law could lead to disparate results in similar cases. Potentially, any particular judicial opinion may meet those goals, even if some results are labor-protective and others are squarely not.

Second, in the United States specifically, sociolegal scholars have shown in a number of important empirical studies that vague law enables employer agents—namely, human resource management professionals—to persuade courts to interpret the laws in ways that most benefit employers, effectively disarming many workplace protections.[87] These studies have thus shown the "endogenous" nature

---

[83] *See* DAVIDOV, *supra* note 19, at 160.

[84] Friedrich Hayek, *El paro y los sindicatos en los años ochenta (El falseamiento de los precios relativos por el monopolio del mercado de trabajo)*, *in* SINDICATOS, ¿PARA QUÉ? 95 (2009) (arguing that unions impede salaries' ability to adjust to market demand, creating a labor market rigidity that increases unemployment).

[85] *See* Janus v. AFSCME, 138 S. Ct. 2448 (2018) (5–4 opinion declaring agency fees in the public sector to be in violation of fundamental free speech rights consecrated under the First Amendment of the U.S. Constitution).

[86] *See* JAMES A. GROSS, A SHAMEFUL BUSINESS: THE CASE FOR HUMAN RIGHTS IN THE AMERICAN WORKPLACE chs. 3–4 (2010).

[87] *See, e.g.*, LAUREN EDELMAN, WORKING LAW: COURTS, CORPORATIONS, AND SYMBOLIC CIVIL RIGHTS 11 (2016) (firms mostly comply symbolically with employment discrimination law because courts readily defer to their human resource management professionals, corporate discrimination policies, and procedures as

of labor law—endogenous, that is, to capitalist organizations, rather than to law as an external force.[88] In this sense, the clearer, simpler, principled method may overall prove better suited for jurisdictions such as the United States with a history of judicial hostility to labor law and deference to employers' legal views.

Moreover, given that we are currently feeling the impact of years of neoliberalism, diminished job quality, and diminished employment opportunities for many workers, there is a need to redouble efforts to protect workers.[89] Principled labor law is particularly useful when such protection is urgently needed.

Finally, principled labor law, in some ways also recognized in Spain, where *in dubio pro operario* has been recognized, and in France and Germany, where somewhat similar rules "of favor," or a "principle of favorability," respectively, exist, makes Davidov's purposivism a bit of a bad bargain.[90] If the law already provides a presumption favoring workers, why complicate it with multiple other goals? In this manner, the purposive approach may be better suited for jurisdictions without clear *pro operario* rules. But whether purposivism can guarantee worker protection given the "endogeneity" problem is an entirely different matter. Given the evidence, we exude little optimism that U.S. courts will consistently protect workers if they adopt an approach with varying purposes.[91]

"evidence" of compliance); FRANK DOBBIN, INVENTING EQUAL OPPORTUNITY (2009) (explaining how human resource management professionals were the institutional actors who ultimately gave meaning to employment discrimination law in the United States). We should note that Lauren Edelman argues that Dobbin diverges from her own perspective inasmuch as Dobbin sustains that ambiguous law lacks real meaning and, therefore, human resource management professionals provide needed meaning to that law. Edelman, however, argues that such employer-provided meaning is expressly and purposefully done in a way to skirt real compliance and merely provides symbolic, cosmetic compliance with the law. EDELMAN, *supra* at 11.

[88] *Id.* at 12. Lauren Edelman explains that:

> Legal endogeneity posits that organizations respond to ambiguous law by creating a variety of policies and programs designed to symbolize attention to law. As these policies and programs become commonplace in organizations, employers and employees alike tend to equate the mere presence of these structures with legal compliance and become less aware of whether the structures actually promote legal ideals. Eventually the ideals underlying law become so closely associated with the organizational structures that legal actors, as well as organizational actors, understand compliance in terms of the presence or absence of these structures and fail to scrutinize their effectiveness. Legal endogeneity theory suggests that the meaning of law evolves through the articulation and resolution of problems not in the halls of Congress but rather in the halls of work organizations.

Id. at 12.

[89] *See* INTERNATIONAL LABOUR OFFICE, REPORT VI, LABOUR PROTECTION IN A TRANSFORMING WORLD OF WORK: A RECURRENT DISCUSSION ON THE STRATEGIC OBJECTIVE OF SOCIAL PROTECTION (LABOUR PROTECTION) 69 (2015), *available at* http://www.ilo.org/wcmsp5/groups/public/---ed_norm/---relconf/documents/meetingdocument/wcms_358295.pdf (underscoring the ILO's purpose to protect workers, especially when an increasing share of workers are falling outside standard forms of employment and traditional labor-protective institutions such as labor unions are declining in influence).

[90] For the rule of favor in France and the principle of favorability in Germany, *see* chapter 2.

[91] *Id.*

AGAINST ECONOMISM

While principled labor law shares at least some common ground with purposivism, it is clearly at odds with libertarian views that call for pure free contract and employment at will.[92] Although these neoliberal voices are marginal in labor law per se, they are pronounced in public policy discussions, especially in the United States. Here, we simply recognize that our method is in direct conflict with laissez-faire. We do not intend to argue with that perspective, since that discussion is of a different nature than the one we take here. Rather, this book intends to open a dialogue with those scholars who accept the premise that state intervention in the regulation of work is an important and valid policy concern.

Perhaps more relevant to the field of labor itself has been a perspective that aims to regulate the labor market by fixing its failures.[93] One strand of this approach, which Professor Hugh Collins calls the "Third Way" of labor law, focuses on improving competitiveness and promoting social inclusion, but rejects equalizing redistributive outcomes, a traditional goal of labor law.[94] In Latin America, labor law is not understood as a law that regulates the market or even tries to make it more efficient or fix its failures. Rather, labor law is, in the traditional sense, an autonomous body of law that attempts to constitute equitable working relationships, themselves required to protect the moral welfare of workers and society in general. As such, principled labor law does not require an adjudicator to consider efficiency concerns. If legislators want adjudicators to make efficiency part of their opinions, legislators need to provide clear rules to that effect.[95] In fact, an entirely different method outside adjudication—a regulatory one—might be in order.

Critics of principled labor law might argue, following the old saying that the "path to hell is paved with good intentions," that a morally concerned law might still lead to foul outcomes. The problem of unintended consequences haunts regulatory processes, especially when done purely on moral and political suasion without the aid of technical experts. Principled labor law might thus overdeter employers from

---

[92] *See generally* Richard Epstein, *In Defense of the Contract at Will*, 51 U. CHI. L. REV. 947 (1984).

[93] *See, e.g.*, Hugh Collins, *Is There a Third Way in Labour Law?*, *in* LABOUR LAW IN AN ERA OF GLOBALIZATION: TRANSFORMATIVE PRACTICES AND POSSIBILITIES 449–69 (Joanne Conaghan, Richard Michael Fischl, & Karl Klare eds., 2002).

[94] *Id.* at 450–52. *See also* SIMON DEAKIN & FRANK WILKINSON, THE LAW OF THE LABOUR MARKET: INDUSTRIALIZATION, EMPLOYMENT, AND LEGAL EVOLUTION (2005); PAUL DAVIES & MARK FRIEDLAND, TOWARDS A FLEXIBLE LABOUR MARKET (2007).

[95] This said, Latin American labor inspectors, who enforce the brunt of the labor codes, apply a level of flexibility to maximize compliance and to develop employer compliance capacities over time. Michael Piore & Andrew

abusing workers and overregulate the workplace, destroying firms and workers' jobs along the way.

But principled labor law does not have to conflict with effective and efficient regulation. Rules can be crafted with efficiency in mind. Experts can get involved in the regulatory process. Principled labor law is simply concerned about ruling on cases where there are vague rules or gaps in the law.

PRINCIPLED LABOR LAW AND THE "CAPABILITIES" PERSPECTIVE

This book's perspective also contrasts with some adherents to the so-called capabilities[96] perspective. This developing strand in labor-law-related scholarship argues that labor law should be to improve the capabilities of human beings to better participate as economic and political agents and, as such, attain true "freedom."[97] While that general view complements labor law, at least one of this view's advocates, Canadian Professor Brian Langille, has argued that labor law should cast aside its entire focus on inequality of bargaining power as both out of date and empirically and analytically problematic[98] and, rather, provide freedom-enhancing rights to everyone regardless of employee status.[99]

While we embrace the idea of improving human capabilities, we disagree with throwing out the baby with the bathwater and ridding ourselves of inequality of bargaining power as an important legal concern. As Professor Judy Fudge has argued, a capabilities approach could incorporate power asymmetries, not reject them, to promote institutions for collective capabilities, including such things as labor organizations.[100] Moreover, casting aside inequality of bargaining power would have a negative effect in the Latin American principle of protection and *in dubio pro*

Schrank, *Toward Managed Flexibility: The Revival of Labour Inspection in the Latin World*, 147 INT'L LAB. REV. 1 (2008).

[96] *See, e.g.*, Simon Deakin, *Capacitas: Contract Law, Capabilities and the Legal Foundations of the Market*, *in* CAPACITAS: CONTRACT LAW AND THE INSTITUTIONAL PRECONDITIONS OF A MARKET ECONOMY (Simon Deakin & Alain Supiot eds., 2009). DEAKIN & WILKINSON, *supra* note 94, at 342–53.

[97] Deakin, *supra* note 96; Brian Langille, *"Take These Chains from my Heart and Set Me Free": How Labor Law Theory Drives Segmentation of Workers' Rights*, 36 COMP. LAB. L. & POL'Y J. 257, 276 (2015). The capabilities approach generally stems from the work of Amartya Sen. *See* AMARTYA SEN, DEVELOPMENT AS FREEDOM (2000) (arguing that economic development should strive to provide effective opportunities for individuals to attain freedom through political liberties, freedom of opportunity, including credit, and freedom from abject poverty).

[98] Brian Langille, *Labor Law's Theory of Justice*, *in* THE IDEA OF LABOUR LAW 105–07 (Guy Davidov & Brian Langille eds., 2011).

[99] *Id.* at 111–14.

[100] Fudge, *supra* note 45, at 120. *See also* Peter Evans, *Collective Capabilities, Culture, and Amartya Sen's Development as Freedom*, 37 COMP. INT'L DEV. 54, 56 (2001) (criticizing the individualist bent of the traditional capabilities approach and calling for a collective capabilities perspective).

operario, which provide clear protections for workers. Let's put it this way: if workers trade the rule of *in dubio pro operario* for a law that aims to promote capabilities, what do they receive, concretely, in return? The bargain appears too uncertain to be a reasonable trade. If they receive Danish-style "flexicurity," universal basic income, and other universal entitlements to de-commodify work, then perhaps that perspective might be on to something, although we still wonder why it needs to *replace* traditional labor law. As we argue in chapter 6, Latin America has been at the forefront of experimenting with noncontributory pensions and welfare programs that help bring millions of people out of poverty—all "capabilities" enhancing—without abandoning labor law and its goal of protecting the weak.

A NECESSARY COUNTERCULTURAL NARRATIVE FOR THE UNITED STATES

Some scholars might claim that U.S. labor law lacks any principles, and, as such, principled labor law makes no sense for the United States. Professor Matt Finkin, for example, describes U.S. labor law as a patchwork that resulted from piecemeal legislation aiming to deal with specific problems of the labor question; it is, according to him, comprehensible only if understood historically.[101] Moreover, as we stated previously, a textual reading of U.S labor law gives the impression of internal inconsistency. The NLRA, for example, states that Congress wants to curb "obstructions to . . . commerce" caused by industrial strife, and maintain "efficiency" while also safeguarding collective bargaining.[102] Protecting collective bargaining may be seen as contradicting the goal of keeping industrial peace, as unions seldom bargain with employers without some conflict erupting in the process. Moreover, employee status tests are different for the NLRA and the FLSA. They also differ in other federal laws and the hundreds of state and municipal laws. Many other concepts will likely also be different across the collage of labor laws. U.S. labor law, then, may appear to be some sort of marauding Frankenstein monster devoid of consistency and principles.

However, we want to underscore that all positive law tends to be empirically inconsistent; law is rife with vague rules and gaps, failing to provide consistent results in all cases. The traditional common law of contract, for example, values individual autonomy as one of its principles.[103] However, contract law also limits individual

---

[101] Matthew W. Finkin, *NAFTA/NAALC Member Countries, United States*, *in* International Labor and Employment Laws, 33a-2 (William L. Keller et al. eds., 3rd ed. 2008).

[102] 29 U.S.C. § 151 (2012).

[103] *See, e.g.*, Fried, *supra* note 36, at 16–17. *See also* Steven J. Burton, Principles of Contract Law v–vi (4th ed. 2012) (describing the principles of contract law as: autonomy, security, justification, fairness, and compensation); Sidney W. Delong, *An Agnostic's Bible*, 20 Seattle U. L. Rev. 295, 307 (1997) (describing

autonomy by acknowledging legal and public policy trappings on contracting activity.[104] Moreover, only contracts where "consideration" is exchanged are generally considered enforceable contracts.[105] "The parties may shout consideration to the housetops, yet, unless consideration is actually present, there is not a legally enforceable [*sic*] contract."[106] And yet, despite legal and public policy exceptions, and the consideration requirement, individual autonomy reigns as a central principle of U.S. common law contracts.[107] Similarly, we argue that labor law has principles despite contradictions, vague terms, or being otherwise silent on some issues. In fact, the whole reason to develop its principles is to clarify rules and extend the law over gaps.

What we propose, then, might be countercultural for U.S. labor law, albeit not for law, generally. We want to find an order for U.S. labor law that is compliant with international labor standards while remaining relevant in today's modern economy. After reading our book, the reader should recognize, for example, as we more fully explain in the following chapters, that employment at will—in which employers may terminate the employment contract for good, bad, or no reason—is a doctrine that legally enshrines freedom of contract in employment.[108] But under principled labor law, the reader can also see employment at will as an anomalous doctrine that is incongruent with labor protection,[109] sustains involuntary servitude in practice, and which, as such, is not part of labor law at all.[110]

---

how some U.S. contracts scholars argue that there are diametrically different principles in contract, or none at all).

[104] *See, e.g.*, Percy H. Winfield, *Public Policy in the English Common Law*, 42 HARV. L. REV. 76, 76–77 (1928) (describing the long history of the public policy exception in the common law).

[105] Melvin Eisenberg, *The Principles of Consideration*, 67 CORNELL L. REV. 640 (1982) (explaining that enforceable promises generally require "consideration," or bargained-for exchange). *See also* RESTATEMENT (SECOND) OF CONTRACTS § 71(1) (AM. LAW. INST. 1981); Hamer v. Sidway, 27 N.E. 256, 257 (N.Y. 1891) (setting forth the bargained-for theory of consideration); Kirksey v. Kirksey, 8 Ala. 131, 133 (1845) (gratuitous promises will not be enforced).

[106] In re Greene, 45 F.2d 428, 430 (S.D.N.Y. 1930).

[107] *See* ROBERT E. SCOTT & JODY S. KRAUS, CONTRACT LAW & THEORY 24–26 (5th ed. 2013).

[108] *See* Bammert v. Don's Super Valu, Inc., 254 Wis.2d 347, 353 (2002) (stating the continued relevance of the employment at will doctrine, where an employer may terminate an employee "for good cause, for no cause, or even for cause morally wrong, without being thereby guilty of legal wrong.").

[109] The Chilean Constitutional Court, for example, has determined that a constitutional right to work under its constitution must mean that workers have a constitutional right to *protected* work, not merely to contract for work willy-nilly. *See* Tribunal Constitucional [T.C.] [Constitutional Court], 26 julio 2011, Rol de la causa: 1852-10 (Chile), *citing* Luz Bulnes, *La libertad de trabajo y su protección en la Constitución de 1980*, 28 REV. DE DER. PÚBLICO U. CHILE 207, 215 (1980); and JOSÉ LUIS CEA, DERECHO CONSTITUCIONAL CHILENO, TOMO II 427 (2004).

[110] Sergio Gamonal C. & César F. Rosado Marzán, *Protecting Workers as a Matter of Principle: A Latin American View of U.S. Work Law*, 13 WASH. U. GLOBAL STUD. L. REV. 605, 659 (2014) (arguing that employment at will is not part of labor law).

THE REST OF THIS BOOK

Different from some other perspectives on the future of labor law, this book adopts a Latin American perspective that is clearly protective of workers and is compliant with international labor standards. We have called it "principled labor law." It complements a labor constitution approach—where collective organization and bargaining serve as key loci of workers' rights—but disagrees with a capabilities approach to the extent the capabilities approach entails erasing inequality of bargaining power as a central matter that the law must remedy. We also propose a method that, while similar to Davidov's purposivism, is simpler and more cogent. It is squarely based on moral tenets to protect weaker parties. It also disagrees with economistic views of the law of work. In all, what we propose is unabashedly countercultural for the United States, where some scholars have even argued that labor law lacks principles. And yet, while countercultural, it may help bring the United States into the framework of international labor standards, with which many of its labor norms conflict.

The book then proceeds in the following way: In chapters 2–5 we take the reader to strange lands, to Latin America, to describe how each labor law principle has been developed there. Because we cannot possibly survey all of the countries of the region, we decided to focus on the countries of Argentina, Brazil, Chile, and Uruguay. Argentina and Brazil are two of the largest countries of the region, which makes them important to include.[111] Chile and Uruguay are much smaller countries but are also among the better performing economies of the region.[112] Moreover, while Argentina and Brazil are state corporatist in orientation, Chile has a longer history with liberal market policies.[113] Uruguay has been much more social democratic; government directly regulates work only slightly because collective bargaining by autonomous employer and worker organizations has played a strong regulatory role.[114] As such, the cases provide sufficient difference—they are big and small, corporatist, liberal, and social democratic—to show how all countries, amid different political

---

[111] *See* World Bank, Gross Domestic Product 2012, http://databank.worldbank.org/data/download/GDP.pdf (last visited July 2, 2013).

[112] For the case of Chile, *see* SEBASTIÁN EDWARDS, LEFT BEHIND: LATIN AMERICA AND THE FALSE PROMISE OF POPULISM 101–21 (2010). For Uruguay, *see* International Finance Corporation and World Bank, Doing Business, http://www.doingbusiness.org/data/exploreeconomies/uruguay/ (last visited July 2, 2013).

[113] *See* MARIA LORENA COOK, THE POLITICS OF LABOR REFORM IN LATIN AMERICA: BETWEEN FLEXIBILITY AND RIGHTS (2007).

[114] *See* Davide Grassi, *Democracy and Social Welfare in Uruguay and Paraguay*, 56 LATIN AM. POL. & SOC'Y. 120 (2014).

economies, follow a principled labor law methodology. We want to underscore the existence of principled labor law in the diverse region and, hence, its probability to survive outside the region.

Many readers, especially U.S. readers, might find some of the cases described as truly different, even odd—a legal Wonderland of sorts—given their own experiences with labor law. They might be surprised, either pleasantly or alarmingly, to read that labor judges in Latin America, trained in the civil law, are all but rule formalists; they commonly apply principles to decide hard cases. Moreover, readers might be surprised to see that in the lands of magical realism, judges and other adjudicators have been facing and deciding contemporary labor law issues similar to those stemming from cutting-edge gig and fissured work. The new seems old for Latin America.

In chapters 2–5 we also try to "find" labor law principles in the United States, namely, in the Thirteenth Amendment, one of the crown jewels of post–Civil War Reconstruction, which bans involuntary servitude and authorizes Congress to legislative in favor of free labor. We also search for the protective principle in the purposes and operative clauses of the NLRA and the FLSA, two key New Deal labor laws. We find that U.S. adjudicators do not always recognize the principles. We argue how cases should have turned out if they had consistently applied them. We also acknowledge that labor law reform, such as derogating employment at will, or constitutionalizing current and future labor law under the Thirteenth Amendment, would more clearly lodge labor law principles in the U.S. legal system.

In chapter 6 we take on likely critics of our principled labor law proposal. Critics might argue, among other things, that even if U.S. labor law reflected the principles outlined, other relevant law—such as tat regarding property rights, free speech, employment at will, and the FAA, among others—crowd out labor law, change its content, or even cancel out labor law entirely. Indeed, we acknowledge that labor law must coexist with other law. We also admit that labor law tends to lose against other law in the United States. However, as we explain in chapter 6, current Supreme Court doctrine on property rights, free speech, and the FAA, as well as the common law courts' historical understanding of employment at will in the United States, are extreme and outlandish, clashing sharply with international labor standards, comparative labor law, and even with U.S. law itself. U.S. labor law jurisprudence appears to inhabit its own Wonderland.

To get back to reality, i.e., to help the United States return from exile and to the labor law legal mainstream, we hold our ground. Principled labor law, we argue, can help adjudicators harmonize labor law with other law, rather than find conflicts where labor law must lose. Labor law need not be in constant conflict with all other law. In doing so, we note that during its golden years, labor law supported liberal democracies where constitutional matters such as property rights and free speech, now supposedly in conflict with labor law, flourished. In labor law's golden years, workers became middle-class property owners and were civically engaged, in part due to labor union strength. Today, workers are increasingly nonunion debtors who are much less civically engaged. In some sense, labor law might have been a victim of its own success. As workers' middle-class status grew, its effects distracted society. Home ownership, car ownership, health insurance, weekends, vacation time, etc., stood more and more in front of labor law, obstructing actors' view of it. Now, many adjudicators, policymakers, political leaders, and even ordinary workers themselves fail to see labor law's importance, and dismantle the very structure of that which made the middle class possible.

So principles matter. Without legal principles, lawyers might as well argue anything they please and take any path, as the Cheshire Cat suggested to Alice when Alice sought his help to find her way in Wonderland. But such lost lawyers should not expect any particular results in their cases. Hence, in the conclusion we summarize our argument and underscore the importance of "sticking to principles," especially as the trek appears more difficult for workers. We also suggest that principled labor law might be useful for jurisdictions outside the United States with similarly "lost" doctrine. If the wildly neoliberal United States, the least likely case of labor protection in the industrialized democracies, has the legal raw materials for a principled labor law, then other jurisdictions should likely also have them. We thus conclude with our main assertion: that labor law's reinvigoration requires promoting the essence of what it does—and that is to protect workers.

2

PROTECTION

INTRODUCTION[1]

In the words of the late Uruguayan legal scholar, Óscar Ermida, labor law's raison d'être is to protect the worker.[2] Like almost all Latin American labor law jurists, he was concerned with remedying subordinated and dependent work in modern capitalist society.[3] When workers are subordinated and dependent, employers can more

[1] Some of the authors' initial ideas in this chapter were originally published in Sergio Gamonal C. & César F. Rosado Marzán, *Protecting Workers as a Matter Principle: A Latin American View of U.S. Work Law*, 13 WASH. U. GLOBAL STUD. L. REV. 605 (2014).

[2] Óscar Ermida Uriarte, *Protección, Igualdad, Dignidad, Libertad y No Discriminación*, 15 CADERNOS DE AMATRA IV 11 (2011) (Braz.) [hereinafter Ermida Uriarte, *Protección*].

[3] For Argentinian scholars, *see* ADRIÁN GOLDIN & JORGELINA F. ALIMENTI, CURSO DE DERECHO DEL TRABAJO Y DE LA SEGURIDAD SOCIAL 3 (2009). For Brazilian scholars, *see* MAURICIO GODINHO DELGADO, PRINCÍPIOS DE DIREITO INDIVIDUAL E COLETIVO DO TRABALHO 33 (2nd ed. 2004); and JOSÉ MARTINS CATHARINO, DIREITO DO TRABALHO 12 (2nd ed. 1976). For Chilean scholars, *see* SERGIO GAMONAL C., FUNDAMENTOS DE DERECHO LABORAL 4 (2008); and JOSÉ LUIS UGARTE C., LA SUBORDINACIÓN EN EL DERECHO LABORAL CHILENO 1–9 (2008). For Uruguayan scholars, *see* AMÉRCIO PLÁ RODRÍGUEZ, LOS PRINCIPIOS DEL DERECHO DEL TRABAJO 63 (3rd ed. 1998); MARIO GARMENDIA ARIGÓN, ORDEN PÚBLICO Y DERECHO DEL TRABAJO 68 (2001); and Óscar Ermida Uriarte, *Crítica de la Libertad Sindical*, 242 REV. DER. LABORAL 226 (2011).

We should underscore that South American labor law scholars will regularly cite comparative sources to buttress their arguments. On the particular point of worker subordination and the need for labor law, they commonly cite OTTO KAHN-FREUND, TRABAJO Y DERECHO 48–49 (1987) (labor law serves as a counterweight easily set the terms and conditions of employment they wish to offer for workers, robbing workers of their autonomy and dignity. Lacking effective autonomy, subordinated and dependent workers come close to involuntary servants. For Professor Ermida, as for labor law generally in Latin America, labor law rebalances the power asymmetry at work, safeguarding workers' human dignity and society's moral interests.[4] A protective principle thus stems from the underlying goal to balance structurally disparate relationships at work. Latin American jurists, as those of many other countries, thus recognize protection as a universal principle of labor law.[5]

---

to employer power in the employment relationship), MANUEL CAMPOS PALOMEQUE, EL DERECHO DEL TRABAJO E IDEOLOGIA 17 (1985) (Spanish labor law scholar who argued that labor law balances the employer-worker relationship); ANTONIO BAYLOS & JOAQUÍN PÉREZ REY, EL DESPIDO O LA VIOLENCIA DEL PODER PRIVADO 40–44 (2009) (Spanish scholars arguing for the need to elaborate a juridical narrative in favor of workers to challenge the neoliberal economic narrative that obscures power relations at work); Bruno Veneziani, *Tre Commenti alla Critique du Droit du Travail de Supiot*, 67 GIORNALE DI DIRITTO DEL LAVORO E DI RELAZIONI INDUSTRIALI 3 (1995) (Italian labor law scholar describes the subordination of the worker to the employer and argues for the need to protect); ALAIN SUPIOT, CRÍTICA DEL DERECHO DEL TRABAJO 133–34 (1996) (French labor law scholar who argued that in employment relations the employer commands the worker and the worker must obey, raising the need for a protective labor law), among many others.

4 Ermida Uriarte, *Protección*, *supra* note 2, at 11.

5 Modern labor protection likely goes back to the English labor laws of the 1800s and to the ideas of Robert Owen. *See* Marc Linder & Ingrid Nygaard, *Rest in the Rest of the World*, 20 COMP. LAB. L. & POL'Y J. 105, 107 (1998). The constitutions of Mexico of 1917 and Weimar of 1919 were also highly influential. *See supra* Chapter 1. Scholars around the world have underscored the central importance of labor protection in labor law. *See* GINO GIUGNI, LAVORO LEGGE CONTRATTI 252 (1989) (arguing that labor law constricts individual autonomy in order to curb workers' exploitation); L. RIVA SANSEVERINO, ELEMENTI DI DIRITTO SINDACALE E DEL LAVORO 78 (1980) (arguing that special protections for workers are necessary because the employment contract concerns an individual's personhood and humanity, which could be threatened at work); ORONZO MAZZOTTA, MANUALE DI DIRITTO DEL LAVORO 16–17 (5th ed. 2017) (pointing out that the history of labor law is based on an image of the worker whose contractual weakness must be balanced through legislative intervention); ANTONIO VALLEBONA, LAVORO E SPIRITO 11 (2011) (labor law stems from the need to protect the worker from the dictatorship of the stronger party); MATTIA PERSIANI & PROIA GIAMPIERO, DIRITTO DEL LAVORO 126–27 (2008) (labor protection is an essential foundation of any society that wishes to respect human values); JEAN-CLAUDE JAVILLIER, DROIT DU TRAVAIL 51–53 (5th ed. 1996) (arguing that labor law historically has been oriented toward protecting workers from all forms of social exploitation, particularly given workers' subordination to employers; NADÈGE MEYER, L'ORDRE PUBLIC EN DROIT DU TRAVAIL 99 (2006) (explaining that the notion of "social public order" inherent to labor law seeks protection of the weaker party); Gerard Vachet, *Le principe de faveur dans les rapports entre sources de droit*, *in* LES PRINCIPES DANS LA JURISPRUDENCE DE LA CHAMBRE SOCIALE DE LA COUR DE CASSATION 79 (2008) (explaining the application of the principle of favor in French jurisprudence); GILLES AUZERO, DIRK BAUGARD, & EMMANUEL DOKÉS, DROIT DU TRAVAIL 3–4 (31st ed. 2018) (explaining that labor law has as its object work executed under the authority and power of another, explaining its public law nature, concerns with power asymmetries, and its connection with human rights law and democratic norms); HUGH COLLINS, EMPLOYMENT LAW 25–26 (2nd ed. 2010) (detailing how British labor law recognizes that labor is not a commodity); DAVID CABRELLI, EMPLOYMENT LAW IN CONTEXT. TEXT AND MATERIALS 7–22 (2nd ed. 2016) (arguing that labor law's mission is to override freedom of contract by protecting workers on the ground that they suffer from an inequality of power).

This chapter focuses on this principle of protection and its crystallization into the rule of *in dubio pro operario*, which mandates that judges and other adjudicators must decide hard cases in favor of workers. While not totally unique to Latin America, since echoes of *in dubio pro operario* exist in other regions, *in dubio pro operario* is the rule that makes Latin American labor law doctrine more firmly protective than other jurisdictions.[6]

The chapter first describes the protective principle and *in dubio pro operario* in Latin America, including the origins of worker protection in International Labor Organization (ILO) instruments and other international human rights texts. It then searches for the protective principle and *in dubio pro operario* in the United States, which we find in the Reconstruction's Thirteenth Amendment, the New Deal's National Labor Relations Act (NLRA), and the Fair Labor Standards Act (FLSA). The Thirteenth Amendment bans involuntary servitude and mandates Congress to protect free labor. Indeed, we even find something akin to *in dubio pro operario* in the general way that U.S. jurisprudence calls for "liberal" interpretations of statutes that derogate the common law. We also find it in U.S. purposive methods of statutory interpretation, applied by some judges. We describe that the U.S. Supreme Court called for a broad reading of the NLRA given its goals to equalize bargaining relationships at work. It also called for broad interpretations of the FLSA given its "remedial and humanitarian" purposes. However, those broad, purposive, worker-protective interpretations of the law have given way to more reluctant and narrow readings of the labor laws—and without good reasons, as we argue here. Finally, we address how employment at will may narrow worker protection in the United States.

THE PROTECTIVE PRINCIPLE IN LATIN AMERICA

This section describes the protective principle in Latin America. First, it anchors the protective principle in ILO documents and other international human rights texts that have influenced labor law in Latin America. Grounding worker protection in international bodies and treaties is what makes worker protection a universal idea

6 For example, German labor law is generally understood to favor the worker in hard cases, coming very close to applying something like *in dubio pro operario*. Roger Blanpain et al., The Global Workplace: International and Comparative Employment Law Cases and Materials 563 (2nd ed. 2012). Moreover, the German "principle of favorability" is used by German courts to determine which contractual terms operate, those in a collective agreement or those in an individual employment contract, when they are in conflict. According to the German rule, the judge must choose the term most favorable to the worker when there are conflicting terms. Manfred Weiss & Marlene Schmidt, Labour Law and Industrial Relations in Germany 187 at § 446 (4th ed. 2008).

that should also be informing all other countries, including the United States. The chapter then describes the protective principle and some examples of its application in the four cases developed throughout the book, Argentina, Brazil, Chile, and Uruguay.

The International Aspects of Worker Protection

Worker protection as a universal idea has important origins in the ILO. The ILO, after a postwar consensus in 1919, managed to issue a series of international agreements with rules regarding child and nocturnal labor, working time, and security measures, among others.[7] The ILO further reinforced the idea of worker protection in the Declaration of Philadelphia of 1944, which states that "labor is not a commodity."[8] Worker protection is also expressly recognized in international human rights texts that have been central in Latin America, especially given the region's leadership in their making.[9] The Universal Declaration of Human Rights of 1948, for example, expressly states social and economic rights protecting workers.[10] In addition to the Universal Declaration of Human Rights, other important human rights instruments with labor rights that influence Latin American countries include the International Covenant on Civil and Political Rights,[11] the International Covenant on Economic,

---

7 The preamble to the ILO constitution states:

> Whereas universal and lasting peace can be established only if it is based upon social justice;
>
> And whereas conditions of labour exist involving such injustice, hardship and privation to large numbers of people as to produce unrest so great that the peace and harmony of the world are imperilled; and an improvement of those conditions is urgently required; as, for example, by the regulation of the hours of work, including the establishment of a maximum working day and week, the regulation of the labour supply, the prevention of unemployment, the provision of an adequate living wage, the protection of the worker against sickness, disease and injury arising out of his employment, the protection of children, young persons and women, provision for old age and injury, protection of the interests of workers when employed in countries other than their own, recognition of the principle of equal remuneration for work of equal value, recognition of the principle of freedom of association, the organization of vocational and technical education and other measures;
>
> Whereas also the failure of any nation to adopt humane conditions of labour is an obstacle in the way of other nations which desire to improve the conditions in their own countries;
>
> The High Contracting Parties, moved by sentiments of justice and humanity as well as by the desire to secure the permanent peace of the world, and with a view to attaining the objectives set forth in this Preamble, agree to the following Constitution of the International Labour Organization . . .

I.L.O. CONST., Preamble.

8 Declaration Concerning the Aims and Purposes of the International Labor Organization (Declaration of Philadelphia), art. 1, para. (a), May 10, 1944, 15 U.N.T.S. 35 (*adopted* Oct. 9, 1946).

9 *See* KATHRYN SIKKINK, EVIDENCE FOR HOPE: MAKING HUMAN RIGHTS WORK IN THE 21ST CENTURY (2017) (describing Latin American contributions to international human rights).

10 G.A. Res. 217A (III), arts. 4, 23–25, Universal Declaration of Human Rights (*adopted* Dec. 10, 1948).

11 International Covenant on Civil and Political Rights (Dec. 16, 1966, *entered into force* Mar. 23, 1976), 999 U.N.T.S. 171.

Social and Cultural Rights,[12] the American Convention on Human Rights ("Pact of San Jose, Costa Rica"),[13] and the European Convention for the Protection of Human Rights and Fundamental Freedoms.[14]

The Protective Principle in Argentina, Brazil, Chile, and Uruguay

Latin American jurists have developed the protective principle, present in the ILO and international human rights texts. For example, take the issue of employee status for contractors—a hot issue of the day given the advent of so-called "gig" work,[15] fissured workplaces,[16] the end of the standard employment contract,[17] and whatnot. Ten years ago, the Court of Appeals of Montevideo, in the small South American country of Uruguay, had to decide whether or not a lead firm could be held liable for the wages of the employees of one of its janitorial contractors. Labor legislation said nothing about lead firm liability. Moreover, under traditional civil law, the lead firm would not be responsible. There was no contract between the lead firm and the workers of its contractors. And yet, the court decided that the lead firm was responsible for the workers' wages. The Uruguayan court based its holding on "principle." It made the lead firm liable as a so-called "complex employer"—a judge-made legal category that resembles the "joint employer"[18] in U.S jurisprudence—in light of the country's constitutional protection of work and the principles that "inform" labor law.[19] As the court stated:

> If we pretend to ignore the legal category of the complex employer merely because there is no rule establishing such legal category, we would introduce an extreme and outmoded positivist paradigm into our court and would show a want of protective constitutional foundation . . . which served as the

[12] International Covenant on Economic, Social and Cultural Rights (Dec. 16, 1966, *entered into force* Jan. 3, 1976), 993 U.N.T.S. 171.

[13] American Convention on Human Rights (Nov. 22, 1969, *entered into force* July 18, 1978), 1144 U.N.T.S. 123.

[14] European Convention for the Protection of Human Rights and Fundamental Freedoms, 213 U.N.T.S. 221 (*entered into force* Sept. 3, 1953, *opened for signature* Nov. 4, 1950).

[15] *See, e.g.*, Jeremias Prassl, Humans as a Service: The Promise and Perils of the Gig Economy (2018).

[16] David Weil, The Fissured Workplace: Why Work Became So Bad for So Many and What Can Be Done to Improve It 189–90 (2014).

[17] *See, e.g.*, Rethinking Workplace Regulation: Beyond the Standard Contract of Employment (Katherine Stone & Harry Arthurs eds., 2013).

[18] For U.S. joint employer doctrine, *see* chapter 3.

[19] Tribunal Apelaciones Trabajo 1ro. [Court of Appeals] Case No. 171 (2008) (Uru.), cited in 233 Der. Laboral: Rev. de doctrina, jurisprudencia e informaciones sociales 120 (2009).

> foundation of Labor Law doctrine and jurisprudence. This is for two reasons. First, principles inform the entire legal system. . . . Second, because the mandate of article 53 of the constitution is directed not only at the legislator but also at [the judge].[20]

The Uruguayan Court of Appeals thereby established that it did not need an express rule forcing responsibility onto lead firms. The constitution's basic guarantees for the protection of work and the general principles of labor law sufficed to make the lead firm liable.

The importance that the Uruguayan court gave to labor protection was remarkable given the inchoate constitutional text from which it partly drew the protective principle; it reads more like a U.S. "right to work" idea than a labor-protective clause. As it states:

> Work is under the special protection of the law. Every inhabitant of the Republic, without prejudice to their freedom, has a duty to apply their intellectual or physical energy in a way that benefits the community, which will seek to offer, giving preference to citizens, the ability to earn a livelihood through the development of an economic activity. [21]

Yet, this seemingly right-to-work clause in the Uruguayan constitution grants the court authority—in fact, a duty—to protect the worker in cases before it, and apply labor principles as legally binding law.

---

[20] *Id.* (translation by authors). The full Spanish original reference says:

> *[P]retender desconocer la figura del empleador complejo bajo el expediente de la inexistencia de norma alguna que lo consagre, importa, una postura positivista a ultranza paradigma de tiempos perimidos y el desconocimiento de las bases constitucionales protectoras que han dado origen y desarrollo a la disciplina del Derecho del Trabajo y a la labor creativa con el mismo designio, de la doctrina y de la jurisprudencia. Ello por dos razones. La primera, porque los principios cumplen un papel informador de todo el ordenamiento jurídico, en tanto expresan los postulados, valores y principios éticos arraigados en la conciencia social cuya vigencia el juez puede constatar mediante mecanismos técnicos que evitan el puro subjetivismo o la arbitrariedad de la decisión. La segunda, porque el mandato constitucional protector del trabajo –arts. 53 y sgtes.- no solo va dirigido al legislador, sino también a los operadores jurídicos. Entre ellos, sin duda al juez en la labor de solución de conflictos a través de la aplicación de las reglas del universo jurídico.*

Id. (internal citations omitted).

[21] Constitución de la República [Constitution of the Republic] (Uru.), art. 53 (translation by authors). The Spanish original text states:

> *El trabajo está bajo la protección especial de la ley. Todo habitante de la República, sin perjuicio de su libertad, tiene el deber de aplicar sus energías intelectuales o corporales en la forma que redunde en beneficio de la colectividad, la que procurará ofrecer con preferencia a los ciudadanos, la posibilidad de ganar su sustento mediante desarrollo de una actividad económica.*

Uruguayan scholars have noted that labor rights in Uruguay are also generally anchored in international human rights norms, perhaps explaining where broad readings of labor protection come from.[22] A widely cited Uruguayan scholar, Óscar Ermida, for example, argued that some labor law principles are common in all human rights protection systems such as, for example, the notion that law must rule in the most favorable way to the person.[23] In fact, this influential scholar argued that labor law was, as a whole, is an instrument to implement human rights.[24]

But small, social democratic Uruguay[25] is not unique in its worker-protective jurisprudence. Big, corporatist Argentina and Brazil[26] also recognize the protective principle. As in Uruguay, Argentina's protective principle stems from the constitution, which provides that work shall be protected.[27] But differently from Uruguay, Argentina's constitution has a very detailed set of social and labor rights.[28] Moreover, Argentina's employment law explicitly states that the protective principle is an inherent part of the country's highest law.[29] Moreover, Argentina recognizes that labor

---

[22] Héctor-Hugo Barbagelata, El Particularismo Del Derecho Del Trabajo Y Los Derechos Humanos Laborales 293 (2nd ed. 2009) (pointing out that since 1948 there has been a transcendental normative change in legal principles, with the enactment of the Universal Declaration of Human Rights, ILO Convention 87, and the various Covenants).

[23] Ermida Uriarte, *Protección, supra* note 2, at 22.

[24] *Id.* at 23.

[25] Davide Grassi, *Democracy and Social Welfare in Uruguay and Paraguay*, 56 Latin Am. Pol. & Soc'y 120, 126 (2014) (detailing the history of left-leaning political parties and welfare state construction in Uruguay).

[26] *See* Maria Lorena Cook, The Politics of Labor Reform in Latin America: Between Flexibility and Rights (2007).

[27] Constitución Nacional [Const. Nac.] (Arg.), art. 14 bis.

[28] The list of enumerated rights in the Argentinian constitution is so extensive that it is better to look at its text. It states:

> Labor in its several forms shall be protected by law, which shall ensure to workers: dignified and equitable working conditions; limited working hours; paid rest and vacations; fair remuneration; minimum vital and adjustable wage; equal pay for equal work; participation in the profits of enterprises, with control of production and collaboration in the management; protection against arbitrary dismissal; stability of the civil servant; free and democratic labor union organizations recognized by the mere registration in a special record.
>
> Trade unions are hereby guaranteed: the right to enter into collective bargaining agreements; to resort to conciliation and arbitration; the right to strike. Union representatives shall have the guarantees necessary for carrying out their union tasks and those related to the stability of their employment.
>
> The State shall grant the benefits of social security, which shall be of an integral nature and may not be waived. In particular, the laws shall establish: compulsory social insurance, which shall be in charge of national or provincial entities with financial and economic autonomy, administered by the interested parties with State participation, with no overlapping of contributions; adjustable retirements and pensions; full family protection; protection of homestead; family allowances and access to a worthy housing.

Id. (translation by authors).

[29] International Labor and Employment Laws 76–4 (William L. Keller et al. eds., 2008), *citing* Ley de Contrato de Trabajo [Ley de C.T.] (Arg.), Law No. (Arg.) 20.744, as amended.

law principles are grounded on an international human rights system. The Supreme Court of Argentina has recognized that the worker enjoys special protections as set forth in the Inter-American Charter of Social Guarantees, which protects workers "of all kinds" and serves for the proper interpretation and development of the standards of the American Declaration of the Rights and Duties of Man.[30]

In Brazil, courts and jurists have distilled the protective principle from the long list of social rights in its constitution.[31] Additionally, Brazil also recognizes that the principles of labor law also emanate from the Universal Declaration of Human Rights, the ILO, and other international instruments.[32]

---

[30] César Arese, Derechos Humanos Laborales. Teoría y Práctica De Un Nuevo Derecho Del Trabajo 37 (2014).

[31] The Brazilian constitution enumerates a number of rights. These are:

- protections against arbitrary dismissal without just cause;
- unemployment insurance;
- minimum wage;
- worker participation in company profits;
- a regular working day not exceeding eight hours and forty-four hours weekly;
- paid weekly rest, preferably on Sundays;
- overtime pay of at least 50 percent of normal pay;
- paid vacations;
- paid maternity leave;
- paternity leave;
- prohibitions against discrimination at work;
- the prohibition of night, hazardous, or unhealthy work for children under eighteen and any work to under fourteen, except as an apprentice.

Constituição Federal [C.F.] [Constitution], art. 7 (Braz.).

We should note, however, that in 2017, the government of Michel Temer relaxed certain rules, including those related to hours, part-time contracting, rest periods, telework, holidays, maternity rights, intermittent work, salaries, contract terms, and collective bargaining. *See* Consolidação das Leis do Trabalho [C.L.T] [Consolidated Labor Laws], Lei No. 13.467 (Brazil). *See also* Jean Marcel Mariano de Oliveira, Direito Constitucional do Trabalho e a Reforma Trabalhista de 2017 (2018). Article 8 of the Consolidation of Labor Laws was also amended so that the "common law" could be a subsidiary source of labor law. Law No. 13.467 of July 13, 2017 (Bra.). The reforms also state that the courts cannot restrict legally envisaged rights or create obligations that are not contemplated in the law. *Id.* Notwithstanding this change, doctrine has emphasized that the principles of labor law, including the principle of protection (Title II to IV), cannot be undermined by the legislature. *See* Gicelli Paixão, Comentários à Reforma Trabalhista 13 (2018). In addition, it has been pointed out that this reform ignores Brazil's constitutional protection of work in Article 7 of its Constitution and ILO Convention 98. Ozéias J. Santos, Reforma Trabalhista Ponto a Ponto: Prática trabalhista 14–22 (2018). Others have argued that the recent reforms are flatly unconstitutional. *Id.* at 192 (internal citations omitted). In other words, these reforms' constitutionality, effectiveness, and permanence await resolution.

[32] Francisco Meton Marques de Lima, Os Princípios De Direito Do Trabalho Na Lei E Na Jurisprudencia 45 (4th ed. 2015).

But even "neoliberal" Chile[33] recognizes the principle of protection. As in Uruguay, the constitutional hook for labor protection branches out from a cryptic, right-to-work-sounding constitutional provision that simply states, "Freedom to work and its protection. Everyone has the right to self-employment and free choice of employment with just remuneration."[34] Interpreting those parsimonious words, the Chilean Constitutional Court noted that:

> Indeed, the constitutional protection . . . is not limited to guarantee[ing] freedom of choice and hiring, but . . . [is a] protection of work itself, in response to the inalienable commitment to respect the worker in the manner in which he or she performs his or her labor and the inescapable social role that work provides.[35]

In reaching this decision the Constitutional Court also referenced human rights instruments signed by Chile.[36] It noted that these international instruments complement Chilean constitutional protections of work.[37] Chilean legal scholars have supported this broad construction of the constitution's labor protections.[38]

In all, these four countries of the region—big and small, corporatist, social democratic, and neoliberal—similarly recognize the importance of protecting workers as a matter of legal principle.

---

[33] *See, e.g.*, VICTIMS OF THE CHILEAN MIRACLE: WORKERS AND NEOLIBERALISM IN THE PINOCHET ERA, 1973–2002 (Peter Winn ed., 2004).

[34] CONSTITUCIÓN [CONSTITUTION] POLÍTICA DE LA REPÚBLICA DE CHILE [C.P.], art. 16 ¶¶ 1–2.

[35] Tribunal Constitucional [T.C.] [Constitutional Court], 26 julio 2011, Rol de la causa: 1852-10 (Chile), *citing* Luz Bulnes, *La libertad de trabajo y su protección en la Constitución de 1980*, 28 REVISTA DE DERECHO PÚBLICO U. CHILE 207, 215 (1980); and JOSÉ LUIS CEA, DERECHO CONSTITUCIONAL CHILENO, TOMO II 427 (2004).

[36] Tribunal Constitucional [T.C.] [Constitutional Court], 26 julio 2011, Rol de la causa: 1852-10 (Chile). Note, however that even though Chile has signed the Additional Protocol to the American Convention on Human Rights, it has not ratified it.

[37] The Constitutional Court, also art. 24 of the Universal Declaration of Human Rights, art. 7 of International Covenant of Economic, Social and Cultural Rights, and art. Additional Protocol to the American Convention on Human Rights. *Id.*

[38] Luz Bulnes, *La libertad de trabajo y su protección en la Constitución de 1980*, 28 REVISTA DE DERECHO PÚBLICO U. CHILE 207, at 209–10 (1980); HUMBERTO NOGUEIRA ALCALÁ ET AL., DERECHO CONSTITUCIONAL TOMO I 281 (1994); GUIDO MACCHIAVELLO CONTRERAS, DERECHO DEL TRABAJO 36 (1986); ALEJANDRO SILVA BASCUÑÁN & MARÍA PÍA SILVA GALLINATO, TRATADO DE DERECHO CONSTITUCIONAL TOMO 13, 222 (Tomo 13 2010); ALAN BRONFMAN VARGAS ET AL., CONSTITUCIÓN POLÍTICA COMENTADA 336 (2012); and PEDRO IRURETA URIARTE, CONSTITUCIÓN Y ORDEN PÚBLICO LABORAL: UN ANÁLISIS DEL ART. 19 NO. 16 DE LA CONSTITUCIÓN CHILENA 52–57 (2006); SERGIO GAMONAL C., INTRODUCCIÓN AL DERECHO DEL TRABAJO 53 (1998) [hereinafter Gamonal C., INTRODUCCIÓN AL DERECHO].

When in Doubt, Rule in Favor of the Weaker Party: The Rule of In Dubio Pro Operario

While questions of employer status today surface given the fissured workplace, questions of employee status also rage from the advent of nonstandard employment contracts. But employee status questions are also not new. Argentina, for example, reckoned with this issue many years ago when physicians demanded employment protections. The Argentinean appellate court held that these physicians were protected workers despite their professional occupation.[39] According to the court, excluding physicians would have violated the protective principle and *in dubio pro operario*.[40]

In dubio pro operario is nothing but the crystallization of the protective principle into a legal rule. It mandates that, in the hard case, the judge or other adjudicator must decide the case in favor of the worker.[41] What are considered hard cases? When the law is ambiguous or vague or when there is a gap in the rules.[42] Importantly, the *in dubio pro operario* rule is mainly used to interpret the law, not assess the facts.[43] Moreover, the function of the rule *in dubio pro operario* is not to modify or amend another rule, but rather to determine its best meaning among several possibilities. We should also note that judges seldom use *in pro operario* as the decisive criterion; it is normally a supporting argument.[44]

---

[39] María del Carmen Piña, La Condición Laboral y el Principio Protectorio 201–02 (2007) *citing* Cámara Nacional de Apelaciones del Trabajo, Sala 1 [National Chamber for Labor Appeals, Room 1], Feb. 28, 1989 (Arg).

[40] *Id.*

[41] Contrary to stylized view that in civil code countries judges do not make law or interpret law, but only "apply" the law, in South American law there is a general "principle of no excuse" (*principio de inexcusabilidad*)." Mario Verdugo Marinkovic et al., Derecho Constitucional 209–10 (1999). The principle of no excuse essentially means that the judge, if competent, must decide a case or controversy even when there is no specific rule resolving the dispute. *Id.* The only exception occurs in penal law, in which the law must establish the criminal conduct to be sanctioned. Bronfman Vargas et al. *supra* note 38, at 116.

[42] Enrique Barros, *Reglas y Principios en el Derecho*, 2 Anuario de Filosofía Jurídica y Social 276 (1984). The application of the rule of *in dubio pro operario* is debatable in the ambit of collective bargaining because some scholars have argued there is no significant imbalance of bargaining power between labor and capital in collective labor relations. Plá Rodríguez, *supra* note 3, at 96–97. Labor unions bargain with employers at a relatively more equal level than that of the individual employee. *Id.* Therefore, most scholars have argued that civil contract interpretation rules are adequate in the collective bargaining context. *Id. But see* Sergio Gamonal C., Derecho Colectivo del Trabajo 448 (2nd ed. 2011) (because collective bargaining agreements have *ergo omnes* effects and may apply to all workers, including nonmembers of the union, the rule of *in dubio pro operario* should apply when there is an interpretative question of the collective agreement).

[43] The main exception to this view of the rule is Argentina. Article 9 of the Employment Contract Law, which provides that the legal interpretation most favorable to the worker must be preferred when in doubt of the facts in concrete cases. Diego Tosca, *Aplicación del Principio 'Pro Operario' en la Valoración de la Prueba en caso de Duda, in* La Relación de Trabajo 210–11 (Mario E. Ackerman & Alejandro Sudera eds., 2009).

[44] Aurelio Desdentado Bonete, *El Principio Pro Operario, in* Los Principios Del Derecho Del Trabajo 73 (Luis Enrique de la Villa Gil & Lourdes López eds., 2003).

In all, *in dubio pro operario* gives the protective principle clear legal weight, calling for labor courts and other adjudicative authorities to take a labor-protective role. Doubt is resolved in favor of the worker. Although not entirely exclusive to Latin America, its clear diffusion and adherence in the region is perhaps what most differentiates Latin American labor law from that of the rest of the world.

However, as we explain below, labor protection exists even in one of the most liberal market economies of the world, the United States. Something like *in dubio pro operario* has been voiced by U.S. courts, at least historically, and certainly unevenly, but latent labor protection does exist and can be revived and even strengthened.

PROTECTION IN THE UNITED STATES: AN EXERCISE IN LEGAL ARCHAEOLOGY

The history and state of labor protection in the United States is complex. Here we focus on the Thirteenth Amendment to the U.S. Constitution and the two hallmark labor law statutes enacted during the New Deal: the NLRA and the FLSA.[45] While our detail of U.S. labor law is incomplete, our partial description shows clear contrast between the labor-protective words in the legal texts—including their stated purposes—some of their early jurisprudence, and the much less labor-protective jurisprudence coming out today from U.S. courts. Thus, we need to underscore the importance of labor law principles to bring back labor protection.

The Protective Principle in the Thirteenth Amendment of the U.S. Constitution

> *"Neither slavery nor involuntary servitude, except as a punishment for crime whereof the party shall have been duly convicted, shall exist within the United States, or any place subject to their jurisdiction. Congress shall have power to enforce this article by appropriate legislation."*[46]

The Thirteenth Amendment provides a basis for worker-protective legislation through the ban of involuntary servitude.[47] It gives Congress the duty to enact

---

[45] There are other U.S. federal labor laws that protect the worker. *See* Employee Polygraph Protection Act of 1988, 29 U.S.C. §§ 2001–09 (2012) (prohibiting employer use of lie detectors); Genetic Information Nondiscrimination Act, 42 U.S.C. §§ 2000ff–2000ff-11 (2012) (prohibiting employers from using genetic tests to discriminate against employers); Family and Medical Leave Act of 1993, 29 U.S.C. §§ 2601–54 (2012) (protecting workers who need to take a leave of absence due to illness, to take care of family member, or when having or adopting a child); Employee Retirement Income Security Act of 1974, 29 U.S.C. §§ 1001–61 (2012) (protecting workers who participate in employee-provided retirement plans).

[46] U.S. Const., amend. XIII.

[47] *See* James Gray Pope, *Labor's Constitution of Freedom*, 106 Yale L.J. 941, 943 (1997); Pope, *Contract, Race, and Freedom of Labor in the Constitutional Law of "Involuntary Servitude,"* 119 Yale L.J. 1474, 1541; María L.

legislation to give effect to that constitutional ban. As Professor Rebecca Zietlow explains, the ban on involuntary servitude aims not only to eliminate chattel slavery but protects workers broadly and gives Congress authority to legislate to enforce those rights.[48] At the time of the Thirteenth Amendment's enactment, during Reconstruction, Zietlow explains that free labor was the exception to the rule.[49] While black slaves were the least free of all workers given that their masters owned them, indentured servants, apprentices tied to their masters, and other forms of bonded work were the norm.[50] After the Civil War, prior slaves and many workers, especially those who fought for the union in the war, struggled against various forms of state-enforced property claims that employers held over their labor.[51] Many joined the nascent labor movement. The Thirteenth Amendment became one of their battle cries.[52] As Professor William Forbath also explained:

> Not liberty of contract alone, but also the legacy of the antislavery movement and the Thirteenth Amendment lent constitutional heft to labor's blows against its court-forged manacles. According to this legacy, the dignity and independence of free labor were inscribed in the Constitution. It smacked of slavery, trade unionists complained, or of feudalism, at best, when courts routinely held that employers had a property right in their workers' returning each day to toil in the employers' plants, or a property right in their workers' non-union status, or a property right in their authority to run the plant without contending with workers seeking to negotiate over union work rules.[53]

Hence, since Reconstruction, ordinary workers and segments of the labor movement attempted to secure an amalgam of rights under the Thirteenth Amendment, including the right to change employers, the right to set wages, the right to refrain from work, the right to practice one's trade, the right to receive fair wages, and the right to strike, all giving credence to claim that the ban against involuntary servitude

---

Ontiveros, *Noncitizen Immigrant Labor and the Thirteenth Amendment: Challenging Guest Worker Programs*, 38 U. Tol. L. Rev. 923, 924–25 (2007); Lea S. VanderVelde, *The Labor Vision of the Thirteenth Amendment*, 138 U. Pa. L. Rev. 437, 441–45 (1989).

[48] Rebecca E. Zietlow, *The Ideological Origins of the Thirteenth Amendment*, 49 Hous. L. Rev. 393, 448 (2012) (*citing Jones v. Alfred H. Mayer Co.*, 392 U.S. 409, 439 (1968)).

[49] Rebecca E. Zietlow, The Forgotten Emancipator: James Mitchell Ashley and the Ideological Origins of Reconstruction 44–45 (2017)

[50] *Id.* at 46.

[51] *Id.* at 63.

[52] William E. Forbath, *The New Deal Constitution in Exile*, 51 Duke L.J. 165, 186 (2001) (internal citations omitted).

[53] *Id.*

provided broad labor protections to workers; the Thirteenth Amendment was meaningful beyond chattel slavery.[54]

Sometimes, workers won in court when they used the Thirteenth Amendment. They found constitutional protection of the right to quit work under the Thirteenth Amendment.[55] The constitutionality of Section 1982 of the Civil Rights Act of 1866,[56] which forbids race discrimination in inheritance, purchase, lease, sale, holding, and conveyance of personal and real property, also found an anchor in the Thirteenth Amendment.[57]

Free Labor in U.S. Reconstruction and Contemporary Latin America

The Thirteenth Amendment broadly corresponds to the Latin American principle of protection, whereby the law needs to protect weaker parties who would otherwise be forced into work, or to accept terms and conditions of employment that they truly object to. For example, in a 1944 case, *Pollock v. Williams*, the U.S. Supreme Court recognized that there might be structural conditions that make it impossible for workers to affect their conditions at work, turning their work into unfree labor that requires special, legal protections.[58] As the Court stated:

> [T]he defense against oppressive hours, pay, working conditions, or treatment is the right to change employers. When the master can compel and the laborer cannot escape the obligation to go on, there is no power below to redress and no incentive above to relieve a harsh overlordship or unwholesome conditions of work. Resulting depression of working conditions and living standards affects not only the laborer under the system, but every other with whom his labor comes in competition.[59]

The constitutional ban on involuntary servitude would legitimize labor-protective legislation that attempts to provide workers with the real, effective right to engage with employers on a more voluntary basis, hence why Professor James Pope argues that the constitutional ban on involuntary servitude requires expanding labor rights currently closed to some categories of employees—e.g., domestic and

[54] Pope, *Contract, Race and Freedom of Labor*, *supra* note 47, at 1478, n.4. *See also* WILLIAM FORBATH, LAW AND THE SHAPING OF THE AMERICAN LABOR MOVEMENT 136–39 (1991) (providing a historical account of how labor framed its defense of strikes and other concerted activities under the Thirteenth Amendment).

[55] Clyatt v. United States, 197 U.S. 207 (1905); Bailey v. Alabama, 219 U.S. 219 (1911).

[56] 42 U.S.C. § 1982 (2012).

[57] Pope, *Contract, Race and Freedom of Labor*, *supra* note 47, at 1518–19; ZIETLOW, *supra* note 48, at 451.

[58] Pollock v. Williams, 322 U.S. 4 (1944).

[59] *Id.* at 18.

agricultural workers.[60] The Thirteenth Amendment could serve to reverse the practice of permanent economic strike replacements, as well as other legal norms that exacerbate worker subordination in the United States and violate international labor standards.[61]

Given the Latin American sensibility toward unequal relationships at work, a Latin American jurist would likely agree with the view that a constitutional protection against involuntary servitude provides a basis to constitutionally legitimize labor-protective legislation. As we read above, unregulated work is understood in Latin America as a condition that easily lends itself to the commodification of labor—to a morally suspect practice of buying and selling labor as a commodity. With such a constitutional basis for ordinary labor laws, interpretation of legal texts would find a much more solid footing in favor of workers. Employer property rights, oftentimes used to limit the scope of labor law, and as more fully explained below, would find their match if labor protections suddenly rose to the same level of constitutional importance.

But such a Reconstruction-era, Labor Republican view of free labor[62] is not the one that reigns today in the United States. By the end of the nineteenth century and the beginning of the twentieth century, many courts began to narrowly interpret the meaning of free labor, constructing a view of it that was individualistic, formalistic, and market-based. As long as employers and workers could formally transact in the market—meaning that employers could hire and fire, and employees would accept or quit work, at will—there was no involuntary servitude. The parties were "free." This view of free labor was especially cemented by the diffusion of employment at will through the various U.S. courts,[63] and by *Lochner v. New York*,[64] where the U.S. Supreme Court struck down a New York law regulating the hours of bakers on the grounds that the law interfered with the constitutional right to contract.

But freedom of contract did not lead to an idyllic market society of free bargainers. Decades of mounting labor strife, a world war, and a depression followed *Lochner*, changing American views on central political questions, including those regarding work. Caught between totalitarian threats—fascism and communism—American New Dealers in the 1930s felt emboldened (or forced) to advocate for labor-protective

---

[60] Pope, *Contract, Race and Freedom of Labor, supra* note 47, at 1541.

[61] *Id.* at 1541. On permanent strike replacements under U.S. labor law, *see* NLRB v. Mackay Radio & Telegraph Co., 304 U.S. 333 (1938) (declaring in *dicta* employers' rights to permanently replace economic strikers, given their right to manage their property).

[62] William E. Forbath, *The Ambiguities of Free Labor: Labor and the Law in the Gilded Age*, 1985 WIS. L. REV. 767, 786–90 (describing the "Free Labor" Republicanism in the United States).

[63] Lea S. VanderVelde, *The At-Will Doctrine in a Laborers' Republic: From Reconstruction's Anti-Subordination to the Gilded Age's Precarity* (unpublished manuscript on file with author).

[64] Lochner v. New York, 198 U.S. 45 (1905).

legislation, among them the NLRA and the FLSA.[65] They constitutionalized the NLRA and the FLSA through the Commerce Clause of the U.S. Constitution given the Lochnerian context.[66] These laws forever changed the employment relationship in the United States, affording rights to workers once thought of as unimaginable. As we will see below, however, a freedom of contract perspective suspicious of labor regulation still pervaded in the legal system, opening spaces for courts to limit the reach of the new laws, and even to rein them in. As a result, we argue that Congress should constitutionalize these and other labor laws through the Thirteenth Amendment to clearly set labor protection as a fundamental constitutional right that can better withstand *Lochner*'s ghost.

The Protective Principle in the NLRA

The Democratic New Dealers' policies aimed against the Great Depression brought laissez-faire to a halt. Promising a new era for the United States, New Dealers got government more involved in economic matters, including work.[67] One of the key pieces of their new agenda was Senator Robert F. Wagner's NLRA. The law, in its Statement of Purpose, called for protecting the right of "employees" to organize and bargain collectively in order to equalize and correct power asymmetries at work.[68] As the law's Statement of Purpose then stated (and still does state):

> Experience has proved that protection by law of the right of employees to organize and bargain collectively safeguards commerce from injury, impairment, or interruption, and promotes the flow of commerce by removing certain recognized sources of industrial strife and unrest, by encouraging practices fundamental to the friendly adjustment of industrial disputes arising out of differences as to wages, hours, or other working conditions, and by restoring equality of bargaining power between employers and employees.[69]

The NLRA thus tries to use state power to protect commerce, safeguard industrial peace, and equalize bargaining relationships. The first two goals were likely included

---

[65] *See* Mark Barenberg, *The Political Economy of the Wagner Act: Power, Symbol, and Workplace Cooperation*, 106 HARV. L. REV. 1379, 1400 and n.9 (1993) (on Senator Wagner's "integrationism" in response to communist alternatives).

[66] *See* IRVING BERNSTEIN, THE TURBULENT YEARS: THE HISTORY OF THE AMERICAN WORKER 1933–1941, at 325 (1969).

[67] *Id.* at 322–23.

[68] 29 U.S.C. § 151 (2012).

[69] *Id.*

by Congress to appease the *Lochner* court,[70] which was concerned about contracting rights.

But even if the NLRA's protections of workers were a means to safeguard the market, the statute has clear labor-protective language. Section 7, the most important clause of the NLRA, states, "[e]mployees shall have the right to self-organization, to form, join, or assist labor organizations, to bargain collectively through representatives of their own choosing, and to engage in other concerted activities for the purpose of collective bargaining or other mutual aid or protection."[71] The NLRA protects workers' rights to engage in collective action for bargaining with the employer and for other reasons related to their "mutual aid and protection." It is not merely a contractual statute.

The law also establishes employer unfair labor practices to protect workers against employers who violate Section 7,[72] dominate labor organizations,[73] discriminate against workers for exercising their Section 7 rights,[74] retaliate against workers who have filed charges or given testimony under the NLRA,[75] or fail to bargain in good faith with a union.[76]

While all but consistent, the U.S. Supreme Court also has held that Section 7 rights provide broad support to employees seeking to act in concert for collective bargaining and for mutual aid and protection. The seminal case of *NLRB v. Washington Aluminum*[77] held that Section 7 of the Act protected a group of employees who walked off the job because the workplace premises were too cold. The Court held that the employer could not summarily dismiss the employees for acting in concert for mutual aid and protection, even if the employees violated company policies when they engaged in such acts.[78] The narrow question before the Court was whether the NLRA protected the employee walkout if the workers had not presented a demand to the employer prior to walking out.[79] According to the employer, the workers' failure to provide a demand made it impossible for the employer to resolve the issue, avoid industrial action, and prevent workers' violation of

---

[70] *See* Jones & Laughlin Steel Corp., 301 U.S. 1, 31 (1937) ("[The NLRA] purports to reach only what may be deemed to burden or obstruct that commerce and, thus qualified, it must be construed as contemplating the exercise of control within constitutional bounds.").

[71] 29 U.S.C. § 157 (2012).

[72] *See id.* at § 158(a)(1).

[73] *See id.* at § 158(a)(2).

[74] *See id.* at § 158(a)(3).

[75] *See id.* at § 158(a)(4).

[76] *See id.* at § 158(a)(5).

[77] 370 U.S. 9 (1962).

[78] *Id.* at 17.

[79] *Id.* at 13–14.

company policies.[80] The employer maintained that the termination was "for cause" under the law and could not be declared an unfair labor practice.[81] The employer argued that the National Labor Relations Board (NLRB) could not order reinstatement, back pay, or other remedies in favor of allegedly aggrieved workers.[82] The Supreme Court disagreed. Basing its decision on Section 7 of the Act, it held that the actions of the employees were protected. The Court reasoned,

> The language of § 7 is broad enough to protect concerted activities whether they take place before, after, or at the same time such a demand is made. To compel the Board to interpret and apply that language in the restricted fashion suggested by the respondent here would only tend to frustrate the policy of the Act to protect the right of workers to act together to better their working conditions. Indeed, as indicated by this very case, such an interpretation of § 7 might place burdens upon employees so great that it would effectively nullify the right to engage in concerted activities, which that section protects. The seven employees here were part of a small group of employees who were wholly unorganized. They had no bargaining representative and, in fact, no representative of any kind to present their grievances to their employer. Under these circumstances, they had to speak for themselves as best they could.[83]

Hence, even though the statute was silent as to whether employees needed to present a demand to the employer prior to engaging in collective action, the Court determined, based on Section 7, that such a demand was not necessary.[84] Any other interpretation of the NLRA would have been likely to render Section 7 rights ineffective by placing obstacles in the way of workers' concerted actions. Here, the Supreme Court resolved a gap in the law in favor of the workers given the protective purposes of the NLRA; a Latin American labor judge would have likely held similarly.

Other concerted activities for mutual aid and protection that may be protected by Section 7 include engaging in political speech at work (as long as it is related

---

[80] *Id.* at 15–16.

[81] *Id.*

[82] *Id.* at 16–17. According to Section 10(c) of the NLRA, "[n]o order of the Board shall require the reinstatement of any individual as an employee who has been suspended or discharged, or the payment to him of any back pay, if such individual was suspended or discharged for cause."

29 U.S.C. § 160(c) (2012).

[83] Wash. Aluminum, 370 U.S. 9, 14 (1962).

[84] *Id.* at 17–18.

to the job),[85] employee postings on social media,[86] and discussing wages with co-workers,[87] among others.

Some American jurists may argue that the NLRA does not provide any substantive worker protections.[88] Rather, they may argue that the NLRA simply lends workers a guarantee that they can organize in the same manner that capital has organized into corporations. The goal of the NLRA, according to this view, is to facilitate formal equality in organizing rights to ease contractual relations, or some sort of formal "freedom of contract" between organized capital and labor. The resilience of this freedom of contract view has some basis in the landmark Supreme Court case *NLRB v. Jones & Laughlin Steel Corp.*,[89] where the Supreme Court found the NLRA constitutional on the grounds that the NLRA simply sought to extend to workers the same rights of organization that employers had.[90] The law did not compel the parties to reach an agreement of any kind. Therefore, neither the NLRB nor the courts could compel any party—a union or an employer—to agree to any term. And as the Supreme Court stated in another case, *H.K. Porter Co. v. NLRB*:[91]

> One of these fundamental policies is freedom of contract. While the parties' freedom of contract is not absolute under the Act, allowing the Board to compel agreement when the parties themselves are unable to agree would violate the fundamental premise on which the Act is based—private bargaining under governmental supervision of the procedure alone, without any official compulsion over the actual terms of the contract.[92]

Here, the Supreme Court is underscoring that parties have to reach *their* agreement. The NLRB can merely supervise the bargaining procedure without compelling any substantive agreement.

---

85 Eastex, Inc. v. NLRB, 437 U.S. 556 (1978).

86 Hispanics United of Buffalo, Inc. and Carlos Ortiz, 359 N.L.R.B. No. 37 (2012).

87 Quicken Loans, Inc. 359 N.L.R.B. No. 141 (2013); Taylor Made Transportation Servs. 358 N.L.R.B. No. 53 (2012): Radisson Plaza Minneapolis, 307 N.L.R.B. 94 (1992).

88 *See* Kenneth Dau-Schmidt et al., Labor Law in the Contemporary Workplace 594 (2nd ed. 2014) ("Collective bargaining statutes reflect a policy determination that favors a privately ordered workplace over one controlled by direct government mandates . . .").

89 301 U.S. 1 (1937).

90 *Id.* at 45 ("The act does not compel agreements between employers and employees. It does not compel any agreement whatever. It does not prevent the employer 'from refusing to make a collective contract and hiring individuals on whatever terms' the employer 'may by unilateral action determine.' ") Moreover, since the Taft-Hartley Act, employers need only to "bargain in good faith" with the union. 29 U.S.C. § 158(d) (2012).

91 397 U.S. 99 (1970).

92 *Id.* at 108 (internal citations omitted).

While we agree that the nature of collective bargaining is to provide for a private ordering of the workplace, an idea that is also central to Latin American labor law under the principle of labor union autonomy,[93] it is also true that such private ordering is collective and is structured and protected by law, a public institution.[94] Employers can agglomerate corporations, partnerships, and other groupings because of laws that legitimize such associations and provide liability limitations and other incentives to its stockowners and managers. Law also facilitates the organization of unions and collective bargaining. It provides legal and hence public support to collective contractual relations and a private ordering of the workplace. Implying that a law that helps workers to get a seat at the bargaining table with employers is merely a "governmental supervision of the procedure alone," i.e., "procedural" and not "substantive," conceals the NLRA's real protections for workers to organize and equilibrate relations with a more powerful actor, the employer.

In fact, even in *H.K. Porter Co.* the Supreme Court recognized the qualified nature of the "freedom of contract" principles inherent in the NLRA.[95] The Court noted that, for example, the NLRA requires under certain conditions that the employer bargain with a specific union,[96] that unions must fairly represent all workers in the bargaining unit,[97] and that employers and unions cannot require bargaining over some terms.[98] As the Court stated:

> [T]he employer is not free to choose any employee representative he wants, and the representative designated by the majority of the employees represents the minority as well. The Act itself prohibits certain contractual terms relating to refusals to deal in the goods of others.... Various practices in enforcing the Act may to some extent limit freedom to contract as the parties' desire.[99]

---

93 *See* Gamonal C., Introducción al Derecho, *supra* note 38, at 60–66.

94 The influential economic historian Karl Polanyi already showed that market societies are embedded in social institutions, including the state, debunking the stylized view that existing market societies were mainly the product of private orderings. For example, modern markets required state law and policies to create money, labor, and land markets—otherwise fictitious markets—required for capitalist development. Karl Polanyi, The Great Transformation: The Political and Economic Origins of Our Time 201–08 (1957).

95 *H. K. Porter*, 387 U.S. at 108, n.6 (internal citations omitted).

96 *See, e.g.*, ILGWU (Bernhard-Altmann Texas Corp.) v. NLRB, 366 U.S. 731, 737–38 (761) (holding that an employer may not bargain with a union claiming to represent a majority of employees without the employer first confirming the union's representativeness).

97 Vaca v. Sipes, 386 U.S. 171, 177 (1967) (exclusive representatives of employees have a duty of fair representation toward all members of the bargaining unit).

98 *See* Fibreboard Paper Products Corp. v. NLRB, 379 U.S. 203, 223 (1964) (categorizing some subjects of bargaining as "mandatory" and some others as "permissive"). *See also* 29 U.S.C. § 158(e) (banning "hot cargoes").

99 *H. K. Porter*, 387 U.S. at 108, n.6 (internal citations omitted).

Yes, there is a collective, private ordering of the workplace, but law, a public institution, shapes that bargaining and sets its limits.

Moreover, and as argued earlier, to the extent labor law facilitates "freedom of contract," it is only because it equalizes bargaining relationships between employers and employees. Otherwise, without this protection, many workers would be treated as commodities; they would be incapable of meaningfully affecting their contractual relationships with employers. In fact, the scholarly authority cited by the Supreme Court in *H.K. Porter* to defend its view of freedom of contract, former Yale Law School professor Harry F. Wellington, mentioned "freedom of contract" but only as a shortened form of the term "*collective* freedom of contract"—a legislative goal inherent in the NLRA. As stated by Professor Wellington: "Among the many competing goals of national labor policy, two have been frequently proclaimed and staunchly defended, almost but never quite to the death, by the Supreme Court of the United States. One is industrial peace; the other is freedom of contract—*collective contract, to be sure*."[100] Thus, the NLRA has a goal to facilitate publicly guarded, *collective* contractual relations by protecting workers to organize and bargain with the employer.[101] These are substantive legal protections.

Moreover, as explained above, the NLRA is not just about collective bargaining. Section 7, as clearly explained in *Washington Aluminum*, also protects workers who lack union representation, have made no prior demands to the employer, and wish to protect themselves from abuse at the workplace.[102] Additionally, the NLRA can be constitutionalized through the Thirteenth Amendment and thereby firmly construed as legislative action to protect labor from involuntary servitude.

Others may argue that while the words of the NLRA and some outstanding cases such as *Washington Aluminum* provide worker protections, American courts have domesticated the NLRA. Professor James Atleson, for example, argued that hidden "values and assumptions" of American decisional labor law stemming from the class biases of judges and the status assumptions that society makes of workers helped to erode the NLRA.[103] These corrosive values and assumptions for labor law have been that employers have a right to maintain production, employees will act irresponsibly if not controlled, employees can only be minor partners in managing an enterprise,

---

[100] Harry H. Wellington, *Freedom of Contract and the Collective Bargaining Agreement*, 112 U. Pa. L. Rev. 467 (1964) (emphasis added) (internal citations omitted).

[101] We should note that the common law understands some circumstances where parties have differing degrees of bargaining power, rendering contracts unenforceable, such as in the doctrine of unconscionable contracts. Joseph M. Perillo, Calamari & Perillo on Contracts § 9.38 (6th ed. 2009). However, labor law does not aim at rendering employment contracts unenforceable, but as we have been arguing here, at protecting workers so that more legitimate contracts can be formed in the employment relationship.

[102] Washington Aluminum, 370 U.S., at 15–18.

[103] Jim Atleson, Values and Assumptions of American Labor Law 5 (1983).

employers own the workplace, and employee participation interferes with the inherent and exclusive managerial rights of employers.[104] According to Atleson, these values and assumptions run in the common law where collective action by workers has been esteemed illegitimate and illegal and where the law only justifies individual action rather than collective self-help.[105] These values have been central in eviscerating the right to organize and to strike in the United States through the doctrine of permanent strike replacements, among others.[106]

Similar to Atleson, Professor Karl Klare argued that the courts and other institutional actors that domesticated the statute hindered a "radical" interpretation of the Wagner Act.[107] According to Klare, the NLRA had six vaguely stated but nevertheless cognizable goals: industrial peace, collective bargaining, equalization of bargaining power, free choice of workers to join a union, rationalization of the market to stop underconsumption, and industrial democracy.[108] Of these goals, the more radical ones were rationalization of the market (which included wealth redistribution), equalizing bargaining power, and industrial democracy.[109] However, the courts increasingly ignored these more radical goals.[110] They eventually recognized much more tamed goals in the NLRA, to wit, "industrial peace, collective bargaining as therapy, a safely cabined worker free choice, and some rearrangement of relative bargaining power."[111] While the Wagner Act had a radical promise, courts went the other way.

As we indicated from our discussions above, we agree with Atleson, Klare, and others that U.S. labor law has been judicially narrowed, hence why worker protection must be further legitimated—constitutionalized—through the Thirteenth Amendment. Judges should find themselves hard-pressed to confirm any immanent

---

[104] *Id.* at 8–9.

[105] *Id.* at 5–9; *see also* Karl Klare, *Judicial Deradicalization of the Wagner Act and the Origins of Modern Legal Consciousness, 1937–1941*, 62 MINN. L. REV. 265; ELLEN DANNIN, TAKING BACK THE WORKERS' LAW, HOW TO FIGHT THE ASSAULT ON LABOR RIGHTS 58–59 (2006).

[106] Pope, *Contract, Race and Freedom of Labor*, *supra* note 47, at 1541. Employers can permanently replace economic strikers. The employer strategy normally goes this way: During contract negotiations, the employer bargains to impasse. The employer then unilaterally implements terms and conditions of employment, legal once impasse occurs. Once the parties are at an impasse, the union may then call a strike to support its bargaining position. In response, the employer permanently replaces the striking workers, which is legal under the law. Finally, the employer may file for a decertification election with the NLRB where the permanent strike replacements can vote. *See* JULIUS GETMAN, THE BETRAYAL OF LOCAL 14: PAPERWORKERS, POLITICS, AND PERMANENT REPLACEMENTS, 31–40, 192–200 (1998). The practice has proven devastating for unions. *See id.* at 224–28. *See also* DAU-SCHMIDT ET AL., *supra* note 88, at 750–53.

[107] *See* Klare, *supra* note 105.

[108] *Id.* at 281–84.

[109] *Id.* at 293.

[110] *Id.*

[111] *Id.* at 292–93.

employer right to permanently replace strikers, for example, given a constitutional protection of workers to quit work and not accept any terms demanded by employers.[112] With such legal foundations, judges would interpret the right to strike as part and parcel of Congress's authority to enforce the constitutional ban on involuntary servitude. Under the language of the statute, the policies on which it is based, and the constitutional ban against involuntary servitude, the Latin American jurist would be similarly hard-pressed to limit workers' freedom willy-nilly to protect employer property interests.

We must also clarify that even if the NLRA has been judicially domesticated, and even without the Thirteenth Amendment, it does not follow that the protective principle is absent from the law. For example, under the current NLRA, workers can act in concert in protest of workplace hazards thanks to the NLRA protective principle. Workers can also proselytize at work in nonworking areas of the employer and during their own time, as long as the issues are related in some fashion to their terms and conditions of employment.[113] And so on, and so forth. To the extent courts have narrowed U.S. labor law protections, they could broaden them in future cases if persuaded that the law lends itself to protective interpretations favorable to weaker parties.

There is also the argument that the NLRA has been significantly amended by the legislature to favor employers, particularly through the Taft-Hartley Act of 1947. Taft-Hartley was decried by organized labor at the time as the "slave labor bill."[114] Its most controversial provisions, or at least the ones most resisted by unions, included the creation of labor union unfair labor practices,[115] which encompass, most importantly, banning secondary strikes and boycotts,[116] protecting employer speech during union elections,[117] excluding certain employees from labor

---

[112] 29 U.S.C. § 163 (2012).

[113] Eastex, Inc. v. NLRB, 437 U.S. 556 (1978).

[114] Risa L. Goluboff, *The Thirteenth Amendment and the Lost Origins of Civil Rights*, 50 DUKE L.J. 1609, n.263 (2001) (internal citations omitted).

[115] 29 U.S.C. § 158(b) (2012).

[116] 29 U.S.C. § 158(b)(4) (2012).

[117] *Id.* at § 158(c). For a review of pro-labor critiques of the employer speech rights clause, *see* Craig Becker, *Democracy in the Workplace: Union Representation Elections and Federal Labor Law*, 77 MINN. L. REV. 495, 516–23 (1993) (employers and workers are locked in unequal bargaining relationships, and the union election model of the NLRA has fostered the wrong impression that unions and employers square off as equals in election campaigns, just as political parties in government elections); James J. Brudney, *Neutrality Agreements and Card Check Recognition: Prospects for Changing Paradigms*, 90 IOWA L. REV. 819, 832 (2005) ("When an employer delivers a series of forceful messages that unionization is looked upon with extreme disfavor, the impact upon employees is likely to reflect their perceptions about the speaker's basic power over their work lives rather than the persuasive content of the words themselves. Captive audience speeches, oblique or direct threats to act against union supporters, and intense personal campaigning by supervisors are among the lawful or borderline lawful techniques that have proven especially effective in diminishing union

law protections,[118] allowing states to enact legislation to permit employee free riding (so-called "right to work laws"),[119] and amending Section 7 so that workers' negative rights of association (to not join a union) would be enforced,[120] among others.[121]

Moreover, the Taft-Hartley Act also excluded independent contractors from NLRA coverage. Congress excluded independent contractors from NLRA protections after it esteemed that in *NLRB v. Hearst Publications, Inc.* the NLRB (with U.S. Supreme Court support) overreached by determining that newspaper boys who bought newspapers and sold them for a profit were employees covered by the Act.[122] In reaching its decision backing the NLRB, the U.S. Supreme Court sanctioned the NLRB's test of employment based on so-called "economic fact"[123]—today recognized as the "economic realities test."[124] The Court sanctioned the test because the NLRA did not define "employees" (except by circular description).[125] The law states: "The term 'employee' shall include any employee, and shall not be limited to the employees of a particular employer."[126] Given the need to better define the term "employee," and given the general purposes of the NLRA to protect workers, the Supreme Court recognized that NLRB's focus on worker dependence on the employer was a reasonable and thus legitimate interpretation of the NLRA.[127] As the Supreme Court stated:

> In this light, the broad language of the Act's definitions, which in terms reject conventional limitations on such conceptions as "employee," 'employer," and "labor dispute," leaves no doubt that its applicability is to be determined broadly, in doubtful situations, by underlying economic facts rather than technically and exclusively by previously established legal classifications.[128]

---

support or defeating unionization over the years."); Roger C. Hartley, *Non-Legislative Labor Law Reform and Pre-Recognition Labor Neutrality Agreements: The Newest Civil Rights Movement*, 22 BERKELEY J. EMP. & LAB. L. 369, 372–73 (2001) (neutrality agreements can redress four disadvantages unions confront when organizing: employer intimidation, harmful delay, inadequate access to employees, and inability to secure a first contract).

118 29 U.S.C. § 152(3) (2012).

119 *Id.* at § 164(b).

120 *Id.* at § 157.

121 *See* DAU-SCHMIDT ET AL., *supra* note 88, at 75–78.

122 NLRB v. Hearst Publications, Inc. 322 U.S. 111 (1944).

123 *Id.* at 129.

124 Marc Linder, *Towards Universal Worker Coverage under the National Labor Relations Act: Making Room for Uncontrolled Employees, Dependent Contractors, and Employee-Like Persons*, 66 U. DET. L. REV. 555, 560 (1989).

125 Hearst Publications, Inc. 322 U.S. 111.

126 29 U.S.C. § 152(3).

127 *Id.*

128 NLRB v. Hearst Publications, Inc. 322 U.S. 111, 129 (1944).

Hence, the Supreme Court recognized something like *in dubio pro operario*. It hinged its holding on legislative purpose. As the Court stated:

> Unless the common-law tests are to be imported and made exclusively controlling, without regard to the statute's purposes, it cannot be irrelevant that the particular workers in these cases are subject, as a matter of economic fact, to the evils the statute was designed to eradicate and that the remedies it affords are appropriate for preventing them or curing their harmful effects in the special situation.[129]

The Supreme Court's *Hearst* decision led to a labor-protective jurisprudence much akin to the Latin American protective principle and *in dubio pro operario*. For example, shortly after *Hearst*, the Tenth Circuit determined that in doubtful cases the court needed to apply the NLRA's labor protections broadly and independently from any common law considerations.[130] As the 10th Circuit held:

> In doubtful situations, coverage is to be determined broadly by reference to the underlying economic realities. Consequently, the control test is not necessarily decisive in a case of this kind, as the Act concerns itself with the correction of economic evils through remedies which were unknown at common law, and if it expressly or by fair implication brings within its ambit workers in the status of these boners, it is immaterial whether under the principles of common law the relationship . . . has been that of employer and independent contractor for other purposes.[131]

Hence, the Supreme Court's "economic realities test" began to diffuse through the lower courts.

The 1947 Republican-controlled Congress, however, was not happy with the growing labor-protective jurisprudence. In its eyes, the Supreme Court and the NLRB were illegitimately covering what appeared to be nonemployees.[132] As a 1947 House of Representatives report stated:

> An "employee," according to all standard dictionaries, according to the law as the courts have stated it, and according to the understanding of almost

---

[129] *Id.* at 127.

[130] Linder, *supra* note 124, at 562, *citing* Walling v. Rutherford Food Corp., 156 F.2d 513, 516 (10th Cir. 1946), *modified sub nom.* Rutherford Food Corp v. McComb, 331 U.S. 772, *reh'g denied*, 332 U.S. 785 (1947).

[131] *Id.*

[132] *Id.* at 566.

> everyone, with the exception of members of the National Labor Relations Board, means someone who works for another for hire. But in the case of *National Labor Relations Board v. Hearst Publications, Inc.* . . . the Board expanded the definition beyond anything that it had ever included before, and the Supreme Court . . . upheld the Board. In this case, the Board held independent merchants who bought newspapers from the publisher and hired people "to sell them" to be "employees." The people the merchants hired to sell the papers were "employees" of the merchants, but holding the merchants to be "employees" of the publisher of the papers was most far reaching. . . . In the law, there has always been a difference, and a substantial one, between "employees" and "independent contractors." "Employees" work for wages or salaries under direct supervision. "Independent contractors" undertake to do a job for a price, decide how the work will be done, usually hire others to do the work, and depend for their income not upon wages, but upon the difference between what they pay for goods, materials and labor and what they receive for the end result, that is upon profits. [C]ongress intended then [1953], and it intends now, that the Board give to words not farfetched meanings but ordinary meanings. To correct what the Board has done, and what the Supreme Court . . . has approved, the bill excludes "independent contractors" from the definition of "employee."[133]

The congressional intent behind Taft-Hartley was, therefore, to exclude from coverage "independent contractors" and to command the NLRB to use the traditional common law tests of employment.

Since Taft-Hartley, the courts have taken notice and stopped using "economic realities" to assess employee versus independent contractor status. In *NLRB v. Town & Country Electric*,[134] for example, the Supreme Court held that the proper standard to assess independent contractor versus employee status is the common law control test.[135] Some courts have gone as far as to say that because the Taft-Hartley Act dis-embedded independent contractors from NLRA coverage, the definition of "employee" should be entirely detached from the Act's purposes.[136] In other words,

---

133 Linder, *supra* note 124, at 566–67, *citing* H. REP. No. 245, 80th Cong., 1st Sess. 18 (1947).

134 516 U.S. 85 (1995).

135 *Id.*

136 Harvey M. Adelstein & Harry T. Edwards, *The Resurrection of Hearst v. NLRB: Independent Contractors under the National Labor Relations Act*, 17 U. KAN. L. REV. 191, 194 (1969); *see also* Linder, *supra* note 124, at 566–76 (describing how some jurists have interpreted Taft-Hartley in a way that dis-embeds the NLRA's labor-protective purposes from issues of employee status).

even in doubtful cases putative employees should not be protected by the NLRA. Taft-Hartley left a wide-open door for principles foreign to labor law to enter into NLRA-related jurisprudence.

While it is empirically accurate that Taft-Hartley led courts to cease using the economic realities test, it does not follow that the NLRA's current purposes are no longer operative in independent contractor versus employee status questions. First, as Professors James Gross and Charles Morris have argued, Congress never significantly modified the Statement of Purpose of the Wagner Act through Taft-Hartley, which provides judges and other adjudicators with the best evidence of what the statute pursues.[137] As Professor James Gross has already detailed, the Republican Congress that enacted Taft-Hartley tried to significantly alter the Statement of Purpose, but could not; the NLRA's Statement of Purpose, still mostly intact, binds courts and the NLRB as it did in 1935.[138] Second, the common law control test is a diffuse multifactor test where no factor is determinative, not even control; it is vague and open ended.[139] Hence, to deal with incessant hard cases, courts still need to guide themselves with statutory purpose. Third, since questions of employee versus independent contractor status may involve statutory employees who should be protected, barring the use of the Statement of Purpose would mean that the adjudicator could err on the side of independent contractor, which is nowhere to be found in the law. In fact, the opposite can be inferred from the Act's still-valid Statement of Purpose: when in doubt, use the Act's broad policy in favor of worker protection to interpret the law in the light most favorable to the worker.

This is all to say the following: The NLRA, even after Taft-Hartley, punishes actions by employers who try to curb workers' collective rights. It protects. Certainly, even though the Taft-Hartley Act slimmed down the Wagner Act's original coverage, the Wagner Act's important protection of workers' rights remains.[140] Additionally, the NLRA has the potential to be more protective if constitutionalized through the Thirteenth Amendment of the U.S. Constitution.

---

[137] Charles Morris, *How the National Labor Relations Act Was Stolen and How It Can Be Recovered: Taft-Hartley Revisionism and the National Labor Relations Board's Appointment Process*, 33 BERKELEY J. EMP. & LAB. L. 1, 6 (2012); JAMES GROSS, RIGHTS, NOT INTERESTS: RESOLVING VALUE CLASHES UNDER THE NATIONAL LABOR RELATIONS ACT, Location 183 (KINDLE ED. 2017).

[138] *Id.* However, the Taft-Hartley Act did include a new paragraph in the Statement of Purposes justifying unfair labor practices by labor unions. KENNETH DAU-SCHMIDT ET AL., STATUTORY SUPPLEMENT TO LABOR LAW IN THE CONTEMPORARY WORKPLACE 46 (2nd ed. 2014).

[139] *See* Bruce Goldstein et al., *Enforcing Fair Labor Standards in the Modern American Sweatshop: Rediscovering the Statutory Definition of Employment*, 46 UCLA L. REV. 983, 1028–29 (1999). *See also* chapter 3.

[140] DANNIN, *supra* note 105, at 71.

The Protective Principle in the FLSA

Congress enacted the FLSA in 1938, once it became clear to the New Dealers that the Court would no longer take a fundamentalist view of freedom of contract to strike down labor law.[141] The FLSA was intended to provide basic minimum wage, maximum hours, and child labor protections in the United States.[142]

In its operative clauses, the FLSA reflects a protective principle. Section 2 of the FLSA states that the main goal of the FLSA is to correct and eliminate commercial practices that perpetuate workers' substandard living conditions.[143] The purpose of said protections are to safeguard commerce from disruptions, obstructions, and similar problems.[144] Resting on Section 2 of the FLSA and its legislative history, the Supreme Court has sustained that the FLSA protects workers to defend the national economy. In one of the key FLSA cases, *Brooklyn Savings Bank v. O'Neil*,[145] the Supreme Court declared that:

> The legislative history of the Fair Labor Standards Act shows intent on the part of Congress to protect certain groups of the population from sub-standard wages and excessive hours which endangered the national health and well-being and the free flow of goods in interstate commerce. The statute was a recognition of the fact that due to the unequal bargaining power as between the employer and employee, certain segments of the population required federal compulsory legislation to prevent private contracts on their part which endangered national health and efficiency and as a result the free movement of goods in interstate commerce. To accomplish this purpose[,] standards of minimum wages and maximum hours were provided.[146]

---

141 29 U.S.C. §§ 201–19 (2012).

142 *Id.*

143 As the FLSA states in Section 2:

> (a) The Congress finds that the existence, in industries engaged in commerce or in the production of goods for commerce, of labor conditions detrimental to the maintenance of the minimum standard of living necessary for health, efficiency, and general well-being of workers . . .
>
> (b) It is declared to be the policy of this chapter, through the exercise by Congress of its power to regulate commerce among the several States and with foreign nations, to correct and as rapidly as practicable to eliminate the conditions above referred to in such industries without substantially curtailing employment or earning power.

29 U.S.C. § 202 (2012).

144 *Id.*

145 Brooklyn Savs. Bank v. O'Neil, 324 U.S. 697 (1945).

146 *Id.* at 706–07 (internal citations omitted). As the Court further substantiated, "The legislative debates indicate that the prime purpose of the legislation was to aid the unprotected, unorganized and lowest paid of the nation's working population; that is, those employees who lacked sufficient bargaining power to secure for themselves a minimum subsistence wage." *Id.* at 707, n.18 (internal citations omitted).

Minimum wage standards, maximum hours, and bars against child labor—all of which are practices regulated by the FLSA—are geared toward protecting workers. In this fashion, the FLSA is a labor-protective statute.

The Supreme Court has also recognized something like the rule of *in dubio pro operario* when interpreting the FLSA. In 1944, in the case *Tennessee Coal, Iron & R. Co. v. Muscoda Local 123*,[147] the Court ruled in favor of workers in a hard case because it recognized "remedial" and "humanitarian" purposes of the FLSA that justified a broad reading of the law.[148] The Court determined that the time spent by miners traveling underground in mines to and from the "working face," i.e., the place in the mine where miners drill and load ore, constituted compensable "work" or "employment" under the FLSA.[149] The legal question was hard because, as the Court determined, the statute failed to define "work" or "employment."[150] A definition was necessary to understand if time spent by workers trying to get to the working face of the mine was compensable under the law. The Court decided that a broad interpretation of those terms favoring workers was required; the Court stated:

> But these provisions, like the other portions of the Fair Labor Standards Act, are remedial and humanitarian in purpose. We are not here dealing with mere chattels or articles of trade but with the rights of those who toil, of those who sacrifice a full measure of their freedom and talents to the use and profit of others. Those are the rights that Congress has specially legislated to protect. Such a statute must not be interpreted or applied in a narrow, grudging manner.[151]

The Court determined that workers were not chattels or articles of trade under the "remedial and humanitarian" purposes of the law. Hence, the FLSA required compensation for all actual work performed by covered employees, including traveling inside the mines to the working face.[152] The Court decided the legal question in the light most favorable to the worker, as a Latin American labor judge would have done adjudicating under the rule of *in dubio pro operario*.

---

147 Tennessee Coal, Iron & R. Co. v. Muscoda Local No. 123, 321 U.S. 590 (1944).

148 *Id.* at 597–98.

149 *Id.* at 598.

150 *Id.* at 597.

151 *Id.*

152 The Court held:

> Viewing the facts of this case as found by both courts below in the light of the foregoing considerations, we are unwilling to conclude that the underground travel in petitioners' iron ore mines cannot be construed as work or employment within the meaning of the Act. The exacting and dangerous conditions in the mine shafts stand as mute, unanswerable proof that the journey from and to the portal involves continuous physical and mental exertion as well as hazards to life and limb. And this compulsory travel occurs entirely on petitioners' property and is at all times under their strict control and supervision.

Id. at 597.

Tennessee Coal has been cited more recently by the Supreme Court precisely to underline why the FLSA's protections deserve a broad interpretation in favor of workers. In *IBP, Inc. v. Alvarez*[153] the Supreme Court stated:

> *In Tennessee Coal, Iron & R. Co. v. Muscoda Local No. 123* . . . we held that time spent traveling from iron ore mine portals to underground working areas was compensable; *relying on the remedial purposes of the statute* and Webster's Dictionary, we described "work or employment" as "physical or mental exertion (whether burdensome or not) controlled or required by the employer and pursued necessarily and primarily for the benefit of the employer and his business."[154]

A broad interpretation of the FLSA was thus warranted given its "remedial" purpose. In this fashion, the Supreme Court validated something akin to *in dubio pro operario*. Additionally, we should underscore that at the time of this writing the phrase "remedial and humanitarian," common in FLSA jurisprudence, was cited over 100 times by U.S. courts of appeals,[155] and over 270 times by U.S. district courts,[156] and not just in cases dealing with the FLSA. Other labor laws are also interpreted with the same purpose in mind.

However, while the U.S. Supreme Court recognized something like *in dubio pro operario* in the FLSA for over seven decades, a recent opinion by Justice Clarence Thomas, *Encino Motorcars, LLC v. Navarro*, almost summarily ended the doctrine of giving the FLSA a broad reading.[157] The case dealt with overtime payments of automobile dealership employees who scheduled service jobs for customers. The job required, at times, that the employees sell a service to a customer. The employer refused to pay overtime to these employees because it argued that the employees were covered by one of the exceptions in the law, the one concerned with a "salesman, partsman, or mechanic primarily engaged in selling or servicing automobiles, trucks, or farm implements."[158] Justice Thomas noted in his opinion that the statute did not explicitly call for a broad reading of the law. Additionally, he averred that since there were over two dozen exemptions to overtime pay, the exceptions were as important as the general rule in favor of overtime pay; the text of the statute appeared

---

153 IBP, Inc. v. Alvarez, 546 U.S. 21 (2005).

154 *Id.* at 25 (emphasis added).

155 Westlaw search on May 6, 2018 (searching for the phrase "remedial and humanitarian" in the U.S. Court of Appeals search engine on Westlaw).

156 Westlaw search on May 6, 2018 (searching for the phrase "remedial and humanitarian" in Federal District Court Cases search engine on Westlaw).

157 Encino Motorcars, LLC v. Navarro, 138 S. Ct. 1134, 1143 (2018).

158 *Id.* at 1138.

to provide equal importance toward who gets overtime pay, and who does not.[159] Moreover, he argued that a broad interpretation of the FLSA would mean that its remedial purpose must be protected "at all costs," which was not the law.[160]

Following the lead of the late textualist Justice Antonin Scalia, and of Professor Brian Garner,[161] Thomas then went on to state that statutes merely deserve a "fair" reading, not a liberal reading.[162] Liberal reading is the opposite of "strict" reading. Strict readings are traditionally associated with textualism. However, strict readings are today renounced by modern textualists who advocate, instead, for fair readings of the law.[163] Under a fair reading, the employees in this case could be classified as exempt, since they sold some services in an auto dealership.[164]

In this way, the Supreme Court quickly got rid of a seven-decade-old method of statutory interpretation for the FLSA. Additionally, it also seems to have dispensed with a centuries-old doctrine that called for liberal construction of remedial statutes. Since at least the eighteenth century, when William Blackstone wrote his *Commentaries on the Laws of England*, jurists recognized that remedial statutes should be construed "liberally."[165] According to Blackstone, remedial statutes are:

> [T]hose which are made to supply such defects, and abridge such superfluities, in the common law, as arise [from] either the general imperfection of all human laws, from change of time and circumstances, from the mistakes and unadvised determinations of unlearned (or even learned) judges, or from any other cause whatsoever.[166]

Laws that correct for unequal bargaining power, such as labor laws, are remedial. In other words, there was centuries-old tradition to interpret remedial statutes, such as labor laws, "liberally." However, Justice Thomas, following his late colleague Antonin Scalia, decided it was better to interpret the law "fairly."

---

[159] This last part of Justice Thomas's opinion, where he gives equal importance to the general rule and its exceptions, has no basis in the text of the law or in its purposes. Rather, it elicits *Lochnerian* aggravation with labor law. *See* John Hart Ely, *The Wages of Crying Wolf: A Comment on Roe v. Wade*, 82 YALE L.J. 920, 937–42 (1973) (describing the manner in which the U.S. Supreme Court "manufactured a constitutional right out of whole cloth [freedom of contract] and used it to superimpose its own view of wise social policy on those of the legislatures").

[160] Encino Motorcars, LLC v. Navarro, 138 S. Ct. 1134, 1142 (2018).

[161] *Id. See also* ANTONIN SCALIA & BRYAN A. GARNER, READING LAW: THE INTERPRETATION OF TEXTS 364–66 (2012).

[162] *Id.* at 364–65.

[163] *Id.*

[164] Encino Motorcars, LLC v. Navarro, 138 S. Ct. 1134, 1142 (2018).

[165] SCALIA & GARNER, *supra* note 161, at 365 (*citing* WILLIAM BLACKSTONE, COMMENTARIES ON THE LAWS OF ENGLAND 86 (4th ed. 1770)).

[166] *Id.* at 365 (*citing* WILLIAM BLACKSTONE, COMMENTARIES ON THE LAWS OF ENGLAND 86 (4th ed. 1770)).

It does not make sense to interpret the FLSA "fairly"—whatever that may mean—but not "liberally" or "broadly." Courts that exempt workers form the FLSA because they might "fairly" fall into an exemption of the FLSA may harm those workers' hours and pay significantly, and maintain or exacerbate substandard living conditions, in contradiction with congressional goals under the FLSA. Moreover, courts should not simply assume that laws have no purposes, as Thomas argued, simply because laws might have exceptions, or because statutory law is the result of political compromises where disparate interests contribute to legal texts. Thomas's purposelessness is a highway to arbitrary and meaningless law, which not only cannot be the law—it is not law at all. The cursory way that the U.S. Supreme Court's conservative majority, with Justice Thomas at its helm, got rid of the American version of *in dubio pro operario* for the FLSA but against the law is precisely the reason why we argue throughout the book for a principled labor law.

WHAT ABOUT EMPLOYMENT AT WILL?

While we argue that a Latin American labor judge would find something like the Latin American protective principle in U.S. labor law, what of employment at will, a peculiar doctrine that exists in all U.S. states except Montana, permitting the employer to fire workers without cause? The Tennessee Supreme Court—in 1884—was the first U.S. court on record to declare employment at will.[167] It stated that employers "may dismiss their employees at will, be they many or few, for good cause, for no cause or even for a cause morally wrong, without being thereby guilty of legal wrong."[168] Since then, the employment-at-will doctrine has diffused to forty-nine states. Only Montana[169] and the territories Puerto Rico[170] and the U.S. Virgin Islands[171] have altered the employment-at-will presumption by enacting statutes prescribing legal causes for termination. As we more fully explain in chapters 5 and 6, employment at will weakens worker protection.[172] And as we also propose in chapter 5, to fully protect workers, Congress and/or the states must extinguish employment at will through statute. Employment at will does

[167] Payne v. W. & Atl. R.R. Co., 81 Tenn. 507, 519–20 (1884), *overruled on other grounds by* Hutton v. Watters, 179 S.W. 134, 138 (Tenn. 1915).

[168] *Id.*

[169] MONT. CODE ANN. §§ 39-2-901–915 (2007).

[170] P.R. LAWS ANN. tit. 29, § 185a–m (2010). *See also* Jorge M. Farinacci-Fernós, *The Search for a Wrongful Dismissal Statute: A Look at Puerto Rico's Act No. 80 as a Potential Starting Point*, 17 EMP. RTS. & EMP. POL'Y J. 125 (2013).

[171] V.I. CODE ANN. tit. 24, § 76 (2017).

[172] *See* chapter 5.

not mean, however, that there are no labor protections in the United States. There are many, as this book shows, and they contain the protective principle.

CONCLUSION

The protective principle in Latin American labor law, its central tenet, stems from constitutional provisions and legislation, some of which are express and detailed, and others more inchoate. The principle of protection posits that the law must protect the worker because workers are weaker parties in employment contracts. Without protection, the worker would be turned into a commodity, and his or her humanity would be threatened. The law, therefore, must aid in correcting this moral problem. We also described how the principle of protection has been crystallized in the rule of *in dubio pro operario*, which means that when deciding hard cases, a judge must interpret the relevant rule in the way most favorable to the worker.

We constructed a protective principle in the United States from the Thirteenth Amendment's mandate against involuntary servitude. Similarly, we argue that labor protection exists in the NLRA and the FLSA, both of which are concerned with the disparate bargaining relationships between workers and employers. The FLSA, furthermore, is humanitarian and remedial in scope, calling for its broad construction. We posit that while in Latin America labor law is concerned about commodification, a moral concern resulting from disparate bargaining positions, in the United States the law is also concerned with market failures and "obstructions to commerce" produced by said inequities. The commercial goals behind U.S. labor law may open opportunities for erosions of worker protection, as have occurred. However, it is also true that the statutes protect workers as their main concern.

We also argued that something similar to the rule of *in dubio pro operario* exists in the United States in the goal to equalize bargaining relationships in the NLRA. Until recently, the Supreme Court also recognized that the FLSA must interpreted broadly given its "remedial and humanitarian" purposes. While current textualists have argued against the relevance of purpose for statutory construction, and Justice Thomas and the late Justice Scalia argued that statutes merely require a "fair" reading—we argued that statutory purpose remains important to help protect statutes as *law*, not arbitrary rules. Finally, while true that employment at will erodes labor protection in the United States, it does not totally destroy it.

In all, we can construct a labor-protective jurisprudence from the Thirteenth Amendment and the New Deal laws favoring basic freedom of association and minimum labor standards for workers. Courts—and Congress and the President—need to recognize and apply it, which, unfortunately, has not been the trend in the United States for decades.

3

PRIMACY OF REALITY

INTRODUCTION: FACT, FICTION, AND PRINCIPLE

> [T]hat grown men and women in robes . . . believe a publisher's claim that a thirteen-year-old boy whom it paid a nickel per paper to deliver its newspaper was "an independent businessman," "essentially acting as a delivery service such as UPS or Federal Express," who must be excluded from workers' compensation coverage after being hit by a truck, poignantly demonstrates an almost willful blindness to reality, common sense, and the purposes of [labor law].[1]

Today's labor market offers workers relatively fewer full-time, long-term employment options than during the post–World War II era through the 1970s, when the American middle class flourished.[2] The growing options of employment, referred

[1] Marc Linder, *Dependent and Independent Contractors in Recent U.S. Labor Law: An Ambiguous Dichotomy Rooted in Simulated Statutory Purposelessness*, 21 COMP. LAB. L. & POL'Y J. 187, 190 (1999), *citing* Johnson v. Workmen's Compensation Appeal Bd., 631 A.2d 693, 697 (1993).

[2] *See* DAVID HARVEY, A BRIEF HISTORY OF NEOLIBERALISM (2005) (explaining how since 1970s neoliberalism surfaced as a countermovement to the gains that workers made after the postwar period, this lead to less desirable outcomes for ordinary workers).

Principled Labor Law. Sergio Gamonal C. and César F. Rosado Marzán.

to as "nonstandard,"[3] "contingent,"[4] "precarious,"[5] or "fissured"[6] jobs, not only offer terms that likely few workers would prefer over full-time, permanent jobs, but also have confounded legal decision makers and some legal scholars as to whether these "nonstandard," "contingent," "precarious," or "fissured" jobs are even covered by existing labor law.[7] Some cases may, in fact, be "hard" ones because the existing laws were made to regulate work in times different than ours. As "nonstandard," "contingent," "precarious," and "fissured" jobs flourish, some scholars argue that there is a crisis in labor law.[8] At other times, and as suggested by the cited epigraph at the beginning of this chapter, some courts have puzzled scholars and others when they refuse to impose employer liabilities on employers, despite the facts. Courts contribute to the misclassification problem.

While we agree that "nonstandard," "contingent," "precarious," and "fissured" work pose challenges to existing labor law, and that positive law needs to change to better fit today's economic realities, here we argue that the principle of "primacy of reality," explicitly developed in Latin America but also existing internationally, including in the United States, provides labor law with some capacity to remain "empirically valid"[9] despite changes in the nature of work. As we will discuss below, the principle has been used in Latin America to determine the threshold issues of employee and employer status, leading adjudicators to find such statuses despite "nonstandard," "contingent," "precarious," or "fissured" work relations formally agreed to by employees and employers. In more recent years, the principle was more clearly applied during Barack Obama's presidency, and his Department of Labor's Wage and Hour Division, headed by David Weil, one of the leading American intellectuals who has studied "fissuring" (in fact, coining the term).[10] As we explain below, the

---

[3] Katherine V. W. Stone & Harry Arthurs, *The Transformation of Employment Regimes: A Worldwide Challenge*, *in* RETHINKING WORKPLACE REGULATION: BEYOND THE STANDARD CONTRACT OF EMPLOYMENT 1, 4, 7 (Katherine V. W. Stone & Harry Arthurs eds., 2013).

[4] Richard S. Belous, *The Rise of the Contingent Workforce: The Key Challenges and Opportunities*, 52 WASH. & LEE L. REV. 863, 865 (1995).

[5] *See* Arne Kalleberg, *Precarious Work, Insecure Workers: Employment Relations in Transition*, 74 AM. SOC. REV. 1, 2, 6–8 (2009); GUY STANDING, THE PRECARIAT: THE NEW DANGEROUS CLASS, 47–49, 52–58 (2011).

[6] DAVID WEIL, THE FISSURED WORKPLACE: WHY WORK BECAME SO BAD FOR SO MANY AND WHAT CAN BE DONE TO IMPROVE IT 189–90 (2014) (defining the fissured workplace, characterized as working relationships mediated by contracting, supply chain management, and franchising).

[7] *See* THE IDEA OF LABOUR LAW (Guy Davidov & Brian Langille eds., 2011) (editors ask whether labor law must change, given transformations in the work world).

[8] *Id.*; Stone & Arthurs, *supra* note 3.

[9] *See* Michel Coutu, *With Hugo Sinzheimer and Max Weber in Mind: The Current Crisis and the Future of Labor Law*, 34 COMP. LAB. L. & POL'Y J. 605, 614 (2013).

[10] U.S. DEPARTMENT OF LABOR WAGE AND HOUR DIVISION, Administrator's Interpretation No. 2015-1, The Application of the Fair Labor Standards Act's "Suffer or Permit" Standard in the Identification of Employees Who Are Misclassified as Independent Contractors (July 15, 2015) (David Weil issuing Administrator). *See also* WEIL, *supra* note 6.

Obama-era National Labor Relations Board (NLRB) also based employee and employer status questions on facts over legal formalities and ramped up its interpretation of the National Labor Relations Act (NLRA) to keep it relevant despite the NLRA's age and the times.

But facts are not the end-all solution to maintain effective labor law. Indeed, some legal opinions simply do not make any sense even with the facts. Parsing through evidence related to the work done by putative employees for a putative employer is not enough to provide consistent legal opinions that, despite the times, protect workers' rights. Ideological blinders also color legal opinions, and may do so in a manner inconsistent with the facts and the law.

Despite being far from perfect and not immune to deficient jurisprudence, courts in Latin America determine employee status not only on primacy of reality but also on the protective principle, discussed in the previous chapter, which informs the overarching logic to hold in favor of the worker when the law is vague or silent on a particular issue. Latin American labor jurisprudence also complements its opinions with other labor law principles, such as nonwaiver and continuity of employment relationships, which will be discussed in later chapters of this book. The principles provide a conceptual "toolkit"[11] that enables decision makers to apply labor law more consistently. Labor law can be capable not only of retaining its character in relationship to other areas of law, such as contract, but also other schools of thought altogether hostile to labor law, such as neoclassical economics.[12]

PRIMACY OF REALITY IN LATIN AMERICA

The Latin American principle of primacy of reality is a labor law principle with a long history, as Américo Plá Rodríguez explained in his treatise *Los Principios del Derecho del Trabajo*.[13] In his treatise, Plá Rodríguez reported cases from Uruguay, his home country, which showed that courts had adopted the principle since at least 1916.[14] The principle posits that facts must be given preference over what is contained in legal texts, documents, or agreements when there is conflict between

[11] *See* Ann Swidler, *Culture in Action: Symbols and Strategies*, 51 Am. Soc. Rev. 273 (1986) (introducing and defining the sociological concept of a "toolkit" as a repertoire of habits, skills, and styles from which social actors build strategies for meaningful social action).

[12] *See, e.g.*, Richard A. Epstein, *In Defense of the Contract at Will*, 51 U. Chi. L. Rev. 947 (1984); Richard Epstein, *A Common Law for Labor Relations: A Critique of the New Deal Labor Legislation*, 92 Yale L.J. 1357 (1983). *See also* Anne Marie Lofaso, *Toward a Foundational Theory of Workers' Rights: The Autonomous Dignified Worker*, 76 UMKC L. Rev. 1 (2007) (explaining the relevance of neoclassical economics on labor law, offering a critique on influence, and advancing a refoundation of labor law based on its own distinct principles).

[13] Américo Plá Rodríguez, Los Principios del Derecho del Trabajo (3d ed. 1998).

[14] *Id.* at 340.

facts and such legal texts, documents, and agreements.[15] Primacy of reality over legal texts, documents, and agreements is grounded in the central principle of labor law, the principle of protection, discussed in chapter 2 of this book. The protective principle, as we discussed in the chapter 2, posits that workers are socioeconomically inferior to employers, and employers may abuse their power and authority over their workers if workers are left without legal protections. Employers may abuse their rights against workers through legal formalities, such as through terms contained in written contracts or employee handbooks, which are bargained in an unequal context and without a real bargain. Conversely, employers may also direct their workers to perform actions that do not conform to their stated agreement, creating problems for judicial reconstruction of the contractual terms.

Moreover, we must note that the employment contract is not a standard agreement where parties make bilateral promises to each other. Rather, it is an agreement in which one party, typically the employer, makes a promise of payment in return for performance by the putative employee. The employment contract, if indeed it is a contract,[16] is also what the modern common law of contract generally refers to as a "relational" contract, where the terms of performance may be in constant flux and negotiation by the parties through principal requests or demands and agent performances.[17] As such, it is important for adjudicators trying to understand the terms of the agreements to inquire into the parties' conduct to decipher the terms. This is why Plá Rodríguez argued, citing Mexican Professor Mario de la Cueva, that

---

[15] *Id.* at 313.

[16] Some American labor law scholars have argued that because of the employment-at-will doctrine, which allows employers to terminate employees for good, bad, or no reason, there is no real contractual element in the employment relationship; workers' most reasonable expectations in the employment relationship, including to remain in employment as long as they are meeting all their expected duties, can be breached at any time by the employer. *See, e.g.*, Jay M. Feinman, *The Development of the Employment at Will Rule*, 20 AM. J. LEGAL HIST. 118, 125 (1976) (employment-at-will rule departs from "pure doctrine"); W. David Slawson, *Unilateral Contracts of Employment: Does Contract Law Conflict with Public Policy?*, 10 TEX. WESLEYAN L. REV. 9, 12 (2003) (arguing courts that enforce employer modifications of binding personnel manuals misunderstand contract law because such modifications defeat employees' reasonable expectations); Clyde W. Summers, *The Rights of Individual Workers: The Contract of Employment and the Rights of Individual Employees: Fair Representation and Employment at Will*, 52 FORDHAM L. REV. 1082, 1098 (1984) ("additional consideration" in the form of continued work is enough to overcome the presumption of employment at will, turning employment at will into a "spurious contractual doctrine"). *But see* Rachel Arnow-Richman, *Mainstreaming Employment Contract Law: The Common Law Case for Reasonable Notice of Termination*, 66 FLA. L. REV. 1513 (2014) (arguing that for jurisprudential and historical consistency, employment should be cast as a bilateral contract terminable at will by either party upon reasonable notice.)

[17] Relational contracts are understood in the United States as a contract where "the parties are incapable of reducing important terms of the arrangement to well-defined obligations. Such definitive obligations may be impractical because of inability to identify uncertain future conditions or because of inability to characterize complex adaptations adequately even when the contingencies themselves can be identified in advance." Charles J. Goetz & Robert E. Scott, *Principles of Relational Contracts*, 67 VA. L. REV. 1089, 1091 (1981).

the employment contract was a "reality contract" (*contrato-realidad*)[18] that required adjudicators to give preference to the parties' conduct over what may have been agreed to in writing or even verbally by the parties.

Primacy of reality becomes most relevant in Latin America when the trier of fact must determine employer and employee status.[19] In these circumstances, courts and other adjudicative institutions must carefully parse through the facts of the case to determine the existence of an employer/employee relationship or an independent contractor relationship under the law.[20] Courts must similarly search the facts when the parties claim different terms in the contracts, such as those regarding pay, scheduling, type of work contracted for, and duration of the employment relationship, among others. In so searching the facts, adjudicators must make sure that the contract conforms to the rules set out for employment established by labor law. Contractual autonomy, as understood by the traditional civil or common law, therefore does not pervade in the field of labor law.

Latin American labor law recognizes that gaps or contradictions between facts and legal texts, documents, or agreements may have different causes.[21] An employer may intentionally feign or simulate a legal condition, or may simply commit an error, have outdated knowledge of the facts, or be unaware of his or her legal duties. However, employment obligations under Latin American labor law hinge on law and facts that lie outside parties' intentions or knowledge.[22] It assumes that the employer commands and controls the workplace; what happens in the workplace is known, or should be known, by the employer.

Moreover, under Latin American doctrine, primacy of reality does not mean that the contractual terms between employers and, for instance, misclassified employees or workers should not be given weight by adjudicative authorities.[23] Under the *pro*

---

[18] Plá Rodríguez, *supra* note 13, at 313–14, *citing* Mario de la Cueva, I Derecho Mexicano del Trabajo 381 (2d ed. 1943).

[19] Independent contracting traditionally lies outside of the protections labor law affords. It involves, for example, the relationship between a physician and his or her patient or between a lawyer and his or her client. Although the physician and attorney perform work, they are not subordinate to patients or clients (who would be the "employers" contracting services). Therefore, independent contracts are relationships governed in Latin America by civil law. *See, e.g.*, Alejandro Castello, Grupos de Empresa y Derecho del Trabajo 86 (Fundación de Cultura Universitaria ed., 2006).

[20] For a comparative view of this principle of the primacy of reality, also called in the literature the principle of transparency, above all in matters, or the fictitious interposition or supply of manpower, *see* Rafaelle de Luca Tamajo & Adalberto Perulli, *Labor Law (individual and collective dimensions) and Decentralization of Production*, *in* General Report, Theme 2, XVIII World Congress on Labour Law 98 (2006).

[21] Plá Rodríguez, *supra* note 13, at 325–26 and n.1.

[22] *See id.* at 326–27.

[23] *Id.*

operario criterion, terms beneficial to the putative employee or worker must be honored.[24]

We should make it clear that the primacy of reality principle is not uniquely Latin American. The International Labor Organization (ILO) has adopted it in its Recommendation 198.[25] It states that when adjudicators face contradictory evidence regarding the threshold question of whether a putative employee has been hired as an employee or for personal services, as would be independent contractors devoid of labor protections, the decision makers need to prioritize the conduct of the parties as ascertained by the facts of the case, and less so by legal, formal documents such as contracts. In this fashion, international labor doctrine gives priority to what parties actually do and how they behave to ascertain the legal status of work relationships under the labor laws.[26] Below, we provide some examples from Argentinian, Brazilian, Chilean, and Uruguayan law and jurisprudence to show how each country understands and applies the principle of primacy of reality.

Argentina

In Argentina, the Employment Contract Law states that an employment contract exists when there is a contract between two parties, and, regardless of its form, one of the parties agrees to perform "acts, execute jobs, or provide services" for the other party "under the dependence of that other party, during a determined or indeterminate

---

[24] *See* chapter 2.

[25] ILO Recommendation 198 of 2006 states:

> For the purposes of the national policy of protection for workers in an employment relationship, the determination of the existence of such a relationship should be guided primarily by the facts relating to the performance of work and the remuneration of the worker, notwithstanding how the relationship is characterized in any contrary arrangement, contractual or otherwise, that may have been agreed between the parties.

International Labour Organization, Employment Relationship Recommendation (No. 198) § II.9 (2006).

[26] We should not confuse the principle of primacy of reality with modern contract interpretation rules that permit adjudicators to ascertain contract terms through written and oral words and the conduct of parties. *See* United Nations Convention on Contracts for the International Sale of Goods (CISG), 19 I.L.M. 669, art. 11 and art. 8(3) (1980). *See also* Restatement (Second) of Contracts §§ 4 and 27 (1981). While true that in common law contracts conduct may create binding legal obligations, formalities and writings still matter and may trump conduct. *See* Restatement (Second) of Contracts §§ 212–17 (1981) (detailing the common law parol evidence rule, where certain statements and conduct made prior to contractual writings may not be included in contract terms); Restatement (Second) of Contracts § 110 (1981) (detailing six types of contracts that require a writing for a court to enforce them: "a contract of an executor or administrator to answer for a duty of his decedent (the executor-administrator provision)"; "a contract to answer for the duty of another (the suretyship provision)"; "a contract made upon consideration of marriage (the marriage provision)"; "a contract for the sale of an interest in land (the land contract provision)"; a contract that is not to be performed within one year from the making thereof (the one-year provision)"; and contracts for goods valued at US$500 or more). *See also* U.C.C. § 2-201 (1).

period of time, in return for payment."[27] Moreover, "clauses regarding form and conditions of the payments are to be mandated by public order dispositions, the statutes, collective bargaining agreements or labor arbitration decisions and orders with the force of law and its uses and customs."[28] Contractual autonomy is therefore significantly curtailed in employment contracts under Argentinian law.

Moreover, the law presumes an employment relationship when an individual provides paid services.[29] As the law states:

> Article 23
> Presumption of the existence of the contract of employment.
>
> The provision of services presumes the existence of a contract of employment, unless circumstances, relations or causes that motivate the contract prove otherwise. This presumption will also operate even when parties use non-employment categories to characterize their contract, insofar as the circumstances do not support qualifying as entrepreneurs those who provide a service.[30]

"Entrepreneurs" are those individuals who run businesses, or "enterprises."[31] Argentinian law defines "enterprises" as: "[T]he instrumental organization of

---

[27] Arg. Law 20.744, art. 21. The original Spanish text reads:

> *Artículo 21 – Contrato de trabajo.*
> *Habrá contrato de trabajo, cualquiera sea su forma o denominación, siempre que una persona física se obligue a realizar actos, ejecutar obras o prestar servicios en favor de la otra y bajo la dependencia de ésta, durante un período determinado o indeterminado de tiempo, mediante el pago de una remuneración. Sus cláusulas, en cuanto a la forma y condiciones de la prestación, quedan sometidas a las disposiciones de orden público, los estatutos, las convenciones colectivas o los laudos con fuerza de tales y los usos y costumbres.*

Law No. 20.744, Sept. 20, 1974, [23.003] B.O., 2 (Arg.) (as amended by Law No. 26.844, Mar. 13, 2013).

[28] *Id.*

[29] *Id.* at art. 23. *See also* International Labor and Employment Laws Vol. IIB § 76-1 (Argentina) (William L. Keller & Timothy J. Darby eds., 4th. ed. 2015).

[30] Arg. Law 20.744 art. 23 (translation by authors). The Spanish original states:

> *Art. 23. Presunción de la existencia del contrato de trabajo.*
> *El hecho de la prestación de servicios hace presumir la existencia de un contrato de trabajo, salvo que por las circunstancias, las relaciones o causas que lo motiven se demostrase lo contrario.*
> *Esa presunción operará igualmente aún cuando se utilicen figuras no laborales, para caracterizar al contrato, y en tanto que por las circunstancias no sea dado calificar de empresario a quien presta el servicio.*

Law No. 20.744, Sept. 20, 1974, [23.003] B.O., 2 (Arg.) (as amended by Law No. 26.844, Mar. 13, 2013).

[31] The original Spanish reads as follows:

> *A los fines de esta ley, se entiende como "empresa" la organización instrumental de medios personales, materiales e inmateriales, ordenados bajo una dirección para el logro de fines económicos o benéficos. A los mismos fines, se llama "empresario" a quien dirige la empresa por sí, o por medio de otras personas, y con el cual se relacionan jerárquicamente los trabajadores, cualquiera sea la participación que las leyes asignen a éstos en la gestión y dirección de la "empresa."*

Id. at art. 5.

personal, material and immaterial means, to accomplish economic or beneficial goals."[32] In this way, "entrepreneurs" are individuals who direct enterprises by themselves or through others.[33] Workers, or employees, are related hierarchically to the "entrepreneur."[34]

Argentinian labor law thus provides an objective standard to determine the existence of an employment contract. It builds a presumption of employee status to any person rendering a service for compensation unless the party rendering the service is an "entrepreneur." Entrepreneurs must be at the top of an enterprise's hierarchy directing the enterprise. In other words, subordinated service providers should be understood as employees under Argentinian law. The law mandates judges and other adjudicators to evaluate the nature of the services rendered according to the facts, regardless of whatever the parties included in their written instruments. [35]

Parties trying to rebut the presumption of an employment contract in situations where someone contracted with another to provide services in return for payment must also prove that the employment relationship was not for an indefinite term, which is also presumed by the law.[36] While written contracts and letters of intent are not customary in Argentina and are not required to establish an employment relationship, it is suggested that parties sign them, especially employers, so that they can better prove the existence of specific type of employment contract or term.[37]

Argentinian courts search for facts to determine issues such as employee status but only against a legal backdrop that presumes an employment relationship. For example, in *Dora Nuñez v. Dirección de Remonta y Veterinaria del Ejército Argentino*,[38] an Argentinian case decided by the National Chamber of Labor Appeals (*Camara Nacional de Apelaciones del Trabajo)*, a civilian worker filed a complaint against her alleged employer, the Argentinian military, alleging that the putative employer terminated her job as a seamstress without cause after sixteen years of uninterrupted employment. The alleged employer, however, argued that the plaintiff was not its employee but an independent contractor who was hired for personal services under successive contracts. According to the Argentinian military, a public institution, the plaintiff was not hired as a civil

---

[32] *Id.*

[33] *Id.*

[34] *Id.*

[35] Keller & Darby, *supra* note 29, at I.A, *citing* Arg. Law 20.744 art. 23.

[36] *Id.*

[37] *Id.*

[38] Cámara Nacional de Apelaciones del Trabajo [CNTrab.] [National Chamber of Labor Appeals], May 13, 2004, Dora Nuñez c. Dirección de Remonta y Veterinaria del Ejército Argentino, No. 37.524 (Arg.).

servant, i.e., a public employee. Public sector employers must hire personnel in Argentina through public service rules set by the legislature. Since the plaintiff was not formally hired as a public servant, she must have been an independent contractor.

Although the plaintiff did not prevail in the trial court, the appellate jurisdiction ruled in her favor. The court held that there was no question that the plaintiff had been hired to perform seamstress duties for a set number of hours of work under the supervision and control of the public authority, in return for a monthly compensation. The court noted that there was no express prohibition in Argentinian law against applying the employment contract protections to those individuals who otherwise met the basic criteria for an employment relationship, even in the public sector. Moreover, the court noted that the legislature did not craft civil servant hiring laws so that the state could flout employer responsibilities by contracting workers through successive civil contracts for personal services. The court was suspicious of what appeared to be an employer's abuse of rights. Second, under the principle of primacy of reality, the seamstress in this case met the elements required to prove employee status: she had a contract to provide seamstress duties under the supervision and control of the military authorities for a set number of hours of work, in return for a monthly compensation. If the court failed to determine employee status and, accordingly, refused to provide her with employee protections, the state would deprive the plaintiff of legal safeguards against arbitrary dismissal. In other words, a recognition that the putative employee was subordinated and dependent to the employer, and suspicions of employer abuse of rights compelled the court to hold that the seamstress was an employee of the Argentinian military.[39] As the court held:

> [T]he plaintiff rendered services under the orders of the defendant and, as it was proved, complied with a schedule of set hours in return for an amount of money paid monthly. There is no doubt that there was an employment relationship between the parties, for which no express, a priori legal regimen had been accorded by the parties. *Therefore, we must apply the principle of primacy of reality.* . . . [S]uccessive contracts are not legally contemplated in public administration. In second place, there exists a *ratio decdendi* or juridical equality in this case; in the employment contract there is no express prohibition against applying its norms, by analogy, to other contexts [such as this one]. Therefore, because the plaintiff was denied employment stability as established by Art 14 bis of the National Constitution, it appears just and equitable, in the particular

[39] *Id.*

> circumstances of this case, to apply by analogy the norms that regulate the less onerous guarantees against arbitrary dismissal [in contrast to those given to public sector workers] and, therefore, provide the plaintiff with identical severance payments as those that would have been given to a worker whose employment relationship ended, as in this case, without fault of his or her own.[40]

Hence, the Argentinian bench applied primacy of reality to better guarantee constitutional employment protections to individuals who met the basic test of employment, namely, rendering services to another party, under the supervision and control of that party, in return for payment. The seamstress received employee protections and could not be terminated without receiving severance pay, which all employees must receive in Argentina.

Brazil

In Brazil, the courts have also applied the principle of primacy of reality to determine employee status. Brazilian law states that an employee is a "person who provides services on a regular basis to an employer, under the orders thereof and for wages."[41] This definition has led courts to develop a five-part test to determine employee status. This five-part test states that an employee is:

- an individual, a physical, or natural person;
- who works regularly, not occasionally;

[40] *Id., citing* Cámara Nacional de Apelaciones del Trabajo [CNTrab.] [National Chamber of Labor Appeals], May 4, 2001, MARQUINEZ C. FAC. ARQUITECTURA Y URBANISMO, No. 34.825 (Arg.) (translation by authors) (emphasis added). The original Spanish states:

> *Empero, en el caso en examen no es necesario develar en profundidad este ultimo supuesto; ello, habida cuenta de que la actora prestó servicios a las órdenes de la demandada y lo hizo, según quedó probado, cumpliendo un régimen de asistencia horaria, y a cambio de una suma de dinero efectivizada mensualmente. Y bien, no quedan dudas entonces, de que entre las partes se ha producido una relación de trabajo, a la que no se le adjudico un régimen jurídico en su momento y por ello corresponde encuadrarlo sobre la base del principio de primacía de la realidad. Entiendo que se cumplen en autos los tres requisitos de procedencia de la analogía ya que el tema de la sucesión de contratos en la administración pública, no está contemplado legalmente, en segundo lugar existe una ratio decidendi o igualdad jurídica en el caso y en el contrato de trabajo no existe prohibición legal expresa de aplicación analógica. Así entonces, privado el agente de la estabilidad que le consagra el Art. 14 bis de la Constitución Nacional, me parece justo y equitativo, en las particulares circunstancias del caso, aplicar analógicamente las normas que reglamentan la garantía menos intensa de protección contra el despido arbitrario y, por tanto, reconocerle una indemnización idéntica a la que un trabajador privado, en sus mismas condiciones, hubiera obtenido al extinguirse la relación de trabajo sin su culpa.*

Id. (internal citations omitted).

[41] Keller & Darby, *supra* note 29, Vol. I.A. § 75-1 (Brazil), at I.C., *citing* CONSOLIDAÇÃO DAS LEIS DO TRABALHO [C.L.T.], art. 3 (Braz.), which states in its original Portuguese that: "Art. 3º – *Considera-se empregado toda pessoa física que prestar serviços de natureza não eventual a empregador, sob a dependência deste e mediante salário.*"

- whose work is carried out dependent upon direction of another;
- who is a salaried or wage worker, rather than one who receives remuneration for services rendered;
- and who personally performs the work.[42]

Independent contractors, occasional workers, temporary workers, domestic workers, rural workers, and child laborers are therefore excluded from any statutory definitions of employee.[43]

As in Argentina, written agreements are not required to establish an employment contract in Brazil; the terms may be inferred from behavior.[44] Moreover, as in Argentina, anyone who knowingly benefits from another's work may be liable toward the worker as an employer.[45] Also, in Brazil, like in Argentina, written contracts are suggested—not required; written contracts help parties to better prove contract terms, especially since the law will presume contracts of indefinite duration in the absence of evidence to the contrary.[46]

While written instruments may provide some evidence of what parties agreed to, they will be put to the test by the facts. Courts will use the principle of primacy of reality not only to determine whether or not an employment relationship exists, as in Argentina, but also what types of contractual terms permeate the agreement. For example, in a case decided unanimously by the Superior Labor Tribunal, the last instance for labor law cases and controversies in Brazil, the court determined that the plaintiff was an English teacher, as she alleged in her complaint, and not a technical assistant of English instruction, as was alleged by the employer and stated in her contract of employment. Being an English teacher and not a technical assistant was important to the worker, since English teachers receive overtime payment, while technical assistants do not. As the court determined:

> In the present case, we are forced to hold, given the facts outlined by the record, that the reality of the contract of employment was that the plaintiff

---

[42] *Id.*

[43] *Id.* at I.C.1–I.C.6.

[44] *Id.* at I, *citing* C.L.T. (Bra.), arts. 442–43 (translation by authors). The original Portuguese text of the law states:

> *Art. 442 – Contrato individual de trabalho é o acordo tácito ou expresso, correspondente à relação de emprego. . . .*
>
> *Art. 443 – O contrato individual de trabalho poderá ser acordado tácita ou expressamente, verbalmente ou por escrito, por prazo determinado ou indeterminado . . .*

C.L.T. (Bra.), arts. 442–43.

[45] Amauri Mascaro Nascimento, *History of Labor Law in Brazil*, *in* PANORAMA OF BRAZILIAN LAW 233, 252 (Jacob Dolinger & Keith Rosenn eds., 1992).

[46] *Id.* at I.A.

> engaged in English teacher activities. . . . Regardless of the title under which the professional was hired—professor, teacher, technician—lies the reality of the contract that defines the functions of the teaching profession and, consequently, the teacher category. It is well known that the contract of employment is a reality contract, and therefore it is in the daily execution of its functions, objectively performed, during the course of the employment relationship, what determines [the contract], as provided for in article 3 of the Consolidated Labor Laws. *The employment contract and the principle of primacy of reality are the elements that should guide the judge's decision*. . . . In this way, when there is divergence between the work done by the worker and the terms set out in the employment contract, reality prevails over what has been agreed [on paper]. The primacy of substance prevails over form.[47]

As in Argentina, primacy of reality is part of the Brazilian labor law.

Chile

Chilean courts have also readily applied the principle of primacy of reality to determine employee status. For example, in *Sociedad Constructora Baical Ltda. with*

---

[47] TST - E-RR: 7000054200851501l4 70000-54.2008.5.15.0114, Relator: Aloysio Corrêa da Veiga, 18.10.2011, Tribunal Superior do Trabalho Jurisprudênica [T.S.T.J.], 28.10.2011, 1, 8 (Braz.) (translation by authors) (emphasis added). In its original Portuguese, the case states:

> *No caso em tela, forçoso é admitir, diante do quadro fático delineado nos autos, que a realidade do contrato de trabalho impõe o reconhecimento das atividades de uma professora de inglês, nos termos previstos nas normas da CLT. Ora, independentemente do título sob o qual o profissional foi contratado—professor, instrutor, técnico—é a realidade do contrato de trabalho que define a função de magistério e, por consequência a categoria diferenciada de docente. É sabido que o contrato de trabalho é um contrato realidade, e portanto, é a execução cotidiana das funções, objetivamente realizadas, durante o curso da relação de trabalho que determina qual a função exercida pelo empregado (que determina a realidade do contrato), conforme disposto no mencionado artigo 3° consolidado. O contrato de trabalho e o princípio da primazia da realidade são os elementos que devem nortear a decisão do Juiz do Trabalho, pois a aplicação do Direito do Trabalho não decorre do acordo de vontades formador do contrato de trabalho, mas da execução diária da relação de trabalho. Sendo assim, em havendo divergência entre o trabalho realizado pelo empregado e os termos firmados no contrato de trabalho, prevalece o primado da realidade sobre o pactuado. Prestigia-se o primado da substância sobre a forma.*

Id.

The decision, furthermore, goes on to cite ILO Recommendation 198 of 2006, the Employment Relationship Recommendation. That Recommendation states in pertinent part that:

> For the purposes of the national policy of protection for workers in an employment relationship, the determination of the existence of such a relationship should be guided primarily by the facts relating to the performance of work and the remuneration of the worker, notwithstanding how the relationship is characterized in any contrary arrangement, contractual or otherwise, that may have been agreed between the parties.

International Labour Organization, Employment Relationship Recommendation (No. 198) § II.9 (2006).

Santibáñez Hugo and others,[48] the Court of Appeals of Antofagasta determined whether a group of putative employees were employed by the employer for an indefinite duration, as the putative employees argued, or were contractors contracted for definite periods (*a plazo*) for specific jobs (*por obra*).[49] The trial level labor court decided in favor of the employees, so the employer appealed. The Court of Appeals affirmed the court below and buttressed its arguments by applying the principle of primacy of reality. First, the court noted that it was well established in Chile that contracts of definite duration or for specific jobs were exceptional and not the norm. When confronted with factual questions of whether employees were hired for set terms or indefinitely, the court applied the principle of employment continuity, which we will explain in the next chapter.[50] That principle generally posits that the court must presume that the employer hired the employee indefinitely.[51] The court also reaffirmed its holding based on the primacy of reality over legal formalities. Here, the court determined that despite successive formal contracts for definite duration, or "for job" contracts, there was *in reality* a "permanent and continuous employment relationship" between the employer and the putative employees.[52] Hence,

---

[48] Corte de Apelaciones de Antofagasta [C. Apel.] [Antofagasta Court of Appeals], Sept. 9, 2013, SOCIEDAD CONSTRUCTORA BAICAL LTDA. CON GONZÁLEZ SANTIBÁÑEZ HUGO Y OTRO, Rol de la causa: 88-2013, derecho del trabajo (Chile).

[49] Chilean law establishes that a for term contract of employment cannot last more than one year, unless the worker is professional or technical, in which case it may last up to two years. CÓD. TRAB. [LAB. CODE] (Chile), art. 159 No. 4. The law also establishes that a second renewal, or if the worker continues working at his post once the contract expires, with the employer's knowledge, the contract becomes indefinite. *Id.* The same effect is provided when the term contracts are interspersed with periods of free work and contract.

On the other hand, the Chilean Labor Code mentions the contract for work or service almost in passing. *Id.* at art. 159 No. 5. The Code does not provide rules on how the contract may become indefinite, or how it may be limited. *Id.*

[50] *See* chapter 4.

[51] The Spanish original portion of the court opinion stated:

> *Que para determinar la naturaleza del contrato que unió a las partes, es pertinente considerar que la contratación por obra o a plazo fijo constituye una excepción, siendo la regla general que los contratos de trabajo tengan una duración indefinida, extendiéndose mientras subsista el trabajo que lo motiva, constituyendo el principio de la continuidad un principio esencial en el derecho del trabajo, razón por la cual en caso de duda en cuanto a que si las prestaciones de servicios fueron continuas o discontinuas, debe estimarse que éstas tienen el carácter de continuas."*

Corte de Apelaciones de Antofagasta [C. Apel.] [Antofagasta Court of Appeals], Sept. 9, 2013, SOCIEDAD CONSTRUCTORA BAICAL LTDA. CON GONZÁLEZ SANTIBÁÑEZ HUGO Y OTRO, Rol de la causa: 88-2013, derecho del trabajo (Chile). *See also* chapter 5.

[52] As the Spanish original stated:

> *NOVENO: Que como es sabido, en el derecho del trabajo tiene aplicación el principio conocido como primacía de la realidad, debiendo privilegiarse lo que ocurre en el terreno de los hechos, incluso sobre lo formalizado por escrito por las partes y en este contexto, la sucesiva existencia de diversos contratos por obra o faena o a plazo fijo, descritos en el considerando octavo de la sentencia recurrida, todos terminados con sus respectivos finiquitos para volver a*

the principle of primacy of reality operates in Chile in much the same manner that it does in Argentina and Brazil.

Uruguay

In Uruguay, courts also readily apply the primacy of reality principle. For example, in *Cabo Guerra, Jorge and others with Banco de Seguros del Estado*,[53] a case similar to *Dora Nuñez*, the Argentinian case previously referenced,[54] the Supreme Court of Uruguay applied the principle of primacy of reality in a unanimous opinion determining the employee status of state workers who the employer argued were mere contractors under the civil code. The courts below determined that the workers had one-year contracts that were renewed each year, followed a specific schedule, and used uniforms provided by the putative employer. While the court held for the plaintiffs in the first instance, the Court of Appeals reversed that initial court opinion and order. The Supreme Court reinstated the trial court's holding. It first noted that the case presented typical questions of employee status already decided by the court. In its jurisprudence, the court noted the essential elements to determine employee status: the personal nature of the services performed by the putative employee, payment by the putative employer in return for said personal services, the duration of the services contracted for, continuity of the putative employment relationship, exclusivity between the putative employer and employee, and, fundamentally, the putative employee's subordination to the employer. Considering the facts, the court concluded that there was an employment relationship and not a civil contract relationship. It held that "applying the principle of reality, which is of no debatable relevance in labor matters," subordination was clearly established by the facts. The putative employer created leave policies and demanded prior authorization before workers could hire transports. The putative employees were dependent on an expert who controlled appraisals, requested and obtained tools from the putative employer, subject to a hierarchy, had to meet a set schedule and punch in and out, and could be disciplined by the employer in case of breach. In this manner, the Uruguayan Court concluded unambiguously, while citing Plá Rodríguez, that what

---

suscribirse otros, demuestra como ya se señaló, que en los hechos y más allá de lo señalado en los finiquitos, se está ante una única relación laboral permanente y continua por parte de ambos actores para la empresa demandada.

Id.

[53] Suprema Corte de Justicia, Feb. 17, 2012, Cabo Guerra, Jorge Alberto y Otros c. Banco de Seguros del Estado/ Demanda Laboral, No. 413/2012, Ficha 2-61192/2006 (Uru.).

[54] Cámara Nacional de Apelaciones del Trabajo [CNTrab.] [National Chamber of Labor Appeals], May 13, 2004, Dora Nuñez c. Dirección de Remonta y Veterinaria del Ejército Argentino, No. 37.524 (Arg.).

happened "in the terrain of fact" superseded what was formally expressed; there was an employment relationship.[55]

PRIMACY OF REALITY IN THE UNITED STATES

U.S. federal labor law, namely, the FLSA and the NLRA, which we covered in the prior chapter, incorporate what we call here "primacy of reality." It is clear that under U.S. law, adjudicators must search the facts over any legal documents, such as contracts, to determine employee or employer status. However, Democrat and Republican administrators oftentimes disagree about employee status even after searching the facts.[56] In other words, more than fact searching may be needed to develop consistent labor law jurisprudence. We argue that the political sensitivity of issues such as employer and employee status requires not only anchoring those legal questions on primacy of reality but also on the protective principle and the rule of *in dubio pro operario*, which mandates worker protection in cases where the law is ambiguous or has gaps. In other words, the Latin American principled method would limit judicial discretion and mandate worker protection, complementing primacy of reality and channeling jurisprudence in a worker protective direction. We argue that especially in jurisdictions known for judicial deference toward employers, principles matter not only as general guidelines but also as nondiscretionary rules compelling worker protection.

Determining Employee and Employer Status

The FLSA generally protects "employees, "which it very broadly defines as "any individual employed by an employer."[57] An employer "includes any person acting directly

---

[55] The Spanish original states:

> *No existen dudas pues, que en la especie, según el material de hecho relevado y de acuerdo al principio de la primacía de la realidad, que establece que al existir discordancia entre lo que sucede en la práctica y lo que surge de documentos o convenios, debe darse preferencia a lo que ocurre en el terreno de los hechos, por sobre las formas, formalidades o apariencias, a la búsqueda de la verdad real sobre lo que las partes hayan acordado de modo más o menos solemne o expreso.*

Id.

[56] Julia Tomassetti, *Who Is a Worker? Partisanship, the National Labor Relations Board, and the Social Content of Employment*, 37 Law & Soc. Inquiry 815, 817–18 (2013) (discussing how Republican-majority National Labor Relations Board decisions have denied labor rights to graduate students, disabled janitors, and many other nonstandard employees, or about 25 percent of the U.S. workforce under the guise that they are primarily not employees but something else).

[57] 29 U.S.C. §§ 203(e), 206–07 (2012).

or indirectly in the interest of an employer in relation to an employee and includes a public agency, but does not include any labor organization (other than when acting as an employer) or anyone acting in the capacity of officer or agent of such labor organization."[58] "Employ," on the other hand, "includes to suffer or permit to work."[59] This standard of "suffer or permit to work" is understood to be a very broad standard of employment that goes much further than traditional common law definitions based on employer control of the employee's work.[60] The Supreme Court itself determined that a "broader or more comprehensive coverage of employees within the stated categories would be difficult to frame."[61]

An Obama-era Department of Labor (DOL) memorandum stated that the "suffer or permit to work" standard was developed originally in child labor laws that aimed to make employers liable for child labor violations even if the employer alleged not knowing that children were working in its property. As the DOL memorandum explained:

> A key rationale underlying the "suffer or permit" standard in child labor laws was that the employer's opportunity to detect work being performed illegally and the ability to prevent it from occurring was sufficient to impose liability on the employer.... Thus, extending coverage of child labor laws to those who suffered or permitted the work was designed to expand child labor laws' coverage beyond those who controlled the child laborer, counter an employer's argument that it was unaware that children were working, and prevent employers from using agents to evade requirements.[62]

Hence, this test was developed to be more inclusive than traditional common law tests for employment that were based on employer control of the workers' work.[63]

---

[58] *Id.* at § 203(d).

[59] *Id.* at §§ 203, 203(g).

[60] Administrator's Interpretation No. 2015-1, *supra* note 10, at *3. *See also* Bruce Goldstein et al., *Enforcing Fair Labor Standards in the Modern American Sweatshop: Rediscovering the Statutory Definition of Employment*, 46 UCLA L. Rev. 983 (describing the history of the meaning of the term "suffer or permit to work," which is much broader than the common law control tests, despite erroneous judicial and administrative narrowing of the term).

[61] U.S. v. Rosenwasser, 323 U.S. 360, 362 (1945); *see also* Nationwide Mut. Ins. Co. v. Darden, 503 U.S. 318, 326 (1992).

[62] Administrator's Interpretation No. 2015-1, *supra* note 10, at 2.

[63] Walling v. Portland Terminal Co., 330 U.S. 148, 149 (1947); Nationwide v. Darden, 503 U.S. at 326 (FLSA's "suffer or permit" standard for employment "stretches the meaning of 'employee' to cover some parties who might not qualify as such under a strict application of traditional agency law principles.").

According to Weil's interpretation of the FLSA, the "economic realities test" used to determine an employment relationship generally entails analyzing the following facts:

- the extent to which the work performed is an integral part of the employer's business;
- the worker's opportunity for profit or loss depending on his or her managerial skill;
- the extent of the relative investments of the employer and the worker;
- whether the work performed requires special skills and initiative;
- the permanency of the relationship; and
- the degree of control exercised or retained by the employer.[64]

However, according to the Obama-era DOL, the degree of control over the employee should not be given too much weight by the decision maker.[65] No factor is supposed to be determinative.[66] The central determinant of whether a worker is an employee is if the putative employee "is economically dependent on the employer. . . ." The memo goes on to state that if the putative employee is essentially operating its own business, then he or she is not an employee but an independent contractor not covered by the FLSA.[67]

Primacy of reality, therefore, exists within the FLSA. Even under the Republican administration of Donald J. Trump, an agreement between employers and employee stating that the latter is an independent contractor is not controlling. As the administration stated:

> There are certain factors that are immaterial in determining the existence of an employment relationship. For example, the fact that the worker has signed an agreement stating that he or she is an independent contractor is not controlling because the reality of the working relationship—and not the label given to the relationship in an agreement—is determinative.[68]
>
> Moreover, the economic realities of the relationship, and not the label an employer gives it, are determinative. Thus, an agreement between an employer and a worker designating or labeling the worker as an independent contractor

---

64 Administrator's Interpretation No. 2015-1, *supra* note 10, at 3.

65 *Id.* at 14.

66 *Id.*

67 *Id.* at 5.

68 United States Department of Labor Wage and Hour Division, Fact Sheet 13: Am I an Employee?: Employment Relationship under the Fair Labor Standards Act (FLSA) (2014).

is not indicative of the economic realities of the working relationship and is not relevant to the analysis of the worker's status.[69]

The NLRA also requires interrogating the facts.[70] It has a broad definition of "employee." Section 2(3) of the NLRA defines "employee" as "any employee, and shall not be limited to the employees of a particular employer . . . ."[71] The statute provides a number of exceptions to the broad rule. These are agricultural workers, domestic workers, individuals employed by parents or spouses, independent contractors, supervisors, individuals employed by an employer subject to the Railway Labor Act, or individuals employed by any other person who is not an employer as defined by the statute.[72]

Because Congress explicitly excluded independent contractors from NLRA coverage, and given that the NLRA does not provide for a standard as broad as "suffer or permit to work" as under the FLSA, the U.S. Supreme Court determined that the NLRB needs to use traditional agency principles and the "right of control test" to determine employee versus independent contractor status under the NLRA.[73] Another test that complements the "right of control test" is the more controversial "primary purpose test," which has been applied by Republican-controlled Boards mostly to deny NLRA rights to workers who otherwise meet the right to control test.[74] But despite controversies surrounding the use and application of these tests, both of them require for adjudicators to base employee status on the facts of the cases.

---

[69] Administrator's Interpretation No. 2015-1, *supra* note 10, at 5, *citing* Scantland v. Jeffrey Knight, Inc., 721 F.3rd 1308, 1311 (11th Cir. 2013) ("This inquiry is not governed by the 'label' put on the relationship by the parties or the contract controlling that relationship, but rather focuses on whether 'the work done, in its essence, follows the usual path of an employee.' "); Brock v. Superior Care, 840 F.2d 1054, 1059 (2d Cir. 1988) ("[E]mployer's self-serving label of workers as independent contractors is not controlling."); Robicheaux v. Radcliff Material, Inc., 697 F.2d 662, 667 (5th Cir. 1983) (explaining that "[a]n employee is not permitted to waive employee status," and affirming that welders were employees despite signing independent contractor agreements). *See also* Rutherford Food Corp. v. McComb, 331 U.S. 722, 729 (1947) ("Where the work done, in its essence, follows the usual path of an employee, putting on an 'independent contractor' label does not take the worker from the protection of the Act.").

[70] National Labor Relations Act (NLRA) §§ 7, 2(3), 29 U.S.C. §§ 157, 152(3) (2012).

[71] *Id.*

[72] 29 U.S.C. § 152 (3).

[73] NLRB v. United Ins. Co. of Am., 390 U.S. 254, 255–58 (1968); FedEx Home Delivery and Int'l Brotherhood of Teamsters, 361 N.L.R.B. No. 55, * 3 (2014), vacated on other grounds by 849 F.3d 1123 (D.C. Cir. 2017) (listing the factors to consider under the common law control test).

[74] *See* Nicholas Fram & T. Ward Frampton, *A Union of Amateurs: A Legal Blueprint to Reshape Big-Time College Athletics*, 60 BUFF. L. REV. 1003, 1032–33 (2012); Tomassetti, *supra* note 56, at 817–18.

The Common Law Control Test

Given that the NLRA's employee definition is broad, even circular, the Supreme Court of the United States has, since the Taft-Hartley Act, defined "employee" by its ordinary meaning. In *NLRB v. Town & Country Electric, Inc.*, the Supreme Court held, citing dictionary sources, that an employee is "any 'person who works for another in return for financial or other compensation,'" or a "'person in the service of another under any contract of hire, express or implied, oral or written, where the employer has the power or right to control and direct the employee in the material details of how the work is to be performed.'"[75] Those definitions reflect the "right of control" doctrine of the common law of agency.[76] The NLRB has thus defined an employee as "a person who performs services *for another* under a contract of *hire*, subject to the other's control or right of control, and *in return for payment*."[77]

Conflicts over employee status arise when employers hire the putative employees as "independent contractors" who are explicitly excluded by the NLRA. Because the NLRA does not define who an independent contractor is, the courts have resorted, again, to the common law of agency to draw the line between employees and independent contractors. Under the common law of agency, an employee is "an agent whose principal controls or has the right to control the manner and means of the agent's performance of work."[78] Courts and the NLRB use a multifactor test to determine whether the principal has a right to control the work of the agent or putative employee. It is worth listing the multifactor test under the common law in full to better grasp its meaning:

- A servant [employee] is a person employed to perform service for another in his affairs and who, with respect to his physical conduct in the performance of the service, is subject to the other's control or right to control.
- In determining whether one acting for another is a servant or an independent contractor, the following matters of fact, among others, are considered:
- the extent of control which, by the agreement, the master may exercise over the details of the work;

---

[75] NLRB v. Town and Country, 516 U.S. 85, 90–91 (1995), *citing* American Heritage Dictionary 604 (3rd ed. 1992) and Black's Law Dictionary 525 (6th ed. 1990).

[76] Restatement (Second) of Agency § 2 (1958) defines a servant, *e.g.*, employee, as "an agent employed by a master to perform service in his affairs whose physical conduct in the performance of the service is controlled or is subject to the right to control by the master."

[77] Brown Univ. and Int'l Union, 342 N.L.R.B. 483, 490 at n.27 (*quoting* NLRB v. Town & Country Elec., 516 U.S. 85, 94 (1995)).

[78] Restatement (Third) of Agency § 7.02(3)(a) (2006).

- whether or not the one employed is engaged in a distinct occupation or business;
- the kind of occupation, with reference to whether, in the locality, the work is usually done under the direction of the employer or by a specialist without supervision;
- the skill required in the particular occupation;
- whether the employer or the workman supplies the instrumentalities, tools, and the place of work for the person doing the work;
- the length of time for which the person is employed;
- the method of payment, whether by the time or by the job;
- whether or not the work is a part of the regular business of the employer; and
- whether or not the parties believe they are creating the relationship of master and servant.[79]

This multifactor test requires the NLRB and the courts to go through detailed factual inquiries and analyses before making a final determination of employee or independent contractor status. For example, after analyzing the facts of the case through a similar multifactor test, the NLRB determined in *Roadway Package Systems Inc.*[80] that drivers of a package-delivery company were not independent contractors under the NLRA, but rather they were employees.[81] It held so because the drivers did not operate independent businesses. They performed functions that were an essential part of the employer's normal operations. They also did not require any prior training or experience but received training from the employer. The drivers also did business in the employer's name, with assistance and guidance from the employer. The agents did not ordinarily engage in outside business either. They constituted an integral part of the employer's business under its substantial control. Even though the agents purchased their own trucks, the NLRB found that the drivers had no

[79] Restatement (First) of Agency § 220 (1933).

[80] 326 NLRB 842 (1998).

[81] The Board's factor test questioned whether the "agents":

> [D]o not operate their own independent businesses, but perform functions that are an essential part of the company's normal operations; they need not have any prior training or experience, but are trained by company supervisory personnel; they do business in the company's name with considerable assistance and guidance from the company and its managerial personnel and ordinarily sell only the company's policies; the "Agent's Commission plan" that contains the terms and conditions under which they operate is promulgated and changed unilaterally by the company; the agents account to the company for the funds they collect under an elaborate and regular reporting procedure; the agents receive the benefits of the company's vacation plan and group insurance and pension fund; and the agents have a permanent working arrangement with the company under which they may continue as long as their performance is satisfactory.

Id. at 849, *citing* NLRB v. United Ins. Co. of Am., 390 U.S. 254, 259–60 (1968).

substantial proprietary interest in the company. They had no significant entrepreneurial opportunity for gain or loss. Given the totality of the circumstances after analyzing the factors in light of the evidence, the agents were statutory employees under the NLRA.

In a similar case, *FedEx Home Delivery*, however, the District of Columbia Circuit court did not agree with the NLRB that a group of home-delivery workers were employees under the NLRA.[82] In the case, the employer petitioned the District of Columbia Circuit Court to review an NLRB decision finding that the employer committed unfair labor practices when the employer refused to bargain with a group of putative employees. The employer argued that it had no duty to bargain with the workers because they were independent contractors, not employees. The District of Columbia Circuit Court agreed with the employer after searching the facts of the case and applying the common law control test. In its holding, it stated that the workers' entrepreneurial opportunities as delivery workers for Federal Express placed them outside employment and in a contractor classification.[83]

What these cases show is that the NLRB and the courts must address the specific facts of cases to determine employee or independent contractor status under the NLRA. However, even after analyzing similar facts in different cases through the multifactor tests, the NLRB and the courts are not always holding consistently. The lack of consistency seems mostly due to what Professor Marc Linder has called the jurisprudential "purposelessness."[84] As we saw above, Latin American courts complement primacy of reality with other principles, especially protection, to better fill gaps and provide meaning to ambiguous or contradictory law. Hence, as we will explain more fully below, it is important for adjudicators to value labor law principles, including that of protection.

The Primary Purpose Test

Another approach to determine employee status under the NLRA is the "primary purpose test," which entails establishing whether the employee in question has primarily an economic relationship with the employer or has some other kind of

---

[82] FedEx Home Delivery v. NLRB, 563 F.3d 492 (D.C. Cir 2009) (vacating the NLRB's decision and holding that small package delivery agents were independent contractors after analyzing similar facts to those in Roadway in light of a similar multifactor test determined by the NLRB). *See also* Crew One Productions, Inc. v. N.L.R.B., 811 F.3d 1305, 1313–14 (11th Cir. 2016) (Eleventh Circuit declines to defer to NLRB's determination of employee status on the grounds that the NLRB has no authority to interpret the common law, which is used to determined independent contractor status versus employee status, and because the court disagreed with the NLRB's interpretation of who is considered an independent contractor versus an employee).

[83] *Id. at* 497.

[84] Linder, *supra* note 1.

relationship, such as that of "student."[85] This "primary purpose test" tends to become more salient in educational settings where the putative employees are an institution's students and, concurrently, work for it.[86] Because of this rather different setting from that of the traditional industrial one, the Supreme Court has held that "principles developed for use in the industrial setting" cannot be " 'imposed blindly on the academic world.' "[87]

One of the most salient questions before the NLRB in recent decades has been whether or not graduate student assistants are employees under the NLRA. The Board has flip-flopped on this question at least twice. In *New York University* (*NYU*), which had a Democratic majority, the Board determined, applying the common law control test, that graduate students could be considered employees under the Act.[88] Later, in *Brown University*,[89] when the Board reverted to Republican control, it changed its opinion on the issue.[90] In *Brown*, the Board determined that the graduate students in question were not employees under the Act because they had a primarily educational, not economic, relationship with their university.[91] The Board based its decision in *Brown* on the grounds that the graduate students must first be enrolled at their university to be awarded a teaching or research assistant position, or to be proctors.[92] The graduate students also only spent a limited number of hours performing their teaching, research, or proctor duties; they spent most of their time being "students."[93] Also, their assistance or proctor duties were "core elements of the Ph.D. degree."[94] Finally, the money they received was not "consideration for work" but financial aid to pursue their degrees.[95] Facts became important to hold for employee status, or against it. In *Brown*, however, the Board did not grant employee status to the putative employees because they were, under the facts described by the NLRB, mostly "students."

The Board changed its mind again in *Columbia University*[96] during Barack Obama's Democratic administration. There, it determined that Columbia University

[85] *See* Fram and Frampton, *supra* note 74, at 95 (*citing* Brown Univ. and Int'l Union 342 N.L.R.B. 483, 488–89 (2004)).

[86] Robert A. McCormick & Amy Christian McCormick, *The Myth of the Student-Athlete: The College Athlete as Employee*, 81 WASH. L. REV. 71, 95–96 (2006).

[87] NLRB v. Yeshiva Univ., 444 U.S. 672, 680–81 (1980) (internal citations omitted).

[88] *New York Univ.*, 332 N.L.R.B. 1205 (2000)

[89] 342 N.L.R.B. 483 at 483 (2004).

[90] *See id.*

[91] *Id.* at 487.

[92] *Id.* at 488.

[93] *See id.*

[94] *Id.*

[95] *Id.*

[96] Columbia University, 364 NLRB No. 90 (2016) (graduate student assistants are employees under the NLRA because they meet the common law control test for employee status and there is no policy justifying their exclusion from NLRA coverage).

exercised sufficient control over student research and teaching assistants to trigger employer liability. Moreover, it asserted that there was no policy justifying exclusion of the graduate student assistants from NLRA coverage. Finally, the NLRB underlined that "policy" could not override clear language in the Act affording collective bargaining rights to all employees.[97]

As in the *Roadway* and *Fed Ex* cases described above, these graduate student assistant cases thus signal two important points. First, factor tests force adjudicators to establish employee or independent contractor status anchored on facts, not labels placed by the parties to their relationship. Second, however, ideological blinders color the ultimate view that adjudicators will arrive at, despite the facts. We will return to this issue further below, as it forces us to discuss other principles detailed in this book, including protection, to limit an adjudicator's ideology from determining threshold questions of employee status under the law.

The Joint Employer

One of the growing problems for labor law lies in the way work is being organized in contemporary capitalist societies. The standard contract of employment, where one employer hires employees to work some sort of regular schedule for it, for an extended period of time, and with vertical promotion schemes, pension benefits, and other benefits provided to promote work and loyalty within the firm while supporting a basic welfare system, appears almost quaint today. "Precarious," "contingent," "nonstandard," and even "fissured" work is becoming more salient in contemporary capitalist work organization. Under such schemes, many lead firms have work done for them through intermediaries, such as contractors, creating a plurality of challenges for traditional labor law. Workers may not be able to organize themselves into unions with ease, for example, since different employers formally employ them. Lead firms may also not be responsible for wage payments and other obligations toward workers because lead firms do not directly employ their contractors' workers. Given that many contractors are undercapitalized, their lack of resources and the limited liability of lead firms may place contemporary workers in situations where no one is de jure or de facto capable to respond for unpaid wages, for example. Not only is the private welfare system created by the standard of employment on the line but also basic liability and responsibilities toward workers.

These problems have motivated U.S. labor advocates and reformers to develop the idea of the "joint employer," who is responsible for the labor obligations of contractors. In the United States, the incapacity of amending existing statutory

[97] *Id.* at 7, *citing* Mertens v. Hewitt Assocs., 508 U.S. 248, 261 (1993).

law led the Obama administration to choose regulatory and adjudicatory strategies to develop the joint employer category and better fit the realities of nonstandard, precarious, contingent, and fissured work relationships into the existing statutory schemes. Both the Wage and Hour Division of the Department of Labor (WHD) and the NLRB developed rules to better understand and expand the notion of joint employers in the United States. Both regulatory advances were based, we argue, on a sharp understanding of subordinated and dependent work and, therefore, on the principle of primacy of reality. Below we explain how the Obama administration understood joint employment.

Joint Employment and the FLSA

The Obama-era WHD established that the FLSA provides for joint employer liability.[98] It underscored two different types of joint employment: horizontal relationships between employers and vertical ones defined by "economic realities," i.e., if employees are dependent and hence employed by more than one employer.[99]

The Obama-era WHD started its analysis of joint employers by making it clear that joint employment has been traditionally recognized by the FLSA.[100] Then, it underscored that the FLSA employment standards are based on "economic realit[ies]," which compels adjudicators to establish whether or not an employer "suffers" or "permits to work."[101] The "suffers" or "permits to work" standard is broader than that of other labor statutes, such as the NLRA (see below), which requires a showing of employer control over the employee.[102]

Horizontal joint employer analysis requires an examination of the relationship between putative joint employers. According to the DOL, "[i]n determining whether a horizontal joint employment relationship exists, the focus should be on the relationship (and often the degree of association) between the two (or more) potential joint employers, with respect to the employee and all of the relevant facts of the particular case."[103] For example, separate employers who share the same managers

[98] The WHD also argued that joint employment could exist under the Migrant and Seasonal Agricultural Protection Act (MSPA), another statute that it administers. Both laws define "employ" in exactly the same manner. Interpretations of either may be useful for the other. *See* U.S. Department of Labor, Wage and Hour Division, Administrator's Interpretation No. 2016-1, Joint employment under the Fair Labor Standards Act and Migrant and Seasonal Agricultural Worker Protection Act (Jan. 20, 2016) (David Weil issuing Administrator), 3.

[99] *Id.*

[100] *Id., citing* Antenor v. D & S Farms, 88 F.3d 925, 929 (11th Cir. 1996); Baystate Alt. Staffing v. Herman, 163 F.3d 668, 675 (1st Cir. 1998); *see also* 29 C.F.R. 791.2(a) (2014).

[101] *Id.* at 4.

[102] *Id.* at 4.

[103] *Id.* at 7. *See* also 29 C.F.R. 791.2(a)(2014).

controlling two or more restaurants may be found to be joint employers.[104] The DOL's regulations provide some guidelines to consider joint employment, including:

- arrangements between the employers to share or interchange the employee's services;
- where one employer acts directly or indirectly in the interest of another employer relation to the employee; or
- the employers directly or indirectly share control of the employee's work;[105]

The Obama-era WHD also provided a long list of factors that could be considered for joint employer determinations. These factors to consider were:

- who owns the potential joint employers (i.e., does one employer own part or all of the other or do they have any common owners);
- do the potential joint employers have any overlapping officers, directors, executives, or managers;
- do the potential joint employers share control over operations (e.g., hiring, firing, payroll, advertising, overhead costs);
- are the potential joint employers' operations intermingled (for example, is there one administrative operation for both employers, or does the same person schedule and pay the employees regardless of which employer they work for);
- does one potential joint employer supervise the work of the other;
- do the potential joint employers share supervisory authority for the employee;
- do the potential joint employers treat the employees as a pool of employees available to both of them;
- do the potential joint employers share clients or customers; and
- are there any agreements between the potential joint employers.[106]

The list was not intended to be all-inclusive.[107] It did show the need, or primacy, of facts or reality in determining horizontal joint employment statuses.

According to the Obama-era WHD, vertical joint employment is when an employee is economically dependent on two or more employers, such as would be the case of the employee hired by a contractor.[108] For these cases, the WHD determined

---

[104] Administrator's Interpretation No. 2016-1, *supra* note 98, at 5.

[105] *Id.*

[106] *Id.* at 8.

[107] *Id.*

[108] *Id.* at 5, *citing* 29 C.F.R. 500.20(h)(5)(2014); Chao v. A-One Med. Servs., 346 F.3d 908, 917 (9th Cir. 2003).

that adjudicators should look into the economic realities of the relationships between the putative joint employer and the employee. The adjudicators must determine if the putative joint employer "employs" individuals under the suffer of permit to work standard discussed previously to find employee status under the FLSA.[109]

Joint Employment and the NLRA

The Obama-era NLRB also recently buttressed primacy of reality.[110] It reaffirmed its prior rule on the issue of joint employer, which posits that two or more statutory employers are joint employers under the NLRA if the employers "share or codetermine those matters governing the essential terms and conditions of employment" of the employees.[111] Unions may compel both joint employers to bargain with them.[112] To determine whether the employers codetermine such terms and conditions of employment, the Board said, inter alia, that it would apply the common law control test.[113] The Obama-era NLRB determined, however, that the employer need not actually control the work of the employees; having the right to do so sufficed to be categorized as a joint employer.[114] This latter condition was underlined in *Browning Ferris*, where the Board noted that in the past thirty years of Board jurisprudence it has found employer status in cases when the employer actually exercised control over employees, a condition that has never existed under the common law.[115]

The Republican majority Board is apt to formally reverse *Browning Ferris* on the issue of employer control.[116] In a 2017 case, *Hy-Brand Industrial Contractors*, it actually reversed *Browning Ferris* on the issue of employer control, holding that actual employer control, and not just the right of control, is required for a finding of joint employer status.[117] The same Board subsequently vacated *Hy-Brand* on the grounds that one of the Republican members had to recuse himself from the case.[118] It is only a matter of time, however, until the Republican-controlled NLRB will reverse *Browning Ferris*.

---

[109] *Id.*

[110] Browning Ferris, Inc., 362 NLRB No. 186 at *2 (2015).

[111] *Id.* (internal citations omitted).

[112] *Id.* (internal citations omitted).

[113] *Id.*

[114] *Id.* at *2 and note 6, *citing* RESTATEMENT (SECOND OF AGENCY) § 2(1) (1958).

[115] *Id.* at *13–14.

[116] Hy-Brand Industrial Contractors, Ltd. and Brandt Construction Co., 365 NLRB No. 156 (2017), *vacated* by Hy-Brand Industrial Contractors, Ltd., N.L.R.B., 366 NLRB No. 26 (2018).

[117] *Id.* at 51.

[118] Hy-Brand Industrial Contractors, Ltd., N.L.R.B., 366 NLRB No. 26 (2018).

We present these NLRA cases here, however, not to show what the precise nature of the law is in the United States, but for the more general point that whichever the formal test, they all require that the Board and the courts look at the facts before making employee and employer status determinations.

PRIMACY OF REALITY AND THE IMPORTANCE OF PRINCIPLES

This chapter has shown how primacy of reality calls for adjudicators to interrogate the facts of cases and not be swayed by legal formalities and labels placed on purported employment relationships, contractual terms, or other employment practices. Primacy of reality makes sense and is necessary, given the protective principle discussed in chapter 2 of this book. If workers require state protection from the market, then adjudicators cannot willy-nilly defer to private contracts and other private documents to ascertain threshold legal questions, such as employee or independent contractor status or an employee's wages and conditions of employment. Deference to labels in a contract or similar documents would essentially provide the employer with the authority to decide those threshold questions, undermining the edifice of labor law. Employer statements must be put to the test of facts and the prescriptions of law.

While primacy of fact exists in the United States, we should underscore, however, that sometimes courts are highly deferential to employer policies and procedures.[119] Stressing primacy of reality can help to rein in such pro-employer, deferential practice among some members of the bench and others.

---

[119] As sociologist Lauren Edelman and her collaborators described in a paper published in the *American Sociological Review*, even the U.S. Supreme Court has deferred to corporate policies as evidence of compliance with labor laws, despite the facts. As Edelman and her collaborators explained:

> On June 20, 2011, the U.S. Supreme Court ruled in *Wal-Mart v. Dukes* that a class action lawsuit against Wal-Mart brought on behalf of its female workers, who alleged widespread discrimination in pay and promotion, could not go forward. The issue before the Supreme Court was whether there were common questions of law or fact such that the female employees could sue as a class rather than individually. Despite statistical evidence showing that women were underrepresented in management and paid less than men, and testimony by sociologist William Bielby that Wal-Mart's corporate culture and discretionary personnel practices make it vulnerable to gender bias, the court maintained that there could be no common experience of discrimination. In a 5–4 decision, with the court divided along ideological lines and Justice Scalia writing for the majority, the court held that the female employees would not be able to establish discrimination across all of Wal-Mart's roughly 3,400 stores. In reaching that conclusion, the majority placed great weight on the fact that "Wal-Mart's announced policy forbids sex discrimination." Thus, despite substantial evidence that the formal policy had little impact on actual practices at Wal-Mart, the presence of a formal policy banning sex bias was an important factor in the court's decision to shut down the class action case.

Lauren Edelman et al., *When Organizations Rule: Judicial Deference to Institutionalized Employment Structures*, 117 AMER. J. SOC. 888, 888–89 (2011).

But even when adjudicators go through facts, many of them end up deciding cases inconsistently.[120] There is a partisan divide on threshold issues of who counts as covered employers and employees, among other issues in labor law.[121] The partisan divide can be breached through principles. President Barack Obama's Democratic administration, for example, made more explicit reference about the need to protect subordinated and dependent work when making employer and employee status determinations.[122] Its WHD explicitly alluded to "principle" to provide guidance on how to determine employee status. As WHD Director David Weil noted in his Interpretation Memorandum 2015-1:

> The factors [to determine independent contractor status] should not be applied as a checklist, but rather the outcome must be determined by a qualitative rather than a quantitative analysis. The application of the economic realities factors is guided by the overarching principle that the FLSA should be liberally construed to provide broad coverage for workers, as evidenced by the Act's defining "employ" as "to suffer or permit to work."[123]

Protective purpose undergirded the Obama-era WHD's views.

Similarly, the Obama-era NLRB alluded to the NLRA's "purposes" to promote employees' rights to act in concert for collective bargaining and their mutual aid and protection, which is as close as mainstream U.S. adjudication comes to the Latin American understanding of legal principles.[124]

CONCLUSION: FOR A LABOR-PROTECTIVE JURISPRUDENTIAL TOOLKIT

This chapter first described the principle of primacy of reality as understood and developed in Latin America. It is a principle with a long history and biography that remains central to answering threshold questions in labor law, including that of employee and employer status and defining the terms of employment contracts. It is

[120] Tomassetti, *supra* note 56 (describing the ideological and partisan underpinnings of employee status).

[121] *Id.*

[122] Administrator's Interpretation 2015-1, *supra* note 10, at 4 (emphasis added).

[123] *Id.*

[124] *See* chapter 1 on how purposive and principled legal methodologies share similar traits, but differ in their level of simplicity and clarity: some purposive methodologies may give more deference to an adjudicator to balance multiple goals, while the Latin American principled methodology is more "rulified," clearly mandating for labor-protective adjudication when the law is vague or has gaps.

also a principle established internationally, since the ILO has alluded to it. It also exists in the FLSA and NLRA. Democratic and Republican Boards, as the courts, recognize the primacy of reality, or fact, to determine threshold employer and employee status questions.

However, this chapter has also shown that primacy of reality is not sufficient for consistent labor law jurisprudence. Other principles that complete decision makers' jurisprudential toolkit, including the principle of protection, from where primacy of reality stems, are important to better channel adjudicators' judgment when making sense of cases. If adjudicators were mandated to consider both primacy of reality and other principles when they have to interpret the labor laws, such as the protective principle and its rule, *in dubio pro operario*, they would likely hold differently, e.g., in favor of the worker.

4

NONWAIVER

INTRODUCTION: A FLOOR OF MANDATORY RIGHTS

Private arbitration of labor cases in lieu of litigation, once a suspect practice, has now become part of the "new normal" in the United States. This contemporary trend has found support in the U.S. Supreme Court's five-out-of-nine conservative bloc,[1] and a legal hook in the Federal Arbitration Act (FAA), a 1925[2] law that favored commercial arbitration at a time when U.S. courts were suspect of arbitration. But American activists, scholars, and policymakers have been swift to criticize the Supreme Court's conservative bloc's apparent and untrammeled extension of the FAA into contracts dealing with economically subordinated parties. The #MeToo movement against sexual harassment and assault has been one of the loudest critics of arbitration agreements. It has described how private arbitration cabins victims and survivors of sexual harassment and assault into a confidential, individual, employer-dominated arbitration process where perpetrators of sexual assault and harassment at work are

[1] *See, e.g.*, Am. Express Co. v. Italian Colors Rest., 570 U.S. 228, 231 (2013) (holding that class action waivers were legal even if the cost of individual arbitration for the plaintiffs exceeded the value of any potential remedy for the plaintiffs if they pursued individual claims through arbitration); AT&T Mobility LLC v. Concepcion, 563 U.S. 333, 347–49 (2011) (finding California law that invalidates class action waivers violates the Federal Arbitration Act).

[2] 9 U.S.C. § 2 (2012).

Principled Labor Law. Sergio Gamonal C. and César F. Rosado Marzán.

shielded from public accountability.[3] It also has a short statute of limitations and typically lower awards for winning plaintiffs.[4] "Gig" economy workers' lawyers have strongly opposed private arbitration, claiming that private arbitration blocks their capacity to represent workers in class actions.[5] In fact, private arbitration is likely making it difficult for many of these workers to seek any redress at all, given how private arbitration is often stacked in favor of employers, who write the agreements and make the rules.[6] Even the threshold issue of who counts as an "employee" with labor rights is threatened by this new trend with five loyal, pro-business Justices on the Supreme Court of the United States.[7]

This chapter supports arbitration agreements' critics from a normative perspective. It provides a Latin American view on the issue of waiver of labor rights, including so-called "procedural" waivers in favor of arbitration. The Latin American principle of nonwaiver generally posits that rights provided to weaker parties in employment relations are not waivable.[8] Waiving labor rights through asymmetric, private agreements, undoes what the legislature has mandated by law. Nonwaiver is a natural consequence of the protective principle, discussed in chapter 2, which mandates the protection of the weaker party in the employment contract.[9] In other words, nonwaiver guarantees the continued validity of worker protection[10] and constitutes a necessary part of workers' rights.[11]

Because nonwaiver implies that employers must comply with labor law as mandated, Latin American judges use the nonwaiver principle to reform agreements destined to diminish workers' rights.[12] Moreover, Latin American labor law scholars argue that labor law is public in character; it intends to protect the individual

---

[3] Philip Galanes, *Catharine MacKinnon and Gretchen Carlson Have a Few Things to Say*, N.Y. Times, Mar. 17, 2018.

[4] *Id.*

[5] Vin Gurrieri, *Uber's Move away from Arbitration Falls Short, Attys Say*, Law360, May 15, 2018.

[6] *See* Charlotte Garden, *Disrupting Work Law: Arbitration in the Gig Economy*, 2017 U. Chi. Legal F. 205 (2017).

[7] *Id.*

[8] Latin American scholars have called the nonwaiver principle the "traveling companion" of the principle of protection. Labor protection would dissipate without the principle of nonwaiver. *See* Luis Roa, *Irrenunciabilidad de derechos: itinerarios de un principio general, in* Estudios de Teoría Crítica de Derecho del Trabajo 241 (Guillermo Gianibelli & Oscar Zas eds., 2006).

[9] *See* chapter 2; Carlos Alberto Etala, Interpretación y aplicación de las normas laborales 141 (2004).

[10] Olga Castillejo de Arias, *Teoría General del derecho del Trabajo*, en Derecho del Trabajo 117 (Carlos A. Livellara & Olga Castillejo de Arias eds., 2004). *See also* Manuel Monsalvo, Los Principios del Derecho del Trabajo, Curso de Derecho del Trabajo y de la Seguridad Social 116 (2009).

[11] Mauricio Godinho Delgado, Princípios de Direito Individual e Coletivo do Trabalho 89 (2nd ed. 2004).

[12] Amauri Mascaro Nascimento, Iniciação ao direito do trabalho 119 (23rd ed. 1997).

worker, third parties, and society as a whole.[13] As such, labor law is a matter of public order. Waiver through individual contract would illegitimately undermine special protections that the legislature has provided to society at large.

As in prior chapters, this chapter distills a labor law principle, here the nonwaiver principle, from the Thirteenth Amendment of the U.S. Constitution, if recognized as a labor-protective constitutional provision, the Fair Labor Standards Act (FLSA) of 1938,[14] and the National Labor Relations Act (NLRA) of 1935.[15] Given the salience of so-called "procedural" waivers in the United States, we also discuss the Norris La Guardia Act (NLGA) of 1932,[16] which bans "yellow dog contracts," or contracts where employers demand that workers do not exercise their freedom to associate. Despite these nonwaiver protections, we show that U.S. courts are enabling employers to demand class or collective action waivers from their employees. U.S. law needs to reverse its overly liberal stance toward arbitration, which is inapposite to the Thirteenth Amendment and basic principles of labor law.

This chapter is organized in the following manner: first, it describes the principle of nonwaiver in Latin America, focusing on Argentina, Brazil, Chile, and Uruguay. It shows how the principle is expressly stated in some positive law, in court opinions, and in legal scholarship. It also details how the principle is typically applied in controversies over contract terms and claim settlements. We show that the principle surfaces in cases related to contract modification or novation, even when such contracts contain terms that meet or exceed minimum labor standards. Second, the chapter finds a nonwaiver principle in the United States, mostly in its protections for free labor under the Thirteenth Amendment and in the positive labor law and jurisprudence. However, we also focus on the particular problem of so-called "procedural" waivers sanctioned by the U.S. Supreme Court. Procedural waivers undermine substantial labor rights and undo labor protections. We argue that such waivers need to either be banned or policed and regulated so as to not undo workers' rights in the United States. We then bring together our conclusions for the chapter.

NONWAIVER IN LATIN AMERICA

Latin American labor law scholars argue that labor law establishes a floor of rights that workers cannot waive. Accordingly, the Uruguayan legal scholar Américo Plá

[13] Ernesto Krotoschin, Manual de Derecho del Trabajo 12–13 (4th ed. 1993).

[14] 29 U.S.C. §§ 201–19 (2011).

[15] 29 U.S.C. §§ 151–69 (2010).

[16] 29 U.S.C. § 101 (2011).

Rodríguez defined the principle of nonwaiver of rights (hereinafter referred to as the "principle of nonwaiver") as "[t]he legal impossibility of denying oneself, voluntarily, benefits provided by labor law, for one's own benefit."[17]

As stated in chapter 2, Latin America premises labor law on the assumption that workers are socioeconomically disadvantaged and subordinate to employers. The state must protect workers given their structural subordination and dependence to employers. Labor law generally provides judges authority to substitute *ipso jure* contract clauses that contravene the nonwaiver principle without invalidating the employment contract in its entirety. Nonwaiver is also grounded on the need to protect "super individual" interests, e.g., collective or social interests, and not just those of the individual worker.[18]

Positive Law

Latin American constitutions, statutory law, and/or scholarship have defined and developed what is known as the principle of nonwaiver. For example, the Argentinian Employment Law (*Ley de Contrato de Trabajo*) expressly states that:

> Art. 7—Less favorable conditions. Nullity.
> In no case may parties agree on terms less favorable to the employee than those provided in legislation, collective agreements, or arbitral decisions with force of law, or which are contrary to them.
>
> Art. 12—Nonwaiver.
> All party conventions to abolish or reduce the rights under this law, professional statutes, collective agreements, or individual contracts of employment, either at the time of their dealing or execution, or the exercise of rights that arise from their extinction shall be null and void. . . .[19]

Argentinian statutory labor law clearly provides against private derogation of labor rights.

In Brazil, the Consolidation of Labor Laws (hereinafter referred to as the CLT, its acronym in Portuguese) states that all acts carried out with the aim of distorting,

---

[17] Américo Plá Rodríguez, Los Principios del Derecho del Trabajo 118 (3rd ed. 1998) (translation by authors). The original Spanish text defines nonwaiver as: "*La imposibilidad jurídica de privarse voluntariamente de una o más ventajas concedidas por el derecho laboral en beneficio propio.*" *Id.*

[18] Alfredo J. Ruprecht, Los Principios Normativos Laborales y su Proyección en la Legislación 60–61 (1994).

[19] Ley de Contrato de Trabajo [Employment Contract Law] (Arg.), Law. No. 20.744 (1974), arts. 7 and 12.

preventing, or defrauding the application of the provisions contained in labor law shall be null and void.[20] In Chile, Article 5, paragraph 2 of the Labor Code provides that labor rights are not waivable.[21] Therefore, the Brazilian and Chilean labor laws underscore the indispensability of legal minimum standards and the principle of nonwaiver.[22]

Uruguay has not expressly legislated a principle of nonwaiver. However, this South American country rarely develops labor law through legislation.[23] Rather, constitutional principles, scholarship, case law, and collective bargaining have been more relevant in developing labor law in Uruguay.[24] As detailed below, the principle of nonwaiver is very present in its jurisprudence.

Jurisprudence

The Supreme Court of Argentina regularly applies the principle of nonwaiver. For example, in *Lichieri, Tulio Franco c. Banco Alas Cooperativo Limitado*, the court applied Employment Contract Law and the principle of nonwaiver, among others, when an employee claimed that the employer owed him overtime wages for work that he performed to service an automatic teller machine (ATM).[25] The employer typically paid the worker for the time the worker spent servicing each ATM. The employer did not pay the employee for any time spent traveling between the machines that he had to service. A lower court determined that the employer did not need to pay the employee for that travel time, especially since the employee had acquiesced to payment only for the time actually spent fixing the machines. The Supreme Court reversed the lower court. It declared that the traveling time was compensable and the employer had to pay the employee for that time, even if the employee acquiesced to not being paid by the employer.[26] The employee could not waive wage and hour laws.

Similarly in *Padín Capella, Jorge Daniel c. Litho Formas S.A.*, the Supreme Court of Argentina reversed an appellate decision against a worker based on the nonwaiver

---

[20] CONSOLIDAÇÃO DAS LEIS DO TRABALHO [C.L.T.], art. 9 (Braz.).

[21] CÓD. TRAB. (LAB. CODE) (Chile), art. 5(2).

[22] The Chilean Labor Code also refers to specific rights that are nonwaivable, such as prohibitions against pay deductions, maternity rights, and the right of the mother to feed her children under two years. *Id.* at arts. 58, 195, 206(2).

[23] SERGIO GAMONAL C., DERECHO COLECTIVO DEL TRABAJO 34 (2nd ed. 2011) (*citing* ÓSCAR ERMIDA URIARTE, INTRODUCCIÓN, CUARENTA ESTUDIOS SOBRE LA NUEVA LEGISLACIÓN LABORAL URUGUAYA 8 (2010)) (explaining the importance of collective bargaining over statutory labor law to set norms in Uruguay).

[24] *Id.* at 35.

[25] Corte Suprema de Justicia de la Nación [CSJN] [National Supreme Court of Justice], Nov. 29, 1988, LICHIERI, TULIO FRANCO C. BANCO ALAS COOPERATIVO LIMITADO, (1988-311-2437) (Arg.).

[26] *Id.*

principle.[27] In *Padín Capella*, the trial court first held that an employer had failed to fully compensate an employee under a collective bargaining agreement.[28] The employee never complained of not being fully compensated until after the employment relationship ended.[29] The appellate court reversed the trial court's ruling because it understood the employee's silence to mean that the employee acquiesced to the alleged lack of payments during his employment.[30] The court concluded that the employee's actions evidenced a legitimate contract modification.[31] The Supreme Court disagreed. It noted that the court of appeals' holding was at odds with the principle of nonwaiver.[32] It held that wage underpayments should be regarded as a down payment toward the total owed to the employee, even if the employee acquiesced to partial payments.[33] The court added that the law did not prevent the employee from waiting until the end of the employment relationship to claim his or her unpaid wages.[34]

In Brazil, the federal Superior Labor Court (hereinafter referred to as the TST, its acronym in Portuguese) heard a case where a collective bargaining agreement waived the legal minimum terms and conditions of employment of workers.[35] The CLT provides that while the employer must pay the employee for the entire time that he or she works, the employer is not liable for de minimis overtime variations of five minutes before or after the regular workday, up to a maximum of ten minutes a day.[36] In other words, if the employee punched in five minutes before the time of entry and punched out five minutes after the regular departure time, the employer does not need to pay that extra time as overtime. If the employee punched in or out more than ten minutes beyond the regular workday—for example thirty minutes—then the employer would have to pay the thirty minutes at the overtime rate.

The issue before the court was whether such overtime rules could be modified against the interest of the worker.[37] In this case, a collective bargaining agreement extended the period that the employer could pay as straight time to fifteen minutes before the regular workday began and ten minutes after it finished. The TST

---

[27] Corte Suprema de Justicia de la Nación [CSJN] [National Supreme Court of Justice], Mar. 12, 1987, Padín Capella, Jorge Daniel c. Litho Formas S.A. (1987-310-558) (Arg.).

[28] *Id.*

[29] *Id.*

[30] *Id.*

[31] *Id.*

[32] *Id.*

[33] *Id.*

[34] *Id.*

[35] WEG Equipamentos Electrico S.A. e Cimara Schwartz Teixeira, Mar. 30, 2011 Processo No. TST RR 367000 (Braz.).

[36] Consolidação das Leis do Trabalho [C.L.T.], art. 58 (Braz.).

[37] *Id.*

determined that the collective bargaining clause was unenforceable. It affirmed the decision of the regional court, which had based its conclusion on the principle of nonwaiver of legal minimums (*indisponibilidade*).

In another Brazilian court opinion, *Caixa Econômica Federal—CEF e Denise Duarte de Oliveira Maia*,[38] the employer classified a bank employee as an "employee of trust" (*empregado de confiança*), or a managerial, exempt employee. The court determined that the employee was nonexempt and could not waive his rights to overtime pay through a private agreement. In that case, the employee initially worked in a "technical" position for six hours a day. He was later promoted to an alleged position of trust where he worked for eight hours a day. However, the employee's job remained the same after he was promoted.[39] The CLT stated that bank employees, such as the employee in this case, must have a regular working day of six hours.[40] The day can be extended up to eight hours, but the last two hours must be paid as overtime. Even if the employee in this case worked for eight hours a day, the employer did not pay him overtime, alleging that he was an "employee of trust."[41]

The law in Brazil considers employees of trust as those employees who perform managerial, leadership, or similar functions.[42] They are exempt from overtime provisions.[43] However, the TST determined that the employee in question was not an employee of trust because he only performed "technical tasks," not any of the managerial or leadership tasks required for a trust position.[44] Even if the worker had agreed to be misclassified and not paid overtime, those contractual terms were unenforceable. Thereafter, the court reformed the employment contract by deleting the illegal terms, and substituting them with the legally mandated ones. It held that the regular working day, since it consisted of technical duties, had to be six hours instead of eight; if the employee worked eight hours, then he had to be paid two hours at the overtime rate. The TST based its decision on the nonwaiver of rights.

Chilean courts also apply the nonwaiver principle. In *Bustos c. Consejo de Defensa del Estado*, the Chilean Supreme Court explained that freedom of contract applies in labor matters to the extent labor rights are not violated through waiver.[45] In

---

[38] *Caixa Econômica Federal—CEF e Denise Duarte de Oliveira Maia* Sept. 29, 2010 Processo No. TST RR 63600-67 (Braz.).

[39] *Id.*

[40] Consolidação das Leis do Trabalho [C.L.T.], arts. 224–25 (Braz.).

[41] *Id.*

[42] *Id.* at art. 224.

[43] *Id.*

[44] *Caixa Econômica Federal—CEF e Denise Duarte de Oliveira Maia* Sept. 29, 2010 Processo No. TST RR 63600-67 (Braz.).

[45] Sergio Gamonal C., *Comentario de la Jurisprudencia Laboral del año 2003*, 1 Revista de Derecho de la Universidad Adolfo Ibáñez 754 (2004), *citing* Corte Suprema de Justicia [C.S.J.] [Supreme Court], Jan. 28, 2003, Bustos c. Consejo de Defensa del Estado, Rol de la causa: 3239-2002 (Chile).

Ingesur c. Navarro, an employer attempted to conceal a contract of indefinite duration with that of a for-term contract—for a project or specific service (*contrato de obra o servicio*).[46] Applying the nonwaiver principle, the Supreme Court of Chile invalidated the for-term clause.[47] It argued that the principle of nonwaiver had a juridical and public purpose that grants the worker conditions that protect his or her life, as well as those of his or her family, among other social concerns.[48] Therefore, the court concluded, the parties violated the labor public order (*orden público laboral*) when they agreed to a for-term employment contract that could be extended beyond the period stipulated by the Labor Code.[49]

In another case, *Reyes c. Empresa PF*, the Chilean Supreme Court held that a worker could not waive her right to maternity *fuero* (job tenure), especially in a case where the protections extended to her unborn child.[50] In *Reyes*, the court below held that the employer terminated the worker without the legally mandated leave of court required from employers prior to terminating pregnant employees.[51] However, it did not find the employer liable for failing to obtain leave of court because the employee waived her *fuero* through an agreement with the employer.[52] According to the court below, the only infraction that the employer committed was failing to provide adequate termination notice to the worker.[53] The Supreme Court reversed the court below and held that protections which protect the rights of the pregnant worker and the unborn child could not be waived.[54]

In another more recent decision, *Araos y otros c. Maquinarias y Equipos Santa Marca Limitada*, the Court invalidated a trial court's judgment deciding that bus drivers had waived their right to be paid for waiting periods.[55] In Chile, employers

---

[46] Sergio Gamonal C., *Comentario de la Jurisprudencia Laboral del año 2004*, 2 Revista de Derecho de la Universidad Adolfo Ibáñez 1234 (2005), *citing* Corte Suprema de Justicia [C.S.J.] [Supreme Court], Mar. 27, 2004, Ingesur c. Navarro, Rol de la causa: 2804-2003 (Chile).

[47] *See* Cód. Trab. [Lab. Code] (Chile.), art. 159, No. 4.

[48] Gamonal C. *supra* note 46, at 1234, *citing* Corte Suprema de Justicia [C.S.J.] [Supreme Court], Mar. 27, 2004, Ingesur c. Navarro, Rol de la causa: 2804-2003 (Chile).

[49] *Id.*

[50] Gamonal C. *supra* note 45, at 757, *citing* Corte Suprema de Justicia [C.S.J.] [Supreme Court], Nov. 4, 2003, Reyes c. Empresas PF, Rol de la causa: 799-2003 (Chile).

[51] *Id. See* Cód. Trab. [Lab. Code] (Chile), arts. 159(4)–(5) and 174.

[52] Gamonal C. *supra* note 45, at 757, *citing* Corte Suprema de Justicia [C.S.J.] [Supreme Court], Nov. 4, 2003, Reyes c. Empresas PF, Rol de la causa: 799-2003 (Chile).

[53] *Id. See* Cód. Trab. [Lab. Code] (Chile), arts. 161–62.

[54] Gamonal C. *supra* note 45, at 757, *citing* Corte Suprema de Justicia [C.S.J.] [Supreme Court], Nov. 4, 2003, Reyes c. Empresas PF, Rol de la causa: 799-2003 (Chile). Most, if not all, Latin American labor law scholars would agree with the decision and, above all, with the argument that the *fuero* does not benefit merely the worker but also the unborn child. *See* Sergio Gamonal C., Introducción Al Derecho Del Trabajo 155–57 (1998).

[55] Corte de Apelaciones de Santiago [C. Apel.] [Court of Appeals], Sept. 13 2013, Araos y otros c. Maquinarias y Equipos Santa Marca Limitada, Rol de la causa: 746-2013 (Chile).

must pay for wait periods, but the parties determine the payment amount.[56] In this case, the workers had a collective bargaining agreement that provided for such payments.[57] However, the workers were seeking wait-period payments predating the existing collective agreement, when it was silent about such payments.[58] The trial judge ruled that because the existing collective agreement did not make any reference to that previous period, the workers waived their right to obtain wait-period payments.[59] The Court of Appeals reversed the trial court and determined that the workers had to receive some sort of payment because the legal minimum rights were not waivable.[60]

Uruguayan courts also apply the principle of nonwaiver, even though no positive law has established it. For example, in the case *Antunez v. Garlux S.A.*, the Supreme Court of Uruguay determined that various terms of a collective bargaining agreement were unenforceable because they diminished legal minimums.[61] The trial court determined that the employer wrongfully dismissed an employee.[62] The Court of Appeals affirmed, and added that the employer had to pay for unpaid overtime, weekly rest, bonuses, and a differential for night work, all of which are mandated by law.[63] According to the employer, these terms were covered by and paid under the collective bargaining agreement, which had altered the legal minimum standards.[64] However, the Court of Appeals disagreed with the employer; it held that those terms were covered by law and could not be reduced by a collective bargaining agreement.[65]

The Supreme Court of Uruguay agreed with the Court of Appeals. It held, inter alia, that the employer failed to demonstrate that the collective bargaining agreement was more favorable to the employees than the legal minimum standards.[66] The Supreme Court was adamant that even collectively bargained agreements must

---

[56] Cód. Trab. [Lab. Code] (Chile), art. 25 bis.

[57] Corte de Apelaciones de Santiago [C. Apel.] [Court of Appeals], Sept. 13 2013, Araos y otros c. Maquinarias y Equipos Santa Marca Limitada, Rol de la causa: 746-2013 (Chile).

[58] *Id.*

[59] *Id.*

[60] *Id.* In the absence of any other agreement, the court assigned payment based on the existing collective agreement.

[61] Suprema Corte de Justicia [SCJ] [Supreme Court of Justice], Antunez Alfonso, Pablo c. Garlux S.A. / Demanda Laboral- Casación, [IUE] (2013-2-27481) (Urug.).

[62] *Id.*

[63] *Id.*

[64] *Id.*

[65] *Id.*

[66] *Id.*

provide more favorable conditions to workers; collective bargaining agreements could not derogate the minimum legal standards.[67]

Another Uruguayan decision, *Plá Regules c. El País S.A.*, also applied the nonwaiver principle.[68] In *Plá Regules*, the question before the court was whether a newspaper photographer's time while "on call" at his home was compensable under the law, even if the employee and employer had a private agreement barring payment during "on call" time, unless the employee was actually performing work.[69] The majority of the Uruguayan Supreme Court applied the principle of nonwaiver and held that because the law mandated payment during on-call time, the private agreement barring such payment was unenforceable.[70]

The facts of the case were straightforward: the photographer was on duty all night until eight in the morning.[71] He was called to work only if there was a need to cover a breaking story during night and early morning hours.[72] But breaking stories were rare.[73] When they happened, and the employer called the journalist to work, the journalist was compensated at the overtime rate of 150 percent, but only when he was called to work.[74] Unhappy with this deal, the worker demanded payment for all hours that he was available to work "on call" for the employer.[75]

The trial court held for the employee.[76] However, the Court of Appeals reversed and dismissed the complaint in its entirety applying the doctrine of *actos propios*,[77] something akin to the common law's estoppel doctrine.[78] It held that the employee had no history of making any overtime pay claims during on-call periods and, as such, tacitly accepted payment only for hours actually worked.[79]

---

[67] *Id.* The court cites to Law No. 15.996, art. 7 (Uru.), which states: "The provisions of this Act shall apply without prejudice to the specific schemes overtime pay that are more favorable to the worker established either by law, arbitration award, or collective bargaining agreement." ("*Las disposiciones de la presente ley se aplicarán sin perjuicio de la validez de los regímenes específicos en materia de remuneración de horas extras más favorables para el trabajador establecidos por ley, laudo o convenio colectivo*"). Law No. 15.996, art. 7 (Uru.).

[68] Suprema Corte de Justicia [SCJ] [Supreme Court of Justice], PLÁ REGULES, AMÉRICO C. EL PAÍS S.A. / DEMANDA LABORAL—CASACIÓN, [IUE] (2013-2-30246) (Urug.).

[69] *Id.*

[70] *Id.*

[71] *Id.*

[72] *Id.*

[73] *Id.*

[74] *Id*

[75] *Id*

[76] *Id*

[77] *Id.* at 2.

[78] WEST'S SPANISH-ENGLISH/ENGLISH-SPANISH LAW DICTIONARY 514 (1992) (defining *actos propios*).

[79] Suprema Corte de Justicia [SCJ][Supreme Court of Justice], PLÁ REGULES, AMÉRICO C. EL PAÍS S.A. / DEMANDA LABORAL—CASACIÓN, [IUE] (2013-2) (Urug.).

The majority of the Supreme Court reversed the appellate court. It argued that when the appellate court applied the theory of *actos propios*, it violated the principle of nonwaiver.[80] The Supreme Court stated that an on-call employee (*guardia de retén*) is subordinated, subject to the employer's orders, and under the direction and control of the employer.[81] Therefore, the court determined that the employee was working and must be paid for the time he was on call.[82]

Unquestionably, Argentinian, Brazilian, Chilean, and Uruguayan courts recognize the principle of nonwaiver.

Regulating Settlements through Nonwaiver

The principle of nonwaiver prohibits any type of act seeking to eradicate labor law rights. It goes beyond mere wage payment laws and applies to legal transactions such as claim settlements.[83] Latin American labor law tries to guarantee that settlements do not conceal an illegal waiver.[84] But some settlements may be enforced by courts if they conform with four requirements: (1) two parties must validly bind themselves; (2) the rights and obligations in the parties' legal claims must be uncertain; (3) the rights claimed by the parties must have accrued; and (4) the parties must extinguish their legal claims through reciprocal concessions.[85]

This all means that if a right is uncertain or is difficult to prove at the time of settlement, the settlement may pass judicial muster and may not violate the nonwaiver

---

[80] *Id.*

[81] *Id.*

[82] *Id.* However, the Supreme Court decided that because the employee exerted less effort during his on-call period than when he is actually working, the employer only needs to provide ordinary, straight pay to the employee when he is on-call but not actually working. *Id.*

[83] PLÁ RODRÍGUEZ, *supra* note 17, at 67; GAMONAL C., INTRODUCCIÓN AL DERECHO, *supra* note 54, at 45.

[84] American legal scholars have made a similar point. *See, e.g.*, Owen M. Fiss, Comment, *Against Settlement*, 93 YALE L.J. 1073, 1076 (1984) (stating "[b]y viewing the lawsuit as a quarrel between two neighbors, the dispute-resolution story that underlies ADR implicitly asks us to assume a rough equality between the contending parties. It treats settlement as the anticipation of the outcome of trial and assumes that the terms of settlement are simply a product of the parties' predictions of that outcome. In truth, however, settlement is also a function of the resources available to each party to finance the litigation, and those resources are frequently distributed unequally. Many lawsuits do not involve a property dispute between two neighbors, or between AT&T and the government (to update the story), but rather concern a struggle between a member of a racial minority and a municipal police department over alleged brutality, or a claim by a worker against a large corporation over work-related injuries. In these cases, the distribution of financial resources, or the ability of one party to pass along its costs, will invariably infect the bargaining process, and the settlement will be at odds with a conception of justice that seeks to make the wealth of the parties irrelevant."). Edward L. Rubin, *Toward a General Theory of Waiver*, 28 UCLA L. REV. 478, 490 (1981) ("The stronger party can induce or compel a waiver, leaving the weaker party in the position that he would have been in if he had never possessed any rights in the first place.").

[85] RUPRECHT, *supra* note 18, at 51 *et seq.* (internal citations omitted).

principle.[86] However, if the parties settle merely to avoid a lengthy lawsuit or to obtain immediate benefits (defraying a larger compensation that is legally owed but that may take longer to obtain because of the legal process), the parties have violated the nonwaiver principle.[87]

To summarize this subsection, the principle of nonwaiver exists in settlements between employers and employees. It does not mean that employees may not settle their claims with employers. It means, however, that employers cannot use settlements to sidestep legal processes to curtail workers' rights. Courts should police settlements.

Waiver of Contractually Acquired Rights

Latin American scholars have also debated whether the nonwaiver principle applies when employees agree with the employer to reduce previously agreed-upon terms that provide better terms and conditions than those afforded by law.[88] Most Latin American scholars have concluded that employees can waive contractual provisions that exceed legal minimum requirements.[89] However, Argentinian Professor Adrian Goldin has argued that in the rare instance where a worker agrees to contractual terms that are less favorable than former contractual provisions, even if those terms exceed legal minimums, judges and other adjudicators should presume that the contractual novation or modification has vices of force or intimidation and, therefore, are unenforceable.[90] In these cases, Goldin argues that the employer must prove to the court

---

[86] *Id.* at 53.

[87] For example, in the Chilean labor court case of *Umaña Gutiérrez c. Fundación Solidaria Trabajo para un Hermano*, a labor court held that a settlement and release agreement entered by the parties after the employment relationship ended was unenforceable. Even though the settlement and release met many contract formalities, the parties needed to obtain a leave of court to settle the controversy because the employee, a pregnant woman, was protected by pregnancy *fuero*. *See* Gamonal C. *supra* note 45, at 772 (*citing* Juzgados del Trabajo [J.T.] [Santiago 4th Labor Court], Jan. 22, 2003, UMAÑA GUTIÉRREZ C. FUNDACIÓN SOLIDARIA TRABAJO PARA UN HERMANO, Rol de la causa: 1.152-01 (Chile)). While Latin American labor law rejects the waiver of labor law rights before and during the term of an employment relationship, scholars debate whether such a right can be waived after the employment contract has terminated. PLÁ RODRÍGUEZ, *supra* note 17, at 103. Some scholars argue that the nonwaiver principle survives after contract termination because the socioeconomic imbalance between the employer and his former worker continues. *Id.* Other Latin American scholars have argued that nonwaiver does not apply after the employment contract terminates. *Id.*

[88] ADRIÁN GOLDIN, CONTRATO DE TRABAJO Y RENUNCIA DE DERECHOS 15 (1987).

[89] *See* GAMONAL C., INTRODUCCIÓN AL DERECHO, *supra* note 54, at 148.

[90] However, some Argentinian judges have held that the worker's intent is a valid form of free expression to amend clauses in individual employment contracts, even in cases where employees consent to less onerous terms than in their previous contract, provided the modifications remained within the legal minimums. *See* Castillejo, *supra* note 10, at 120; M. ZURETTI, PRINCIPIOS, CURSO DE DERECHO DEL TRABAJO Y DE LA SEGURIDAD SOCIAL 60 (Jorge Rodriguez Manicini ed., 4th ed. 2000); *see also* Diego Tosca, *La regla de la irrenunciabilidad*, 1 TRATADO DE DERECHO DEL TRABAJO 360 (Mario E. Ackerman & Diego M. Tosca eds., 2005).

that he or she made a "functional" and "regular" use of his or her prerogatives and rights, such that the act *in pejus* (reducing benefits) is to ensure the survival of the company or of the employment contract, which was threatened by adverse and unforeseeable economic events.[91] According to Goldin, the employer need not prove that there was no intimidation or force, which would be difficult to demonstrate in practice.

Sometimes, however, the mere threat of termination could be considered sufficient intimidation or force to invalidate a contractual modification. For example, in an important Chilean opinion by the Santiago Labor Court of Appeals (*Corte del Trabajo de Santiago*),[92] *Andreani et al. v. the Registro Nacional de Comerciantes, Pequeños Industrials y Artesanos de Chile*, the court voided an employment contract modification that attempted to eliminate severance benefits that exceeded those required by law.[93] The lower labor court held that the employee acquiesced to the change under the threat of termination.[94] According to the facts, the employer notified its workers that if they wished to continue working for the company, they had to sign a new employment contract without extralegal severance rights.[95] The severance clause provided for two months' salary over the stated legal severance requirements provided by the Chilean Labor Code.[96] In its decision, the Santiago Labor Court of Appeals stated, "it is a fact that a great majority of workers can only count with the proceeds of their work for their subsistence and that of their family."[97] It added that "from that viewpoint, the loss of a job causes great damage to the employee as he and his family are exposed to the very serious wrong of not being able to count on the only source of income for livelihood, aggravated by the difficulty of finding a new job."[98] The Court of Appeals also stated that:

> [I]t is illegitimate to put pressure on a worker to force him to waive a contractual benefit—such as a special indemnity for time of employment—under the

[91] Goldin, *supra* note 88, at 51.

[92] The Santiago Labor Court of Appeals was one of various courts of labor appeals in Chile. These specialized courts of appeals for labor cases and controversies existed from 1927 to 1981. They were eliminated during Augusto Pinochet's dictatorship. Since then the Court of Appeals of general competence has reviewed the opinions of the trial level labor courts. *See* Guido Macchiavello Contreras, Manual de Derecho Procesal del Trabajo 44–46 (1997).

[93] Corte Suprema de Justicia [C.S.J.] [Supreme Court], July 10, 1980, Andreani y otros c. Registro Nacional de Comerciantes, Rol de la causa: 4240 (Chile). *See* 77 Revista de Derecho y Jurisprudencia y Gaceta de los Tribunales 61 (1980).

[94] *Id.*

[95] *Id.*

[96] *Id.*

[97] *Id.*

[98] Corte Suprema de Justicia [C.S.J.] [Supreme Court], July 10, 1980, Andreani y otros c. Registro Nacional de Comerciantes, Rol de la causa: 4240 (Chile) (*citing* the Court of Appeals below).

threat of termination because it deprives him of a freely bargained for right, and causes a strong impression [on the worker] since unemployment prevails at this time and it is not easy to find a job, regardless of the age, sex or condition of individuals. Consequently, that pressure constitutes a vice of sufficient force so as to invalidate consent. . . .[99]

The court invalidated the contract even though the terms otherwise met the legal minimums.[100]

* * *

To summarize, Latin American labor law provides for mandatory employment contract terms that cannot be waived by workers through individual, private agreements with the employer. Such waivers would undo the legal protections provided by the legislature for the benefit of the worker and society. Nonwaiver does not mean, however, that the law prohibits all agreements between workers and employers from having some impact on workers' legal and contractual rights. Some out-of-court settlements are permitted in Latin America, as are agreements to reduce previously agreed-upon terms and conditions of employment, so long as the new terms do not effectively waive workers' rights or are used for the benefit of mostly, or only, the employer. Below we will see how the principle of nonwaiver operates in a truncated fashion in the United States and how Latin American law may help us think of ways to better implement the nonwaiver principle in the United States.

NONWAIVER IN THE UNITED STATES

A principle of nonwaiver exists in theory in the United States, but not entirely in practice. We can distill it in the FLSA and its jurisprudence and in collective labor law, and can distill it from the U.S. Constitution's Thirteenth Amendment. But while workers generally may not waive "substantive" legal rights, the U.S. Supreme Court

[99] *Id.* at 61 (translation by authors). The original Spanish states: "*la presión que se ejerce sobre un trabajador para obligarlo a renunciar a un beneficio contractual -como es una indemnización especial por antigüedad- bajo amenaza de despido, es ilegítima porque le priva de un derecho libremente pactado, y es capaz de producir una impresión fuerte en una persona de sano juicio, ya que en las actuales circunstancias existe cesantía y no es fácil encontrar trabajo, independiente ello de la edad, sexo o condición de las personas. En consecuencia, la referida presión constituye el vicio de fuerza suficiente para invalidar el consentimiento, en los términos del art. 1456 del Código Civil.*" *Id.* On July 10, 1980, the Supreme Court upheld the decision by the Santiago Labor Court, confirming the trial judge's decision in favor of the worker. Although many rules have changed, the substance of the decision and the doctrine of the ruling fully apply to the Labor Code currently in force in Chile.

[100] *Id.*

has held that workers may waive their so-called "procedural" rights to present individual and collective complaints in court and, instead, choose to arbitrate disputes individually.[101] As explained more fully below, the U.S. Supreme Court has eclipsed considerations of disparate bargaining positions and protection of workers when holding that workers can waive their rights to sue employers in court and participate in class and collective actions. Given that the U.S. Supreme Court has sanctioned such waivers, Congress needs to act under its authority and duty enshrined in the Thirteenth Amendment to curb so-called procedural waivers, regulating them to better protect workers' rights.

Waiver under the FLSA

The FLSA has express provisions regarding waiver. It clearly states, for example, that no employee may waive his or her right to not be retaliated against for attempting to enforce his or her rights under the FLSA or participating in proceedings related to the enforcement of the law regarding other employees.[102] The text of the FLSA allows for employee waivers in some limited and specific circumstances, as long as policed by government authorities.[103] For example, it allows for employee waivers in wage and hour settlements as long as they are supervised by the Department of Labor.[104] In cases where employees are represented solely by a private attorney, and not by the Department of Labor, then the Court must supervise the settlement.[105]

Positive law does not expressly mention the nonwaiver principle. The Supreme Court read it into the law in *Brooklyn Savings Bank v. O'Neil*[106] and *D. A. Schulte, Inc. v. Gangi*.[107] In those cases, the Court searched the text of the statute, the legislative purposes, and history to determine the scope of waiver under the Act.[108] It concluded that the FLSA's purpose was to protect workers from substandard

---

[101] *See* Epic Systems Corp. v. Lewis, 138 S. Ct. 1612 (2018) (holding that class action waivers are enforceable under the Federal Arbitration Act and do not conflict with the National Labor Relations Act).

[102] The FLSA states: "The rights and remedies in this section may not be waived by any agreement, policy, form, or condition of employment." 29 U.S.C. § 218c(b)(2).

[103] For example, some agricultural employers may request the Wage and Hour Division of the Department of Labor to exempt them from certain child labor provisions. *See* 29 U.S.C. § 213(c)(1)(A)(ii).

[104] 29 U.S.C. § 216(c).

[105] *See* D. A. Schulte, Inc. v. Gangi, 328 U.S. 108, 113 n.8 (1946) (Supreme Court agreed, in *dicta*, that there was a distinction between unsupervised, illegal settlements and stipulated, legitimate judgments where, after bringing suit under the FLSA, employees settle with the employer under supervision of the court).

[106] 324 U.S. 697 (1945).

[107] 328 U.S. 108 (1946).

[108] *See generally* D. A. Schulte, Inc. v. Gangi, 328 U.S. 108 (1946); Brooklyn Sav. Bank v. O'Neil, 324 U.S. 697 (1945).

wages and oppressive working hours.[109] To effectuate this purpose, the Supreme Court held that the Act's provisions are mandatory and could not be waived.[110] If employees could waive their right to minimum wages by accepting wages under the legal minimum, this would be completely contrary to the Act.[111] The Court also determined that other rights granted by the law, such as "liquidated damages"—additional damages available to plaintiffs beyond standard back pay—should be mandatory and nonwaivable to keep with the purposes of the Act.[112] As the Court held in *Brooklyn Savings Bank*:

> Neither the statutory language, the legislative reports nor the debates indicates that the question [of waiver of liquidated damages] was specifically considered and resolved by Congress. In the absence of evidence of specific Congressional intent, it becomes necessary to resort to a broader consideration of the legislative policy behind this provision as evidenced by its legislative history and the provisions in and structure of the Act . . . Such consideration clearly shows that Congress did not intend that an employee should be allowed to waive his right to liquidated damages.[113]

The FLSA's purpose thus recognizes a principle of nonwaiver for similar reasons that Latin American labor law incorporates it: to protect weaker parties from accepting contractual terms that could cancel the workers' legal protections.

Waiver under Collective Labor Law

U.S. collective labor law also contains nonwaiver principles. The NLGA of 1932,[114] perhaps the first federal labor-protective statute in the United States, instituted a principle of nonwaiver. Through the Act, Congress barred federal courts from enforcing so-called "yellow dog contracts," where employers prohibited workers

---

[109] D.A. Schulte, Inc. v. Gangi, 328 U.S. 108, 116 (1946); Brooklyn Sav. Bank v. O'Neil, 324 U.S. 697, 707 (1945); *see also* 29 U.S.C. § 202(a); Barrentine v. Arkansas-Best Freight System Inc., 450 U.S. 728, 739 (1981).

[110] D. A. Schulte, Inc. v. Gangi, 328 U.S. 108, 112 n.8 (1946); Brooklyn Sav. Bank v. O'Neil, 324 U.S. 697, 707 (1945).

[111] Ellen C. Kearns et al., The Fair Labor Standards Act 18–198 (Ellen C. Kearns et al. eds., 2010).

[112] The statute provides: "Any employer who violates the provisions of section 206 or section 207 of this title shall be liable to the employee or employees affected in the amount of their unpaid minimum wages, or their unpaid overtime compensation, as the case may be, and in an additional equal amount as liquidated damages." 29 U.S.C. § 216(b).

[113] Brooklyn Sav. Bank v. O'Neil, 324 U.S. 697, 705–06 (1945).

[114] 29 U.S.C. §§ 101–15 (1995).

from joining labor organizations.[115] The National Labor Relations Board applied the nonwaiver principle present in the NLGA in very recent cases, *D. R. Horton, Inc.*[116] and *Murphy Oil USA, Inc.*[117] Though these cases did not deal with labor unions, they dealt with workers' rights to join class or collective actions in pursuit of FLSA claims. *D.R. Horton* and *Murphy Oil* determined that such employee waivers, where they agreed not to participate in class or collective actions and agreed, instead, to relief through individual, private arbitration, were contrary to the NLRA's guarantees in favor of employee concerted, protected action for mutual aid and protection. The Fifth Circuit reversed *D. R. Horton* and *Murphy Oil* on the grounds that the FAA states a strong federal policy in favor of arbitration, which courts must respect despite the NLGA and the NLRA. On the other hand, on two other cases dealing with identical legal questions, the Seventh and Ninth Circuits held that employees could not waive their right to participate in class and collective actions because to do so would violate the NLRA.[118] The Circuit split led the U.S. Supreme Court to grant *certiorari* to the line of cases. A five-member conservative majority of the Court upheld the class waivers.[119] It held that another federal statute, the FAA, specified a strong federal policy in favor of arbitration. Moreover, it held that the FAA and federal labor law do not conflict because federal labor law only protect species of activities related to collective bargaining and union organizing, such as strikes and pickets, not filing suits in court. In its holding, the five-member conservative majority held that such agreements to arbitrate had coexisted with U.S. labor law for decades. As fully explained below, however, the path toward waiver of so-called "procedural" rights has a protracted and contradictory history. In fact, arbitration of employee claims is a rather novel thing in the United States. It follows a contemporary deterioration in U.S. labor jurisprudence in favor of employers.

---

[115] 29 U.S.C. §§ 103 & 104 (b). Professor Katherine Stone describes yellow dog contracts in the following manner: "'Yellow dog contracts' are employment contracts in which workers promise not to join a union in order to obtain employment. They were prevalent in the early decades of the twentieth century and were approved by the Supreme Court in the Hitchman Coal and Coppage cases . . . After decades of agitation by organized labor, in 1932 Congress declared yellow dog contracts unenforceable in [§] 3 of the Norris-LaGuardia Act. . . ." Katherine Van Wezel Stone, *Mandatory Arbitration of Individual Employment Rights: The Yellow Dog Contract of the 1990s*, 73 DENV. U. L. REV. 1017, 1037 n.146 (1996). *See also* Hitchman Coal & Coke Co. v. Mitchell, 245 U.S. 229 (1917); Coppage v. State of Kansas, 236 U.S. 1 (1915).

[116] D. R. Horton, Inc., 357 N.L.R.B. 2277 (2012), *rev'd in part*, 737 F.3d 344 (5th Cir. 2013).

[117] 361 NLRB No. 72 (2014), at *10; *rev'd*, 808 F.3d 1013 (5th Cir. 2017), *cert granted* 137 S. Ct. 809 (2017).

[118] Lewis v. Epic Systems Corporation, 823 F.3d 1147 (7th Cir. 2016), *rev'd*, 138 S. Ct. 1612 (2018). Morris v. Ernst & Young, LLP, 834 F.3d 975 (9th Cir. 2016), *rev'd*, 138 S. Ct. 1612 (2018).

[119] Epic Systems Corp. v. Lewis, 138 S. Ct. 1612 (2018) (holding that class action waivers are enforceable under the Federal Arbitration Act and do not conflict with the National Labor Relations Act).

The Perilous American Journey to Arbitration

Employers' demands for arbitration in lieu of court-based litigation has crystallized from a long line of cases dealing with the FAA, a 1925 statute aiming to facilitate arbitration agreements between commercial parties. That statute states in relevant part:

> A written provision in any maritime transaction or a contract evidencing a transaction involving commerce to settle by arbitration a controversy thereafter arising out of such contract or transaction, or the refusal to perform the whole or any part thereof, or an agreement in writing to submit to arbitration an existing controversy arising out of such a contract, transaction, or refusal, shall be valid, irrevocable, and enforceable, save upon such grounds as exist at law or in equity for the revocation of any contract.[120]

Hence, the statute, as passed in 1925, states that courts of law should treat arbitration agreements as if they were traditional contracts. Courts may not enforce them based on traditional contract doctrines such as fraud, duress, or unconscionability. Congress enacted the FAA because courts at the time frowned on arbitration agreements. Such agreements enabled private parties to remove themselves from the jurisdiction of the courts. Congress understood, however, that merchants should decide if courts should handle their disputes. Moreover, courts should respect parties' agreements.[121]

However, it took many years for courts to apply the FAA to contracts that involved economically subordinated parties such as workers. The FAA's language strongly suggests that it does not apply to workers.[122] The FAA states that any "contracts of employment of seamen, railroad employees, or any other class of workers engaged in foreign or interstate commerce" are exempted from the Act.[123] Because of that language, courts disagreed about the applicability of the FAA to employment contracts.[124] The leading U.S. Supreme Court case enforcing an arbitration agreement in the employment context was a 1991 case, *Gilmer v. Interstate/Johnson Lane Corp.*[125] In that case, the U.S. Supreme Court green-lighted agreements

---

[120] 9 U.S.C. § 2.

[121] *See* Jeffrey W. Stempel, *Reconsidering the Employment Contract Exclusion in Section 1 of the Federal Arbitration Act: Correcting the Judiciary's Failure of Statutory Vision, 1991*, J. DISP. RESOL. 259, 259–62 (1991).

[122] Matthew W. Finkin, *"Workers' Contracts" under the United States Arbitration Act: An Essay in Historical Clarification*, 17 BERKELEY J. EMP. & LAB. L. 282, 282–83 (1996).

[123] 9 U.S.C. § 1.

[124] Martin H. Malin, *The Arbitration Fairness Act: It Need Not and Should Not Be an All or Nothing Proposition*, 87 IND. L.J. 289, 293 (2012).

[125] 500 U.S. 20 (1991).

to arbitrate age discrimination claims absent a congressional statement to the contrary.[126]

Since *Gilmer*, U.S. courts have increasingly supported a broad federal policy favoring arbitration agreements in the employment context.[127] In *Circuit City Stores, Inc. v. Adams*,[128] the Supreme Court emboldened its view that the statute applied to employees.[129] It held that Section 1 of the FAA applied only to employees involved in moving goods across state lines or with foreign jurisdictions.[130] That narrow interpretation of Section 1 of the FAA has been criticized by legal scholars as inapposite to the plain meaning of the statute and Congress's purpose,[131] but those critiques have failed to move the Supreme Court against its trend to broadly enforce agreements to arbitrate in the employment context. As of 2018, estimates show that more than half of U.S. workers are covered by agreements to arbitrate claims.[132]

Agreements to arbitrate have become so commonplace today in the United States that workers only need to provide what amounts to constructive assent to be bound.[133] These waivers are often drafted in small print by employers' attorneys and in legalese.[134] Courts have even enforced such agreements to arbitrate when merely made in pre-employment applications with boilerplate waivers[135] or employment manuals.[136] The parties do not even need to sign such waivers to make them go into effect.[137] Not even state law, which provides the common law foundations for contract law, including agreements to arbitrate, may undo agreements to arbitrate

---

126 *Id.* at 26. For a sarcastic view on how courts and primarily the current Roberts Court's conservative majority have created de facto rules that presume arbitrability of many claims, including employment claims, *see* Charles A. Sullivan & Timothy P. Glynn, *The FAA Triumphal: A Modest Opinion*, 19 EMP. RTS. & EMP. POL'Y J. 103 (2015).

127 Gilmer, 500 U.S. 20 at 25 (*citing* Moses H. Cone Mem'l Hosp. v. Mercury Constr. Corp., 460 U.S. 1, 24 (1983)). In fact, the policy is so broad that even labor unions can waive employee individual statutory rights. 14 Penn Plaza LLC v. Pyett 556 U.S. 247 (2009).

128 Circuit City Stores Inc., v. Adams, 532 U.S. 105 (2001).

129 *Id.* at 112–19. *See also* Tenney Engineering, Inc. v. United Elec. Radio & Mach. Workers, 207 F.2d 450, 452 (3rd Cir. 1953) (divided court of appeals holds that the employment contract is covered by FAA because only employees directly involved in the movement of goods in interstate commerce were excluded).

130 Circuit City Stores Inc., v. Adams, 532 U.S. 105, 114 (2001).

131 *See, e.g.*, Finkin, *supra* note 122, at 282; Stempel, *supra* note 121, at 259; Stone, *supra* note 115, at 1017.

132 Editorial Board, *The Supreme Court Sticks It to Workers, Again*, N.Y. TIMES, May 24, 2018.

133 Jean R. Sternlight, *Disarming Employees: How American Employers Are Using Mandatory Arbitration to Deprive Workers of Legal Protection*, 80 BROOK. L. REV. 1309 (2015).

134 *Id.*

135 KEARNS ET AL., *supra* note 111, at 18–12.

136 *See, e.g.*, Lang v. Burlington N. R.R. Co., 835 F. Supp. 1104, 1106 (D. Minn. 1993) (employee constructively assented to an arbitration agreement when employer promulgated a new employee manual with an arbitration clause and the employee did not object to it, and remained working for the employer).

137 *See* Caley v. Gulfstream Aerospace Corp., 428 F.3d 1359, 1368–69 (11th Cir. 2005) (stating that while an arbitration agreement is required to be in writing, it need not be signed by the parties).

employment claims. In another recent case, the Supreme Court validated a commercial agreement to arbitrate even though California state law explicitly stated that agreements to arbitrate statutory rights were unconscionable.[138] According to the Supreme Court, the FAA preempted California's unconscionability rule if the rule targeted arbitration specifically and not all contracts.[139] The U.S. Supreme Court has thus made arbitration the rule, not the exception, for employment and many other claims. In the words of two U.S. labor law scholars, the FAA reigns "triumphal."[140]

The Empirical Evidence against Arbitration

Arbitration agreements suffer from more than just doctrinal deficiencies, such as assent and violations of party autonomy. The evidence also shows that it leads to less stringent enforcement of workers' rights. Professor Jean R. Sternlight has argued, for example, that employees win less often and win less money in arbitration than in litigation, attorneys are less willing to take employee claims that are heard in arbitration rather than in litigation, and arbitration is an inhospitable venue for *pro se* plaintiff-employees.[141] She further argued that arbitration is being used to eradicate class actions, collective actions, and even group litigation, which are all essential for an effective system of labor law justice where individual workers can suffer significant collective action problems.[142]

---

[138] AT&T Mobility v. Concepcion, 563 U.S. 333, 340 (2011). As the Supreme Court recognized: "Under California law, courts may refuse to enforce any contract found 'to have been unconscionable at the time it was made,' or may 'limit the application of any unconscionable clause.'" *Id.* (*citing* Cal. Civ. Code Ann. § 1670.5(a)). The U.S. Supreme Court added, "Under California Supreme Court precedent: '[W]hen the waiver is found in a consumer contract of adhesion in a setting in which disputes between the contracting parties predictably involve small amounts of damages, and when it is alleged that the party with the superior bargaining power has carried out a scheme to deliberately cheat large numbers of consumers out of individually small sums of money, then . . . the waiver becomes in practice the exemption of the party 'from responsibility for [its] own fraud, or willful injury to the person or property of another.' Under these circumstances, such waivers are unconscionable under California law and should not be enforced." *Id.* (*citing* Discover Bank v. Superior Court, 113 P.3d 1100, 1110 (Cal. 2005) (alterations in original)).

Even though the California Supreme Court and American courts used essentially the same test for unconscionability of contracts generally, the U.S. Supreme Court deemed California law to be particularly hostile to arbitration, in conflict with the FAA, and held the *Discover Bank* rule against federal public policy and the FAA. *Id.*

[139] AT&T Mobility, 563 U.S. at 359 (dissent argues that arbitration agreements under the FAA's text and purposes allows "courts to refuse to enforce arbitration agreements on grounds that exist 'for the revocation of any contract.'"). *See* 9 U.S.C. § 2.

[140] Sullivan & Glynn, *supra* note 126, at 103.

[141] Sternlight, *supra* note 133, at 1312.

[142] *Id. See also* David S. Schwartz, *Enforcing Small Print to Protect Big Business: Employee and Consumer Rights Claims in an Age of Compelled Arbitration*, 1997 Wis. L. Rev. 33, 36 (1997) (criticizing the Supreme Court's broad endorsement of adhesive pre-dispute arbitration agreements, which have created "a monster"). For a more middle-of-the-road critique against mandatory arbitration *see* Malin, *supra* note 124, at 311-312 (arguing that not all arbitration clauses in employment contracts need to be completely banned, but, rather, regulated

Sternlight reports that win rates for employees are much lower in arbitration than in litigation. While the win rate is 21.4 percent in arbitration for employees, it is 36.4 percent in federal court employment discrimination cases, 57 percent in state court noncivil rights cases, and 59 percent in California state court common law discharge claims.[143] The data also showed that employees win much lower awards in arbitration. Median damages in arbitration were only $36,500 in AAA arbitration, while they were $176,426 in federal court employment discrimination cases, $85,560 in state court noncivil rights employment cases, and $355,843 in California state court common law discharge cases.[144] The difference in mean damages was also stark: $109,858 in AAA arbitration, $394,223 in federal court employment discrimination, and $575,453 in state court noncivil rights employment cases.[145]

Sternlight also reports studies that have shown that only a minuscule number of employees covered by mandatory employment arbitration agreements ever present a complaint in arbitration.[146] As she recounts: "although the American Arbitration Association handles roughly 50% of all employment arbitration claims that are filed, in 2008 it received only 946 claims involving employees. And roughly 10% of those claims were brought by employers against employees rather than employees against employers."[147] These low numbers mean that only 0.008 percent of covered employees, or 1 of every 12,000 covered employees, files an arbitration claim each year.[148] While some may argue that the claims are not being filed simply because there are no claims to file, that argument falls on its face once we compare rates of arbitration with those of courts. On average, employees file 30,000 cases based on the FLSA or Employee Retirement Income Security Act (ERISA) each year, of which roughly 560 are class actions, meaning that they involve many individual workers per suit.[149] Sternlight estimated that if arbitration were to follow a similar rate of frequency for employees covered by private arbitration, employees should be filing 75,000 cases per year (7,500 if we ignored the class actions, which is still a much higher frequency than the measly 2,000 arbitration claims brought by employees,

in ways that better protect the due process rights of employees, like appointing the arbitrator in ways to reduce pro-employer bias and providing disclosure rules for arbitrations).

143 Sternlight, *supra* note 133, at 1326.

144 *Id.*

145 *Id.*

146 *Id.* at 1332. *See also* Alexander Colvin & Mark D. Gough, Comparing Mandatory Arbitration and Litigation: Access, Process and Outcomes, Research Report to the Robert L. Habush Endowment of the American Association for Justice 34–35 (2014) (on file with author); Alexander J. S. Colvin & Kelly Pike, *Saturns and Rickshaws Revisited: What Kind of Employment Arbitration System Has Developed?*, 29 Ohio St. J. on Disp. Resol. 59 (2014).

147 Sternlight, *supra* note 133, at 1329–30.

148 *Id.* at 1330.

149 *Id.*

roughly).[150] The existing evidence does not seem to support arbitration as an effective system for worker justice.

An important part of the reason employees do not pursue claims through arbitration is that they are uneconomical for plaintiff-employees' attorneys; the damages sought are generally lower than the cost of representing the worker in the arbitration process.[151]

Finally, the hostility of arbitration to *pro se* plaintiff-employees also matters if employees cannot find lawyers to represent them. Research by Alexander Colvin and his collaborators, on which Professor Sternlight based much of her own reported evidence, has shown that though represented parties fare ill in arbitration winning 27.9 percent of their cases, *pro se* plaintiffs fare even worse, winning only 17 percent of their cases.[152] *Pro se* plaintiffs also recovered much lower awards, even if they won: an average of $11,071 compared to the $99,217 recovered on average by represented plaintiffs.[153]

Individual employment arbitration, as it exists today in the United States, seems to be an ineffective procedure to enforce labor law. It has become a de jure and de facto means to eradicate workers' rights.

Buttressing Nonwaiver in the United States: The Thirteenth Amendment, Statutory Reform, and Regulating Arbitration

Under our Latin American view agreeing that the Thirteenth Amendment is a constitutional labor-protective provision, as explained in chapter 2, labor rights, which guarantee workers' freedom, should not be waived. Employers who willy-nilly require that their workers sign boilerplate provisions and contracts of adhesion nullifying labor rights may be forcing onto workers terms and conditions of employment, effectively undoing the ban on involuntary servitude. Political philosopher Elizabeth Anderson calls this kind of employer power, which can undo public order norms, a "private government."[154] We simply cannot sanction this kind of untrammelled employer power in a modern, democratic republic.

In line with some U.S. scholars of the Thirteenth Amendment, we argue that courts and the U.S. Congress should read the Thirteenth Amendment as a general constitutional protection of work. As such, courts need to be more attentive

---

150 *Id.*

151 Sternlight, *supra* note 133, at 1336.

152 *Id.* (*citing* Colvin & Pike, *supra* note 146, at 78).

153 *Id.* at 1341.

154 Elizabeth Anderson, Private Government: How Employers Rule Our Lives (and Why We Don't Talk about It) (2017).

to workers who waive their labor rights, as these are rights that guarantee worker freedom, autonomy, and dignity. The U.S. Congress, under its duty to safeguard workers' freedom under the Thirteenth Amendment, and to better cement the nonwaiver principle, should amend the NLRA to clearly include employee participation in class and collective actions as part of its protections for concerted activities for mutual aid and protection. It should also amend the FAA to exclude workers from it, i.e., so that workers cannot waive their labor rights to file suits in court and join class and collective actions. In the alternative, and perhaps a better solution than outright banning arbitration given that judicialization of workers' rights has never been a panacea for U.S. workers,[155] Congress could create rules to regulate employment arbitration and, as such, sponsor a system of labor courts through private arbitration where workers' due process rights are better protected.

Scholars have already argued the need to regulate boilerplate and contracts of adhesion where weaker parties waive their rights.[156] Professor Margaret Jane Radin argues that the abuse of boilerplate documents has provided powerful contracting parties the capacity to rewrite laws, including those in the workplace, generating a dangerous democratic deficiency in the United States.[157] According to Professor Radin, courts could help fix the democratic imbalance through stricter scrutiny of boilerplate contracts, including agreements to arbitrate. She also argues that the powerful parties who write boilerplate contracts and induce others to assent to them without the waiving parties' express informed consent should be held liable for tort.[158]

Professor Martin Malin has also argued for a regulatory approach to employment arbitration. He calls for better protections of employees' due process rights when they waive rights, appointing arbitrators in ways that reduce pro-employer bias, and disclosure rules for arbitrations.[159] He also argues that the law should outright ban class and collective action waivers because they exist to erase these procedural mechanisms from the employment context.[160]

---

[155] *See, e.g.*, Ellen Barry et al., Rights on Trial: How Workplace Discrimination Law Perpetuates Inequality (2017) (arguing that the adversarial character of litigation in the United States imposes considerable personal and financial costs on plaintiffs of sexual harassment that make them feel like they have lost, regardless of the case's outcome).

[156] *See* Margaret Jane Radin, Boilerplate: The Fine Print, Vanishing Rights, and the Rule of Law 155 (2013).

[157] *Id.*

[158] *Id.* at 156 (arguing that because unsuspecting parties agree to boilerplate in the form of an accident, not contract, tort law could provide a remedy to its victims). *But see* Eric A. Posner, *ProCD v Zeidenberg and Cognitive Overload in Contractual Bargaining*, 77 U. Chi. L. Rev. 1181, 1194 (2010) (arguing that consumers seem to assume the risk of partial disclosure of boilerplate terms because they do not contain any real surprises for consumers).

[159] Malin, *supra* note 124, at 294.

[160] *Id.* at 313–14.

From a Latin American perspective, regulatory strategies for so-called "procedural" waivers resemble the regulatory rules pertaining to settlement of employee claims and contracts that diminish or constrict existing rights. Procedural waiver regulations are similar to such settlement rules in that their aim is not to ban all waivers, but to regulate waivers in a manner where the integrity of the so-called "substantive" legal protections remains.

There is some evidence supporting bilateral benefits of arbitration. Arbitration can be faster, simpler, and more economical for employees.[161] While employment claims that go through arbitration take only about one year to be adjudicated after filing, litigation takes twice as long.[162] Moreover, as Professor Malin has argued, existing research may underestimate the speediness of arbitration given that employers seek appeal of trial court orders half of the time, a strategy that employers may easily undertake given the American liberality toward appealing judicial decisions.[163] On the other hand, the grounds to appeal arbitration decisions are extremely limited.[164]

Moreover, the evidence appears to suggest that arbitration may be more accessible as a forum to seek redress of employment claims for workers with modest means and relatively smaller claims. After analyzing data from the American Arbitration Association (AAA), which handles half of all employment arbitrations in the United States, Professor Alexander Colvin found out that 82.4 percent of the claimants reported salaries under $100,000.[165] Median claims amount to a little over $105,000, while 25 percent of the claims were for $36,000 or less.[166] Moreover, because employers must pay 100 percent of the arbitration fees 97 percent of the time, access to arbitration as a forum to seek redress of workplace claims may actually be feasible for workers.[167]

We should note that the importance of speedy, simple, and cheap forums for the redress of workplace claims is particularly important in the United States because the United States does not have a comprehensive system of labor courts or employment tribunals that provide effective justice to workers, unlike many foreign jurisdictions.[168] Therefore, we must consider the strong principle of nonwaiver

---

[161] Alexander J. S. Colvin, *An Empirical Study of Employment Arbitration: Case Outcomes and Processes*, 8 J. EMPIRICAL LEGAL STUD. 1, 8 (2011) [hereinafter Colvin, *Case Outcomes*]; Alexander J. S. Colvin, *Empirical Research on Employment Arbitration: Clarity Amidst the Sound and Fury?* 11 EMP. RTS. & EMP. POL'Y J. 405, 426 (2007) [hereinafter Colvin, *Clarity Amidst the Sound and Fury?*].

[162] Colvin, *Case Outcomes, supra* note 161; Colvin, *Clarity Amidst the Sound and Fury?, supra* note 161.

[163] Malin, *supra* note 124, at 294 (internal citations omitted).

[164] *Id.*

[165] Colvin, *Case Outcomes, supra* note 161, at 10–11, table 2.

[166] *Id.*

[167] *Id.* at 9.

[168] The existence of labor courts or employment tribunals in Europe and Latin America may also help explain why the United States has been almost unique in providing for private arbitration of labor and employment claims.

against a procedural background where specialized labor tribunals do not exist. Arbitration may be the American labor court. Even so, we cannot give employers all the authority to create, fund, and otherwise institutionalize it.

CONCLUSION: GETTING OUT OF THE "PROCEDURAL" TRAP THROUGH PRINCIPLES

This chapter has described the principle of nonwaiver in Latin America. It also has compared it with the U.S.'s "substantive" and "procedural" waiver jurisprudence. It has shown that Latin American labor law eschews waiver of workers' rights because workers are weaker parties in bargaining relationships. As such, waiver, a private agreement, could undo what the law has attempted to correct. While the United States has a similar principle, today it relates mostly to waivers of so-called "substantive" rights. Procedural rights can be generally waived under Supreme Court liberal interpretations of the FAA. Individual employees may waive their rights to sue employers in courts. Additionally, employers might require collective and class action waivers from employees.

From one perspective, the strong policy in favor of employment arbitration as a procedural but not substantive waiver may make sense because arbitration may offer quicker, simpler, and less expensive procedures to resolve employment disputes, goals that are also inherent in procedural labor law in Latin America. However, the existing empirical evidence suggests that employees seek legal redress much less frequently, prevail less, and obtain lower sums when they waive their rights to seek judicial redress and participate in class and collective action. This evidence is damning for individual employment arbitration. Hence why amending the FAA to clearly exclude employees from the federal policy in favor of arbitration, and amending the NLRA to include class and collective actions as part of its protections of concerted, protected activity may be in order. Such amendments should be based on the Thirteenth Amendment of the U.S. Constitution, which gives Congress the right and authority to protect workers' freedom and protect them from involuntary servitude.

See Sternlight, *supra* note 133, at 843–44. We should stress that Latin American legal scholars recognize special principles of procedural labor law: economy, swiftness, and simplicity. Héctor-Hugo Barbagelata, *Tendencias de los Procesos Laborales en Iberoamérica*, 21 Revista Facultad de Derecho de la Universidad de la República 37 (2002). Other procedural rights include orality, immediacy, primacy of reality (of facts), and the judge's active participation in the process. *Id.*

However, while we argued that outright bans of individual arbitration in the employment context would better enshrine nonwaiver, perhaps a better alternative to protect workers' rights is to regulate arbitration. Judicial processes have been all but a panacea for labor rights in the United States, which lacks a comprehensive system of labor courts that can provide simple, cheap, and fast labor justice. Arbitration in the collective bargaining context has been effective in providing workplace justice for many years in the United States. A legitimate space for individual employment arbitration could exist in that country. Latin American countries sometimes take such regulatory strategies. For example, in this chapter we read that when workers agree to reduce existing contractual rights, Latin American law may establish a rebuttable presumption stating that the agreement is detrimental to workers and, therefore, unenforceable. Employers may rebut the presumption by convincing a court that the agreement benefited the worker. In the United States, we could also create a rebuttable presumption that the agreement to arbitrate is illegal and against public policy, unless the employer can prove that the agreement benefited the worker, providing effective, quicker, cheaper, and simpler procedures than those provided by courts of law. The process may also have to provide economic incentives for lawyers to represent employee-plaintiffs. As Professor Malin already argued, regulatory strategies may also include the creation of panels of state or tripartite-sanctioned employment arbitrators with a reputation for legal expertise, impartiality, and fairness. In fact, employment arbitration could be fashioned as U.S.-style labor courts or employment tribunals if carefully crafted. Something good might come out of the otherwise scandalous judicial sanction of labor rights waivers in the United States.

5

CONTINUITY

INTRODUCTION: PRESUMING STABILITY AND CONTINUITY

This chapter concerns the continuity principle of employment relationships. Jurists have also referred to it as the principle of employment "stability"[1] or "permanence."[2] Essentially, Latin American jurists presume that the employment contract has an indefinite duration. Therefore, employers must provide cause to terminate the employment contract and/or pay the employee some form of severance. But the continuity principle in Latin American labor law is not merely concerned with termination. It also serves to provide employees with the benefits of their employment contracts and to subsequently bind employers to their obligations, despite changes in the contract terms (resulting from contractual modifications) or a change in the parties to the contract (such as when predecessor employers are acquired by successor employers). In addition, judges also use the continuity principle to reform precarious contracts, under certain conditions, into more stable, permanent employment contracts.

The continuity principle is perhaps the first principle that should be discussed in this book after protection, given that it is the principle that substantively protects

[1] Américo Plá Rodríguez, Los Principios del Derecho del Trabajo 220 (3rd ed. 1998).

[2] Inmaculada Baviera, *Employment Stability in Spanish Labor Law: Between Regulatory Tradition and Social Reality*, 34 Comp. Lab. L. & Pol'y J. 677 (2013) (describing the erosion of employment stability in Spain).

Principled Labor Law. Sergio Gamonal C. and César F. Rosado Marzán.

workers at dismissal and during other stages in the employment contract (e.g., contract modification) where workers are particularly vulnerable. However, we discuss the continuity principle toward the end of this book because the United States, unlike most other countries, and certainly unlike any Latin American country, generally does not have laws that presume employment stability. The United States, through its common law courts, has adopted a peculiar rule of "at-will" employment since about the end of the nineteenth century.[3] Only the state of Montana[4] and the territories of Puerto Rico[5] and the Virgin Islands[6] have altered employment at will through statute. As such, of all the principles that we discuss in this book, the principle of continuity is weakest in the United States.

The absence of general statutory protections for employment stability does not mean, however, that the continuity principle is totally absent in the United States. The U.S. public sector, which employs about 9 percent of the U.S. workforce, generally requires some sort of "cause" for termination.[7] Moreover, workers with more bargaining power, particularly unionized workers, have collectively bargained out of at-will employment and for "just-cause" termination.[8] In workplaces covered by collective bargaining agreements arbitrators have developed a "common law of the shop."[9] Dismissal protections under the U.S. "common law of the shop" are stronger than in most of Latin America because employees may request reinstatement with back pay as remedies for unjustified dismissals, while in Latin America most terminations without cause may merely imply that the employer is liable for

---

[3] *See, e.g.*, Payne v. W. & Atl. R.R. Co., 81 Tenn. 507 (1884) (Supreme Court of Tennessee holds that the employment relationship can be terminated by any party at will "for any cause, good or bad, or without cause, and the other cannot complain in law").

[4] Montana Wrongful Discharge from Employment Act (WDEA), MONT. CODE ANN. §§ 39-2-901 to -915 (2007).

[5] P.R. LAWS ANN. tit. 29, §§ 185a-m (2010). *See also* Jorge M. Farinacci-Fernós, *The Search for a Wrongful Dismissal Statute: A Look at Puerto Rico's Act No. 80 as a Potential Starting Point*, 17 EMP. RTS. & EMP. POL'Y J. 125 (2013). As of this writing, however, the congressionally appointed and unelected Fiscal Control Board, which is managing Puerto Rico's finances in light of a fiscal crisis, is pressuring the local government to derogate its just-cause termination law and legislate for employment at will. Joanisabel González, EL NUEVO DÍA, *La Junta Fiscal Accede a los Pedidos de Ricardo Rosselló: El Ente Fiscal No Tocará el Presupuesto de la Legislatura a Cambio de la Ley 80*, May 22, 2018, https://www.elnuevodia.com/negocios/economia/nota/lajuntafiscalaccedealospedidosdericardorossello-2423632/#cxrecs_s.

[6] U.S. Virgin Islands Wrongful Discharge Act. 24 V.I.C. § 76.

[7] *See* Michael Greenstone & Adam Looney, *A Record Decline in Government Jobs: Implications for the Economy and America's Workforce*, BROOKINGS (Aug. 3, 2012), http://www.brookings.edu/blogs/jobs/posts/2012/08/03-jobs-greenstone-looney (explaining how in 2012, government employment represented less than 9 percent of the total U.S. workforce).

[8] *See, e.g.*, Clyde W. Summers, *Individual Protection against Unjust Dismissal: Time for a Statute*, 62 VA. L. REV. 481 (1976).

[9] *Id.*

some sort of severance pay.[10] Hence, the continuity principle applies unevenly to U.S. workers since only a small minority has strong protections against dismissal. Labor law reformers should try to extend it further through statute. Additionally, despite employment at will, there is a doctrine of wrongful dismissal in the United States that protects workers against terminations that are discriminatory, retaliatory, tortious, or violate public policy.[11] For those workers, a much softer version of continuity protects them, but it does exist.

This chapter is organized in the following way: First, we describe the principle of continuity in Latin American doctrine and law, particularly in Argentina, Brazil, Chile, and Uruguay, the four countries that we have been surveying throughout this book. We describe how the principle is relevant to protect workers against unfair dismissal, reinforce employer obligations despite contract modification and successorship, and give judges the authority to reform precarious contracts into standard contracts of employment. Second, we describe the uneven and weaker presence of continuity in the United States. While we recognize its weakness and unevenness, we also underscore its existence, which sometimes may be understated by labor adversaries and labor allies alike. We also argue that while collective bargaining is the historically and institutionally most congruent manner to extend continuity in the United States, extending continuity through collective bargaining today would require federal legislation to strengthen collective bargaining protections and unionization, a highly unlikely scenario.[12] Increasing public employment would also buttress dismissal protections in the United States since government employers' jobs provide for just-cause termination. However, massive increments in public employment in the United States also appear unlikely given political interests to diminish public sector employment and a generalized skepticism of government in the United States, among other reasons.[13] "Flexicurity" schemes, where workers have rights to generous unemployment compensation benefits, lifetime training, and where government tries to match workers to jobs, also appear too inimical to the U.S. political

---

[10] *See* Samuel Estreicher & Jeffrey M. Hirsch, *Comparative Wrongful Dismissal Law: Reassessing American Exceptionalism*, 92 N.C. L. REV. 343, 457–58 (2014) (describing how most countries with for-cause dismissal rarely order reinstatement, even if available as a remedy, and damages are capped by statute).

[11] *See, e.g.*, Cynthia L. Estlund, *Wrongful Discharge Protections in an At-Will World*, 74 TEX. L. REV. 1655, 1691 (1996).

[12] KENNETH DAU-SCHMIDT ET AL., LABOR LAW IN THE CONTEMPORARY WORKPLACE 115–16 (2nd ed. 2014) (describing the political near impossibility of reforming labor law given decades-old legislative deadlock on the issue).

[13] Richard J. Pierce, Jr., *Valuing Bureaucracy Is a Quixotic Project*, THE REGULATORY REVIEW, Dec. 13, 2017, https://www.theregreview.org/2017/12/13/pierce-valuing-bureaucracy-quixotic-project/ (explaining the reason why increasing the ranks of professional civil servants is politically and economically unfeasible); PAUL R. VERKUIL, VALUING BUREAUCRACY: THE CASE FOR PROFESSIONAL GOVERNMENT 47–48 (2017) (explaining political opposition to public sector employment in the United States).

economy to be a realistic option.[14] Federal repeal through a just-cause termination law would also end employment at will, but that solution also appears politically difficult. Therefore, we argue that the most likely way of expanding the continuity principle in the short to medium term in the United States is through state-by-state statutory repeal of the employment at will doctrine.[15] We then conclude the chapter.

CONTINUITY IN LATIN AMERICA

As Professors Katherine Stone and Harry Arthurs have already explained, in the twentieth century, especially after World War II, the standard employment contract, "was conceived as a continuing, stable, long-lasting, full-time legal relationship that would provide a career for the worker with his or her employer."[16] Employment stability was understood to benefit workers and employers, especially those employers organized vertically.[17] Employers used employment stability as a strategic resource to build their internal labor markets, including the firm-specific skills of their workers, which workers strove to improve upon in return for advancement opportunities and seniority rights.[18] Continuity also helped to guarantee certain economic security for workers so that they could consume, thereby benefiting the overall economy.[19]

With the advent of precarious work, the diffusion of the standard employment contract appears over, alongside optimism about labor law.[20] However, the growth of nonstandard work and pessimism in labor law seem to be more of a developed world problem.[21] In Latin America, despite the fact that the standard employment contract has truly never covered most workers due to economic informality, labor

[14] Thomas Bredgaard, *Flexibility and Security in Employment Regulation: Learning from Denmark*, *in* Rethinking Workplace Regulation: Beyond the Standard Contract of Employment 213 (Katherine V. W. Stone & Harry Arthurs eds., 2013) (explaining the Danish system of flexicurity). *See also* Kathleen Thelen, Varieties of Liberalization and the New Politics of Social Solidarity (2014) (describing the United States and other Anglo-American countries as liberal market economies that differ markedly from coordinated market economies more common in Northern and Central Europe).

[15] *See* Moshe Z. Marvit, *The Way Forward for Labor Is Through the States*, The American Prospect, Sept. 1, 2017, http://prospect.org/article/way-forward-labor-through-states (explaining that progressive labor law reform is available today in the United States almost exclusively through the states, not the federal government).

[16] *See* Rethinking Workplace Regulation: Beyond the Standard Contract of Employment (Katherine V. W. Stone & Harry Arthurs eds., 2013).

[17] *Id.* at 2.

[18] *Id.*

[19] *Id.* at 2–3.

[20] *See id.*

[21] *Id.* at 4.

laws have always presumed a continuing, full-time employment contract, and generally continue to do so unless explicitly legislated to the contrary. In other words, despite gaps in coverage, Latin American law has striven to provide workers with stable employment relationships and continues to do so, at least generally. To that end, the employment laws of most Latin American countries protect the employment relationship from interruptions and limit the rights of employers to terminate the employment relationship or substitute it for a different one.[22]

As we argued in Chapter 1, the principle of continuity stems from the protective principle. In essence, it posits that while the employer is bound to maintain its employment relationships with employees, employees can resign from their jobs without generally facing liability.[23] If employers could indefinitely bind workers to their jobs, workers would be strapped into some type of forced servitude.[24]

Since the publication of Américo Plá Rodríguez's treatise on labor law principles, Latin American jurisprudence has understood the principle of continuity to operate in three ways: (1) it provides rules for the termination of the employment contract; (2) it provides continuity despite contractual dynamics—e.g., contract modification and successorship—in the employment relationship; and (3) it provides judges with the authority to reform precarious contracts into more stable ones.[25] Below we discuss each of these three main ways in which the principle operates in the Latin American countries surveyed in this book: Argentina, Brazil, Chile, and Uruguay.

Contract Termination

Latin American employers cannot freely fire their employees. Unfair termination, or termination without cause, generally results in liability, which may include, at a minimum, severance pay based on how long the employment relationship lasted.[26]

For example, in the case of Argentina, Article 14 of the constitution protects workers from arbitrary dismissals.[27] Moreover, under Article 28, the state may not legislate in any way that diminishes a worker's right to be protected against arbitrary dismissals.[28] Additionally, the Employment Contract Law expressly establishes the continuity principle and the presumption of a standard employment contract terminable only for cause.[29]

---

[22] Sergio Gamonal C., Introducción al Derecho del Trabajo 159 (1998).

[23] Plá Rodríguez, *supra* note 1, at 220.

[24] *Id.* at 220.

[25] Gamonal C., *supra* note 22, at 159 *et seq.*

[26] Juan Raso Delgue, La Contratación Atípica del Trabajo 99 (2nd ed. 2009).

[27] Constitución Nacional [Const. Nac.] (Arg.), art. 14 bis.

[28] *Id.* at art. 28.

[29] Law No. 20.744, Sept. 20, 1974, [23.003] B.O. 2 (as amended by Law No. 26.844, Mar. 13, 2013) (Arg.).

In Chile, employers may only terminate employees for just cause.[30] Even employers who terminate employees for "business necessity" must pay employees severance equaling one month of salary per year worked, capped at eleven months of pay.[31] Moreover, employers may not terminate employees in a manner that threatens workers' fundamental rights, e.g., privacy, free speech, right to life, physical integrity, religious liberty, and nondiscrimination, among others.[32] Employers who terminate employees in violation of fundamental rights incur added penalties.[33]

Uruguayan law does not define which causes justify employment termination.[34] However, the law states that employers must pay severance to terminated employees, which may equal up to six months of salary.[35] Moreover, Uruguayan courts have developed a doctrine of unfair dismissal where employers may be penalized if they terminate the employee in an abusive fashion.[36] Uruguayan doctrine and rulings have imposed penalties on employers who act in bad faith and disloyally toward workers.[37] However, flagrant misconduct by workers will excuse employers from paying severance.[38]

Brazil is the only Latin American country surveyed here that is anomalous about employment stability, albeit not historically. The present-day Brazilian constitution, adopted in 1988, states that all workers are protected against arbitrary dismissals.[39] Moreover, for many decades, Brazilian labor law provided for just-cause termination rules and additional protections for workers laid off due to economic reasons.[40] However, the government of President Michel Temer, which came into power in 2016 through a legislative vote following removal of the elected president,

---

[30] Cód. Trab. [Lab. Code] (Chile), arts. 159-61, 163 bis, 168.

[31] *Id.* at arts. 161–63.

[32] *Id.* at art. 489. The employer will be liable for moral damages, which may equal six to eleven months of employee pay. Moreover, severance pay may be further increased 30–100 percent. *Id.* If the labor court determines that the discriminatory termination was "grave," then the employee may request reinstatement or the payments described. *Id.*

[33] *Id.*

[34] Plá Rodríguez, *supra* note 1, at 252–53.

[35] *Id.* at 252–53.

[36] *Id.* at 255–56. Abusive dismissals are exceptional dismissals where employers act in bad faith, such as when triggered when an employee refuses sexual advanced by the employer, or when the employer terminates the employee to not pay commissions due before the date of termination. *See* Plá Rodríguez, *supra* note 1, at 255–56.

[37] *See* Informe Relasur, Coleccíon Informes de Organización Internacional del Trabajo, Las Relaciones Laborales en Uruguay 245–47 (Centro de Publicaciones Ministerio de Trabajo y Seguridad Social, 1995). Law No. 10.489, June 6, 1944 (Uru.); Law No. 10.542, Dec. 15, 1944 (Uru.); Law No. 12.597, Dec. 30, 1958 (Uru.); Decree-Law No. 14.188, Apr. 5, 1974 (Uru.).

[38] Plá Rodríguez, *supra* note 1, at 253–54.

[39] Constituição Federal [C.F.] [Constitution] (Braz.), art. 7.I.

[40] *See* Estreicher & Hirsch, *supra* note 10, at 367 (2014).

Dilma Rousseff, enacted a new labor law in 2017[41] that provides for employment terminations by "mutual accord" between employers and employees.[42] Worker advocates are currently challenging the new law's constitutionality, stating it violates Article 7 of the Brazilian constitution.[43] Therefore, it is still difficult to gauge what this new law and the constitutional challenge will mean for employment stability in Brazil.

Contractual Dynamics: Continuing Obligations Despite Changing Terms and Parties in the Employment Contract

The Latin American labor law principle of continuity also protects the worker from contractual modifications and successorship, e.g., contractual dynamics, which may alter rights employees have attained through the employment contract.[44]

In Latin American labor law, changes in the terms of the contract generally do not extinguish the employment contract.[45] Changes in the parties to a contract also do not extinguish the employment contract unless the worker is the new party in the contract.[46] In other words, successor employers inherit the employment obligations of predecessor employers. In this manner, labor law contrasts with traditional private law, where changes in terms or parties extinguish the contract and give rise to a new one.[47]

---

41 Consolidação das Leis do Trabalho [C.L.T.] [Consolidation of Labor Laws] (Braz.) Law No. 13.467, July 13, 2017.

42 *See* Ozéias J. Santos, Reforma Trabalhista Ponto a Ponto: Práctica trabalhista 14–22 (2018).

43 *Id.*

44 Plá Rodríguez, *supra* note 1, at 236–37.

45 *Id.* at 234–35.

46 *Id.*

47 Plá Rodríguez, *supra* note 1, at 236–37; Gamonal C., *supra* note 22, at 165–67. Latin American law expressly legislated for successor liability. For example, the Argentinian Labor Contract Law expressly states that successor employers acquire all employment obligations of the predecessor employer. Law No. 20.744, art. 225, Sept. 20, 1974, [23.003] B.O. 2 (Arg.) (as amended by Law No. 26.844, Mar. 13, 2013). Moreover, the predecessor and successor employers are jointly liable for any employment obligations arising under the employment contracts entered into by the predecessor employer. *Id.* at art. 228. Similarly, Brazil's C.L.T. establishes that a change in the property or the legal nature of an employer does not affect the employment contracts, and therefore, the employer's obligations toward the employees continues. C.L.T (Bra.), arts. 10 and 448. Given this law, the TST has declared on numerous occasions that the employment obligations of predecessor employers are transferred to the successors. C.L.T (Bra.), arts. 10 and 448. In Chile, the Labor Code is clear that successor employers retain all of the obligations of the predecessor employer toward employees. Cód. Trab. [Lab. Code] (Chile), art. 4(2). The Labor Code provides: "Total or partial amendments relative to the ownership, possession or mere holding of the enterprise do not alter the rights or obligations of workers arising from their individual contracts or collective labor instruments, which will remain in effect and continue with the new employers." *Id.* Therefore, when there is a change in employer, the contractual relationship between the workers and the successor employer remain in effect. The exception, however, is Uruguay; it has no express legislation codifying continuity. However, scholars and the courts have uniformly recognized successor employer

Reforming Contracts in Favor of Nonprecarious Work

Latin American jurisprudence prefers employment contracts of an indefinite duration rather than precarious employment.[48] According to Latin American jurists, contracts of indefinite duration provide workers with contracts that last longer and are more stable.[49] They also provide workers with contractual liberty, as they can also quit their jobs at any time and seek better opportunities.[50] Under the *pro operario* criterion, continuity binds the employer but not the worker.

Continuity also usually works together with the primacy of reality principle to provide high evidentiary bars for parties who want to prove that a contract is something other than that of indefinite duration.[51] Courts also invoke the principle of nonwaiver—that an employee may not voluntarily waive his or her right to a permanent contract of employment—when employers may have abusively demanded that employees agree to modify their standard employment contract into something else.[52]

Argentina's preference for indefinite term contracts is clear. Its constitution states: "In case of doubt, situations must be resolved in favor of the continuity or survival of the contract."[53] Other articles of the same law reaffirm continuity, such as Articles 90 through 95.[54] These articles give authority to courts

---

liability. *See* ALEJANDRO CASTELLO, GRUPO DE EMPRESAS Y DERECHO DEL TRABAJO 55 (2006) (*citing* ANUARIO DE JURISPRUDENCIA LABORAL (AJL) 1340–45 (2000), AJL 668–69 (2002), and AJL 1064 (2001)).

48 PLÁ RODRÍGUEZ, *supra* note 1, at 223–24.

49 *Id.* at 224.

50 *Id.* at 225.

51 *See* chapter 3.

52 *See* chapter 4.

53 The original Spanish text reads: "*Artículo 10. – Conservación del contrato. En caso de duda las situaciones deben resolverse en favor de la continuidad o subsistencia del contrato.*" LEY DE CONTRATO DE TRABAJO [EMPLOYMENT CONTRACT LAW] Law No. 20.744 of 1976 art. 10 (Arg.).

54 *Id.* at arts. 90–95. For example, in *Sánchez, Carlos c. Auditoria General de la Nación*, the National Labor Court of Appeals reformed a government employee's for-term contract into one of indefinite duration despite a gap in the law; it was not clear whether public sector employers were bound by employment stability norms. The court held that the government was so bound. It stated:

> When the State breaks with public law duties and contracts with private persons for the provision of personal services, it must comply with the norms that regulate private activities, more exactly with the rules of the employment contract to avoid the violation of workers' rights. . . . In this case, the plaintiff worked for the General Audit Office through a series of successive contracts which lasted for eight years, in excess of the objective requirement referred to in paragraph b) of art. 90 of the employment contract law, which would then mean that the contract should be understood as permanent, since the plaintiff was not hired for a specific purpose and for a limited period of time that could have justified the implementation of the exceptions set out in the [law]. . . .

to reform for-term contracts into contracts of indefinite duration, subject to certain conditions.[55]

Similarly, the Brazilian Consolidated Labor Law (CLT) establishes that for-term employment contracts cannot last more than two years.[56] Thereafter, the law states that if a for-term contract is renewed more than once, the employment relationship is legally converted into an indefinite term contract.[57] Complementing this rule, the law states that the for-term contract will only be valid if it is for transitory entrepreneurial activities, a probationary contract, or for a service whose nature justifies the term.[58]

The Chilean Labor Code similarly states that a for-term contract becomes a contract of indefinite duration if the employee worked for the employer for more than twelve months in a fifteen-month period through three or more temporary contracts, if the employer renews the for-term contract at least twice, or if the employee remains working for the employer beyond the agreed-upon term.[59] Based on these legal rules, the Chilean courts have on numerous occasions reformed formally successive contracts of fixed duration into indefinite contracts.[60]

While the Chilean Labor Code gives clear authority to courts to convert successive contracts of definite duration to contracts of indefinite duration, it is silent about what happens when a contract for a specified job or service (*contrato para obra o servicio*), which are legal in Chile, extend beyond the time required to perform that job or service.[61] Despite the statutory silence, the Supreme Court of Chile presumed continuity based on principle.[62] However, rather than finding that contracts for a specified job or service convert to indefinite contracts by operation of law, the Court

---

Cámara Nacional de Apelaciones del Trabajo [CNAT], June 29, 2005, Sánchez, Carlos c. Auditoria General de la Nación s. despido (Arg.). Sala VII Expte No. 24015/03 Sent. 38.601 del 29/6/05 (Ruiz Díaz—Rodríguez Brunengo) (translation by authors).

In another case, the same court determined that when parties create an expectation of an indeterminate employment term despite the existence of discrete, successive contracts, it recognizes the relationship as one structured by an uninterrupted and permanent relationship. Cámara Nacional de Apelaciones del Trabajo [CNAT], Argibay, Lidia y otros c. Estado Argentino s/ despido (Arg.). Sala III Expte No. 48894 Sent. 37368 del 26/3/79.

[55] *Id.*

[56] C.L.T. (Bra.), art. 445.

[57] *Id.* at. 451.

[58] *Id.* at 443.2. The probationary contract is regulated by C.L.T. (Bra.), art. 445; it can only last ninety days.

[59] Cód. Trab. [Lab. Code] (Chile), art. 159.

[60] Sergio Gamonal C., Introducción al Derecho, *supra* note 22, at 161–63.

[61] Cód. Trab [Lab. Code] (Chile), art. 159, No. 5.

[62] Corte Suprema de Justicia [C.S.J.] [Supreme Court], Palma c. Nuet Latour, Rol de la causa: 677-03 (Chile). *See also* Sergio Gamonal C., *Comentario de la Jurisprudencia Laboral del Año* 2003, 1 Revista de Derecho de la Universidad Adolfo Ibáñez 758, 774 (2004).

determined that there was an *implied term* in the parties' agreement stipulating a conversion of the contract into one of indefinite duration if the worker continues to work after the job or service concludes.[63]

In Uruguay, there are no statutory rules regarding contract reformation when employers keep workers laboring beyond contracted terms. However, Uruguayan jurisprudence has recognized the practice.[64] One court held, "[T]he typical employment contract is an expression of the principle of continuity[.] It has a vocation for durability without a term. Hence, when any parties argue that there exists an atypical employment contract, whichever it may be, which may displace the typical contract, the burden of proof lies in the party making that claim."[65] Uruguayan labor law scholar Américo Plá Rodríguez also explained that courts in Uruguay will reform successive, for-term contracts into permanent contracts of employment.[66]

* * *

As we have seen, the principle of continuity is clearly recognized in the countries surveyed. Brazil seems to have recently weakened it by providing employment contract terminations based on mutual accord. However, the meaning and constitutionality of that new law is under litigation. Generally, and historically, the continuity principle protects against unfair dismissal, provides employees with acquired contractual rights despite changed terms or parties, and shields workers from possible contractual subterfuges used by employers to deny workers the benefits of stable employment.

---

[63] Corte Suprema de Justicia [C.S.J.] [Supreme Court], PALMA C. NUET LATOUR, Rol de la causa: 677-03 (Chile). *See also* Sergio Gamonal C., *Comentario de la Jurisprudencia Laboral del Año 2003, supra* note 62, at 774. In *Palma v. Nuet Latour*, a Chilean court determined that successive contracts for a job or service consisting of the same type of work are one continuing employment contract even though the parties stipulated otherwise in signed releases. *Id.* The court determined that the releases were not sufficient to disprove the presumption of continuity because the types of work contracted for by the parties were not of the kind involved on contracts for a specified job or service. *Id.* Similarly, in *Guerra v. Maestranzas Navales*, the Chilean Supreme Court held that when an employer terminates a contract for a specified job or service it must do so at an opportune or reasonable time, or it may be bound to a contract of indefinite duration. Corte Suprema de Justicia [C.S.J.] [Supreme Court], GUERRA C. MAESTRANZAS NAVALES, Rol de la causa: 3110-02 (Chile). Where an employment relationship remained in effect after the job contracted for was completed, the court found that when the employer terminated the contract extemporaneously and without reasonable notice, it was unjustified in severing the relationship. *Id.* The fixed-term contract thus becomes a permanent contract of employment when the employee continues working for the employer after the job contracted for is completed. Continuity is implied in the contract terms by the parties' conduct.

[64] PLÁ RODRÍGUEZ, *supra* note 1, at 227–28.

[65] ANUARIO DE JURISPRUDENCIA LABORAL, Asociación Uruguaya de Derecho del Trabajo, 472–74 (2011).

[66] PLÁ RODRÍGUEZ, *supra* note 1, at 228–30.

CONTINUITY IN THE UNITED STATES

The principle of continuity in employment relations exists as an exception to the rule in the United States due to the preeminence of the employment-at-will doctrine.[67] From a Latin American perspective, it is the least present principle of labor law in the United States. We argue, however, that even in its limited form, exceptions to employment at will such as just-cause termination in the collective bargaining context and in the public sector, limitations placed on employers' rights to fire workers by antidiscrimination and anti-retaliation law, some torts, and public policy are not de minimis. There is a present, albeit unevenly applicable and weaker version of continuity in the United States. This section describes employment at will and its exceptions and how to extend and strengthen continuity by statute, specifically through state-by-state derogation of employment at will.

The Peculiar Doctrine of Employment at Will

The U.S. employment-at-will doctrine stands almost alone among the industrialized democracies, and perhaps even among all other countries of the world.[68] It posits that the employer and employee may terminate the employment relationship without notice, for any reason, or for no reason at all, and without any severance payment.[69]

U.S. courts modified traditional English master-servant law almost out of plain cloth to create employment at will as it is known today.[70] The English rule traditionally asserted that a master had the duty to keep his or her servant employed for at least one year, unless the parties expressly agreed for a different term, which the master had to prove.[71] The American rule morphed during the course of the nineteenth century when courts allowed indefinite term contracts to presume that parties agreed to end the employment contract for good cause, no cause, or bad cause; the party asserting anything other than employment at will had the burden of proving otherwise.[72]

---

[67] Estlund, *supra* note 11, at 1691.

[68] Estreicher & Hirsch, *supra* note 10, at 347. SAMUEL ESTREICHER & MIRIAM CHERRY, GLOBAL ISSUES IN EMPLOYMENT LAW 56 (2008).

[69] *See, e.g.*, Bammert v. Don's Super Valu, Inc., 646 N.W.2d 365 (Wis. 2002).

[70] As William Blackstone described it: "If the hiring be general without any particular time limited, the law construes it to be a hiring for a year; upon a principle of natural equity, that the servant shall serve, and the master maintain him, throughout all the revolutions of the respective seasons; as well when there is work. . . ." WILLIAM BLACKSTONE, COMMENTARIES ON THE LAWS OF ENGLAND, VOL. 1, *413 (1765–69). *See also* Jay M. Feinman, *The Development of the Employment at Will Rule*, 20 AM. J. LEGAL HIST. 118, 127–29 (1976).

[71] BLACKSTONE, COMMENTARIES, *supra* note 70, at *413.

[72] Estlund, *supra* note 11, at 1670. We must underscore that employment at will developed in the United States in part as a challenge to Reconstruction's Labor Republicanism, an ideology that favored government intervention in labor matters to facilitate worker freedom. Lea S. VanderVelde, The At-Will Doctrine in a Laborers'

The Tennessee Supreme Court was the first known U.S. court to publish an opinion adopting employment at will.[73] It stated that: "All may dismiss their employees at will, be they many or few, for good cause, for no cause or even for cause morally wrong, without being thereby guilty of legal wrong."[74] Since then, the employment-at-will doctrine diffused to forty-nine states. Only Montana[75] and the Puerto Rican[76] and U.S. Virgin Islands[77] territories have altered the employment-at-will presumption by enacting statutes prescribing legal causes for termination.

Wrongful Dismissal Law under the Shadow of Employment at Will

Despite employment at will, the United States has developed a doctrine of wrongful dismissal law based on labor-protective statues, public policy, and contract.[78] As stated in prior chapters, the National Labor Relations Act (NLRA),[79] the Fair Labor Standards Act (FLSA),[80] and Title VII of the Civil Rights Act of 1964,[81] as well as other federal and state labor and employment laws, prohibit employment discrimination based on union-related activities, race, and sex, among others. Further, employers may not retaliate against employees for attempting to get their rights enforced under most labor laws, or participating in proceedings where a jurisdictional entity is investigating a matter under those laws.[82]

The rest of the wrongful dismissal cases can be grouped into four types: (1) the public policy exception; (2) intentional infliction of emotional distress; (3) the good faith exception; and (4) the exception of implied terms. The first two exceptions reside in the law of torts. The public policy exception is a tort pertinent only to employment, while intentional infliction of emotional distress is a general tort that may prevail, at times, in the employment context.[83] The latter two are contractual exceptions. They require the employee to sustain that the employer breached the

Republic: From Reconstruction's Anti-subordination to the Gilded Age's Precarity (unpublished manuscript on file with author). Legal scholars at the time favored doctrines requiring cause for employment termination, but their positions did not prevail in the courts given the influence of employers on judicial institutions. *Id.*

[73] Payne v. W. & Atl. R.R. Co., 81 Tenn. 507, 519–20 (1884), *overruled on other grounds by* Hutton v. Watters, 179 S.W. 134, 138 (Tenn. 1915).

[74] *Id.*

[75] MONT. CODE ANN. §§ 39-2-901–915 (2007).

[76] P.R. LAWS ANN. tit. 29, § 185a–m (2010). *See also* Farinacci-Férnós, *supra* note 5, at 125.

[77] V.I. CODE ANN. tit. 24, § 76 (2017).

[78] Estlund, *supra* note 11, at 1656.

[79] 29 U.S.C. § 151 (2012).

[80] 29 U.S.C. § 201 (2012).

[81] 42 U.S.C. §§ 2000e–e-17 (2012).

[82] *See* Estlund, *supra* note 11, at 1559–60.

[83] ROGER BLANPAIN ET AL., THE GLOBAL WORKPLACE: THE INTERNATIONAL AND COMPARATIVE EMPLOYMENT LAW 143–44 (2nd ed. 2012).

employment contract's implied covenant of good faith and fair dealing, or some other implied term that limited the employer's ability to terminate employment.[84]

Jurists have traced the public policy exception to a 1959 California decision, *Peterman v. International Brotherhood of Teamsters*.[85] In *Peterman*, an employer fired a worker because the worker refused to commit perjury.[86] The California District Court of Appeals decided that allowing an employer to dismiss a worker for refusing to commit perjury would be contrary to public policy and state interests.[87] The court declared that to hold otherwise would be unreasonable and against the spirit of the criminal laws of California.[88]

Since *Peterman v. International Brotherhood of Teamsters*, various state courts have fashioned a law of wrongful dismissal based on public policy exceptions. These cases fall into three categories. The first category is when employers terminate an employee for exercising a clear legal right (such as filing a workers' compensation claim).[89] The second category pertains to when the employer terminates the employee for performing a clear public duty (such as reporting to jury duty).[90] The third category pertains to when the employer terminated the employee because the employee refuses to violate the law (such as refusing to engage in perjury, as in *Peterman*[91]). Some jurisdictions have also extended the public policy exception to whistleblowing.[92]

The general tort of intentional or reckless infliction of emotional distress may also be available to an employee who suffered from an extraordinarily abusive dismissal.[93] Some courts have ruled that abusive investigations or interrogations, veiled threats, violent or aggressive dismissals, dismissals that include racial slurs, telephone harassment, or physical attacks all may serve as the bases for intentional or reckless infliction of emotional distress.[94] However, cases based on this general tort are more exceptional than the wrongful termination cases based on public policy.[95] In essence, only the most outrageous of cases fall within the tort because U.S. courts assume that employers have the right to treat workers in ways that are emotionally painful,

---

84 *Id.*

85 Peterman v. International Brotherhood of Teamsters, 344 P.2d 25 (Cal. Ct. App. 2d Dist. 1959).

86 *Id.* at 27.

87 *Id.* at 27–28.

88 *Id.* at 27.

89 Estlund, *supra* note 11, at 1660.

90 *Id.*

91 *Id.*

92 *Id.*

93 *See* Agis v. Howard Johnson Co., 355 N.E.2d 315, 318–19 (Mass. 1976).

94 *Id.* at 49.

95 Blanpain et al., *supra* note 83, at 143–44.

offensive, and insulting.[96] As Professor Regina Austin found, U.S. courts generally assert that parties assume that workers can suffer pain, insults, and indignities at work and, therefore, should meet these employer actions with "acquiescence and endurance."[97]

Some U.S. state courts have held that terminated workers may sue employers for violating the covenant of good faith and fair dealing.[98] It is another limited exception to the at-will rule.[99] It posits that employers may not dismiss employees in bad faith.[100] Bad faith is normally recognized when parties fail to act honestly "in fact," and in ways that are reasonably commensurate with contracting or business practices.[101] A 1977 case decided in Massachusetts, *Fortune v. National Cash Register Company*, describes an example of an actionable, bad faith

---

[96] *See* Regina Austin, *Employer Abuse, Worker Resistance, and the Tort of Intentional Infliction of Emotional Distress*, 41 STAN. L. REV. 1 (1988).

[97] *Id.* at 1. *But see* David C. Yamada, *Workplace Bullying and American Employment Law: A Ten-Year Progress Report and Assessment*, 32 COMP. LAB. L. & POL'Y J. 251 (2010) (describing that the doctrine of "bullying" has been creeping slowly into the United States, providing some modicum of dignity at work).

[98] *See* Lea VanderVelde, *Where Is the Concept of Good Faith in the Restatement of Employment*, 21 EMP. RTS. & EMP. POL'Y J. 335 (2017). A 2007 study reported that twenty-nine U.S. states declined to recognize the duty of good faith and fair dealing in employment. CLYDE W. SUMMERS ET AL., LEGAL RIGHTS AND INTERESTS IN THE WORKPLACE: STATUTORY SUPPLEMENT AND MATERIALS 193–200 (2007).

[99] *See* VanderVelde, *supra* note 98, at 335 (internal citations omitted).

[100] *Id.*

[101] The Restatement of Contracts defines good faith as " 'honesty in fact in the conduct or transaction concerned.' " RESTATEMENT (SECOND) OF CONTRACTS § 205 (AM. LAW INST. 1981). The Uniform Commercial Code adds that parties must act in a manner reasonably commensurate with commercial standards in the prevailing context. It states that in the case of a merchant, good faith means: " 'honesty in fact and the observance of reasonable commercial standards of fair dealing in the trade.' " U.C.C. § 1-201(19) (2014). The Restatement of Contracts also includes such contextual considerations in its comments when it states: "The phrase 'good faith' is used in a variety of contexts, and its meaning varies somewhat with the context. Good faith performance or enforcement of a contract emphasizes faithfulness to an agreed common purpose and consistency with the justified expectations of the other party; it excludes a variety of types of conduct characterized as involving 'bad faith' because they violate community standards of decency, fairness or reasonableness. The appropriate remedy for a breach of the duty of good faith also varies with the circumstances." RESTATEMENT (SECOND) OF CONTRACTS § 205 cmt. a.

Taking a more economic view on the matter, Professor Steve Burton has argued: "Bad faith performance occurs . . . when discretion is used to recapture opportunities forgone upon contracting—when the discretion-exercising party refuses to pay the expected cost of performance." Steven J. Burton, *Breach of Contract and the Common Law Duty to Perform in Good Faith*, 94 HARV. L. REV. 369, 373 (1980) (footnote omitted). Good faith, on the other hand, is when the parties act in ways commensurate with the bargain, or as Professor Burton explains, "when a party's discretion is exercised for any purpose within the reasonable contemplation of the parties at the time of formation—to capture opportunities that were preserved upon entering the contract, interpreted objectively." *Id.* (footnote omitted). This view of good faith breach is derived from the concept of "economic opportunism" by Oliver Williamson; his concept of opportunism means "self-interest seeking with guile." Charles J. Goetz & Robert E. Scott, *The Mitigation Principle: Toward a General Theory of Contractual Obligation*, 69 VA. L. REV. 967, 982 n.38 (1983) (*citing* Oliver E. Williamson, *Transaction-Cost Economics: The Governance of Contractual Relations*, 22 J.L. & ECON. 233, 234 n.3 (1979)).

termination.[102] There, the court held that an employer breached an implied covenant of good faith and fair dealing when the employer terminated a salesman shortly after the salesman negotiated a multimillion dollar sale.[103] Since the salesman's commissions accrued only when the employer installed machines he sold and the employer fired the worker before the company installed the machines, the salesman would not make a commission from his multimillion-dollar sale.[104] The court determined that the termination was in bad faith.[105] In another case, the same court found bad faith when an employer terminated an employee because the employee refused sexual advances by her supervisor.[106]

Tacit stability clauses, or implied terms for just-cause termination, also abrogate the presumption of employment at will. Some states have recognized such clauses in written documents and verbal commitments, or derived from practices or company policies.[107] One of the leading cases where a court determined that an implied stability clause could defeat the at-will presumption is *Pugh v. See's Candies, Inc.*[108] In *Pugh*, a lower court held against an employee who argued that an implied stability clause could override the default at-will presumption in employment relationships.[109] After analyzing the cases' facts, the appellate jurisdiction reversed the lower court.[110] The facts suggested, among other things, that the company president had assured the employee that "if you are loyal to [the employer] and do a good job, your future is secure."[111] The same president also had the practice of terminating employees without showing cause.[112] Looking at the evidence, the California Court of Appeals overturned the lower court and held that the employer could have made an implicit promise of stability that became part of the contract. The employer could have breached it when it fired the employee without cause.[113] The court remanded

---

This said, however, Professor Burton agrees that bad faith may be motivated by noneconomic considerations, but these appear much less frequently in reported cases. Burton, *supra* at 387 n.80 (*citing* Monge v. Beebe Rubber Co., 316 A.2d 549 (N.H. 1974)).

[102] Fortune v. Nat'l Cash Register Co., 364 N.E.2d 1251 (Mass. 1977)).

[103] *Id.* at 1257–58.

[104] *Id.*

[105] *Id.*

[106] Monge v. Beebe Rubber Co., 316 A.2d 549 (N.H. 1974); *see also* Peggie R. Smith et al., Principles of Employment Law 39, n.117 (2009).

[107] *But see* VanderVelde, *supra* note 72 (noting that the current trend is towards nonrecognition of stability terms unless expressly accorded in writing).

[108] Pugh v. See's Candies, Inc., 171 Cal. Rptr. 917 (Cal. Ct. App. 1st Dist. 1981).

[109] *Id.* at 918.

[110] *Id.* at 927.

[111] *Id.* at 919.

[112] *Id.*

[113] *Id.* at 927.

the case to the lower court to determine if under the facts of the case such an implied term existed.[114]

Despite this case, and many other similar ones that have followed *Pugh*, sophisticated employers have refashioned their handbooks, other documents, and what they say to employees to make it explicit that employees have been hired "at will," with no implied stability terms.[115] Therefore, as with other exceptions, the implied stability exception remains a limited one.[116]

A Stubborn Presumption

Given the continued relevance of the employment-at-will rule in the United States, the principle of continuity of employment relations sits in an extremely uneasy position there. U.S. law presumes noncontinuity, i.e., that an employer may freely terminate employees, and the worker has an equal right to resign from the job. Parties may expressly contract out of the at-will presumption, and some do. For example, most collective bargaining agreements signed by employer and labor unions have dismissal clauses for just cause.[117]

However, because the at-will rule serves as a legal presumption or default rule, the party claiming anything other than employment at will in an employment relationship must prove that other regime to the court.[118] Even with burden-shifting tests under employment statutes that protect workers from discriminatory termination, or when workers make prima facie cases of wrongful dismissal, employees retain the final, practical burden to prove their cases.[119] The employment-at-will backdrop is different from "for-cause" or "just-cause" regimes because in those jurisdictions, employers, rather than employees, must prove that the termination was lawful.[120]

Continuity in the Public Sector and Unionized Contexts

Despite the general applicability of at-will employment, employment at will is not pervasive in the U.S. public sector.[121] There, employers can generally only fire

---

[114] *Id.* at 927.

[115] *See* Jonathan Fineman, *The Inevitable Demise of the Implied Employment Contract*, 29 Berkeley J. Emp. & Lab. L. 345 (2008).

[116] Implied stability terms might even be recognized by courts, for practical purposes. *See* VanderVelde, *supra* note 72.

[117] *See* Summers, *supra* note 8.

[118] *See* Estlund, *supra* note 11, at 1670–74.

[119] *Id.* at 1671.

[120] *Id.* at 1670–74.

[121] The U.S. Supreme Court determined that public sector employees with an expectation of continued employment have a property right to employment and, therefore, a constitutional right to procedural protections before termination. As the U.S. Supreme Court stated: "[T]his Court has made clear that even though a person

employees for cause, as stated in civil service rules. Because of such rules prescribing termination for cause, public sector employees also have the right for a hearing before termination.

If we assume that public sector workers—those who are hired by some form of government entity—cannot be terminated without legal cause, this means that about 9 percent of the U.S. workforce is not subject to employment at will.[122] Between that 9 percent, and the 6 percent private sector union membership rate, perhaps about 15 percent of the U.S. workforce, plus those who obtain it through individual contracts, is not under the employment-at-will regime.[123] While not irrelevant, employees covered by something other than employment at will are nevertheless a minority.

Modifying Contracts and Successorship

As we discussed above, the continuity principle in Latin America makes it impossible for employers to unilaterally modify employee contract terms without facing liability. Moreover, continuity generally pervades even in the face of corporate restructurings or when others acquire employers. However, because of employment-at-will presumptions in the United States, employers can more freely modify their employees' contracts.[124] Most American courts have held that continued at-will employment itself, despite unilaterally modified terms, is sufficient consideration to make unilateral modifications binding.[125] Very few courts have held that employers must provide additional consideration, such as a salary raise or promotion, in exchange for the modified terms.[126]

Moreover, successor employers are not bound to a predecessor's contracts with their employees unless the successor had agreed to be bound. The contractual matter is simple: the successor employer has no contractual relationship with the

has no 'right' to a valuable governmental benefit and even though the government may deny him the benefit for any number of reasons, there are some reasons upon which the government may not rely. It may not deny a benefit to a person on a basis that infringes his constitutionally protected interests—especially, his interest in freedom of speech. For if the government could deny a benefit to a person because of his constitutionally protected speech or associations, his exercise of those freedoms would in effect be penalized and inhibited. This would allow the government to 'produce a result which (it) could not command directly.' . . . Such interference with constitutional rights is impermissible." Perry v. Sindermann, 408 U.S. 593, 597 (1972).

[122] *See* Greenstone & Looney, *supra* note 7.

[123] *See* Stanley Aronowitz, *The Last Good Job in America*, 51 SOC. TEXT 93 (1997).

[124] *See* Rachel Arnow-Richman, *Modifying At-Will Employment Contracts*, 57 B.C. L. REV. 427, 428 (2016) (arguing that employers should have the duty to provide reasonable notice before making unilateral, midterm contract modifications).

[125] *Id.* at 429.

[126] *Id.* (*citing* Demasse v. ITT Corp., 984 P.2d 1138, 1145 (Ariz. 1999) (en banc); J.M. Davidson, Inc. v. Webster, 128 S.W.3d 223, 228 (Tex. 2003); Labriola v. Pollard Grp., Inc., 100 P.3d 791, 796 (Wash. 2004)).

predecessor's employees.[127] In the case that the successor agreed with the predecessor to be bound to the predecessor's employees, the employees of the successor employer are considered to be intended beneficiaries and, as such, would retain those contractual rights.[128]

Despite no real successor obligation in employment other than that provided by contract, U.S. law establishes that successor employers may have a duty to bargain with the union of the predecessor's employees if the employees are unionized.[129] Successor employers have this duty only if the new company acquired substantial assets of the predecessor and continued the predecessor's business operations without interruption or substantial change.[130] To determine if there has been an interruption or substantial change, the National Labor Relations Board (NLRB) examines whether each employer's business of was essentially the same, whether the employees of the new company were doing the same jobs in the same working conditions and under the same supervisors, and whether the new entity had similar production processes, products, and a similar body of customers.[131] Moreover, the successor must have hired a majority of its workforce from the predecessor's employee pool, or what the NLRB has termed a "substantial and representative complement" of employees from the predecessor employer.[132] Despite this limited duty to bargain, successor employers are not bound by the substantive terms of any preceding collective bargaining agreement between the union and the predecessor employer.[133] Hence, these successorship limitations on employers further underline the freedom of successor employers to modify contracts between predecessor employers and their employees. Successorship rules are limited to the narrowly circumscribed protections afforded by the statute, in this case, the employees' representative's right to bargain with the employer.

While the FLSA and the NLRA do not explicitly state a rule regarding successorship, various trial and appellate courts have taken the lead from NLRA jurisprudence to fashion a federal common law of successorship, including for other

---

[127] Restatement (Second) of Contracts § 302 cmt. e (Am. Law Inst. 1981). *See also* John Wiley & Sons, Inc. v. Livingston, 376 U.S. 543, 550 (1964); Upholsterers' Int'l Union Pension Fund v. Artistic Furniture of Pontiac, 920 F.2d 1323, 1325–26 (7th Cir. 1990).

[128] Restatement (Second) of Contracts § 302 cmt. e (Am. Law Inst. 1981).

[129] Fall River Dyeing & Finishing Corp. v. N.L.R.B., 482 U.S. 27 (1987). *See also* Golden State Bottling Co. v. N.L.R.B., 414 U.S. 168 (1973); N.L.R.B. v. Burns Int'l Sec. Serv. Inc., 406 U.S. 272 (1972); John Wiley & Sons, Inc. v. Livingston, 376 U.S. 543 (1964).

[130] Fall River Dyeing, 482 U.S. at 43.

[131] *Id.*

[132] *Id.* at 49. *See also* N.L.R.B. v. Burns Int'l Sec. Serv. Inc., 406 U.S. 272, 278 (1972).

[133] *Id.* at 282.

federal labor laws.[134] For example, the Seventh Circuit has determined that successor liability should attach to employers in the FLSA context, given the labor-protective goals behind the law.[135] It determined that the NLRB and the Supreme Court fashioned the successorship doctrine in the NLRA context to effectuate the policies of the NLRA, inter alia, to "avoid labor unrest and provide some protection for employees against the effects of a sudden change in the employment relationship."[136] The Seventh Circuit, citing other circuits, underlined the relevance of importing the doctrine of successorship from the NLRA to other labor-protective statutes "to avoid undercutting Congressional purpose by parsimony in provision of effective remedies."[137] Based on the successorship doctrine created by the NLRB, the Supreme Court, and several courts of appeals, the Ninth Circuit held that there was successor employer liability under the FLSA, but three basic circumstances must be present: the subsequent employer must be a bona fide successor,[138] the subsequent employer had notice of the potential liability,[139] and the predecessor employer cannot provide effective relief to the aggrieved employees.[140] Moreover, the Ninth Circuit determined that equitable considerations, including effectuating the policies of the labor-protective statutes and the interests of the aggrieved parties, will matter greatly in successorship cases.[141] In this fashion, at least some circuit courts in the United States have made successor employers liable for the minimum wage payments owed to employees by predecessor employers.[142] Again, continuity

---

[134] *See* Steinbach v. Hubbard, 51 F.3d 843, 845 (9th Cir. 1995) (creating a successorship doctrine for the Multiemployer Pension Plan Amendments Act (MPPAA) (*citing* Upholsterers' Int'l Union Pension Fund v. Artistic Furniture of Pontiac, 920 F.2d 1323 (7th Cir. 1990))); Sec'y of Labor, Mine Safety & Health Admin. v. Mullins, 888 F.2d 1448 (D.C. Cir. 1989) (creating a successorship doctrine for the Mine Safety and Health Act); Criswell v. Delta Air Lines, Inc., 868 F.2d 1093 (9th Cir. 1989) (creating a successorship doctrine for the Age Discrimination in Employment Act); Trustees for Alaska Laborers–Constr. Indus. Health & Sec. Fund v. Ferrell, 812 F.2d 512 (9th Cir. 1987) (creating a successorship doctrine for the Employee Retirement Income Security Act); Musikiwamba v. ESSI, Inc., 760 F.2d 740 (7th Cir. 1985) (creating a successorship doctrine for 42 U.S.C. § 1981); Bates v. Pac. Mar. Ass'n, 744 F.2d 705 (9th Cir. 1984) (creating a successorship doctrine for Title VII of the Civil Rights Act of 1964).

[135] Steinbach, 51 F.3d at 845 (*citing* Golden State Bottling Co. v. N.L.R.B., 414 U.S. 168, 182–85 (1973)). *See also* John Wiley & Sons, Inc. v. Livingston, 376 U.S. 543, 549 (1964).

[136] Steinbach v. Hubbard, 51 F.3d 843, 845 (9th Cir. 1995).

[137] Wheeler v. Snyder Buick, Inc., 794 F.2d 1228, 1237 (7th Cir. 1986).

[138] Steinbach, 51 F.3d at 846 (*citing* Golden State Bottling Co. v. N.L.R.B., 414 U.S. 171–72 n.2 (1973)).

[139] *Id.*

[140] *Id.* (*citing* Criswell v. Delta Air Lines, Inc., 868 F.2d 1094 (9th Cir. 1989); Bates v. Pac. Mar. Ass'n, 744 F.2d 709–10 (9th Cir. 1984)).

[141] *Id.* (*citing* Howard Johnson Co. v. Detroit Local Joint Exec. Bd., 417 U.S. 249, 262–63 n.9 (1974); Baker v. Delta Air Lines, Inc., 6 F.3d 632, 637 (9th Cir. 1993); Criswell, 868 F.2d at 1094; Musikiwamba v. ESSI, Inc., 760 F.2d 740, 750 (7th Cir. 1985); Bates v. Pac. Mar. Ass'n, 744 F.2d 709 (9th Cir. 1984)).

[142] Here we can see the principle of continuity interacting with the principle of primacy of reality. In this fashion, U.S. successorship is a doctrinally created outgrowth of U.S. labor-protective law.

exists in the United States albeit fragmented—applying unevenly—and in a weaker version.

EMPLOYMENT AT WILL IS NOT LABOR LAW

Some may argue that employment at will renders U.S. labor law wholly unprotective. Unlike the law in most other industrial democracies, the U.S. employment-at-will doctrine does not require "cause" or "just cause" for terminating the employment contract. Even if some statutes such as the NLRA and FLSA protect workers, these seem to be mere islands of protection in a wide, lonely sea of nonprotection. Employment at will is the backdrop against which wrongful discharge causes of action are litigated. In such a backdrop, workers suing employers, not employer-defendants, are the ones who must prove that "bad" causes—i.e., illegal or against public policy—motivated terminations.[143] Even with burden-shifting tests available under some statutes and wrongful discharge law,[144] employees retain the final, practical burden to prove their case. Hence, considerations related to burden of proof, delay, and cost of the litigation make it difficult for workers to bring suit and win cases, even under statutory labor laws that protect workers.[145]

We agree with these critics but go even deeper. Employment at will erodes labor law because it is not labor law at all.[146] It is master-servant law—and a bastardized version of it—that encroaches on labor law.[147] As we discuss further in the next chapter, four U.S. doctrines, employment at will, permanent strike replacements, compulsory arbitration, and the deregulatory First Amendment, defeat labor law in the United States. What is most tragic about the role of employment at will, like permanent strike replacements, compulsory arbitration, and the deregulatory First Amendment, is that those legal doctrines have encroached labor law through judicial fiat despite hard laws, including the Thirteenth Amendment, the NLRA, and the FLSA, which provide for different legal rules and principles. Unquestionably, employment at will, a rule that mutated from master-servant law in the United

---

[143] Estlund, *supra* note 11, at 1670–74.

[144] *Id.* at 1671.

[145] *Id.* at 1670–74.

[146] Sergio Gamonal C. & César F. Rosado Marzán, *Protecting Workers as a Matter of Principle: A Latin American View of U.S. Work Law*, 13 Wash. U. Global Stud. L. Rev. 605, 659 (2014) (arguing that employment at will is not part of labor law).

[147] *See* Laura A. Turczanski, *Closing the Door on the Public Policy Exception to At-Will Employment: How the Washington State Supreme Court Erroneously Foreclosed Wrongful Discharge Claims for Whistleblowers in* Cudney v. ALSCO, Inc., 36 Seattle U. L. Rev. 2025, 2027 n.11 (2013).

States, must be derogated in the United States with labor law so that courts can have a clear mandate to protect workers.[148] Legislative repeal of employment at will, to be robust, should be federal and anchored in the Thirteenth Amendment of the U.S. Constitution. Since such federal laws may be politically unfeasible today, we argue that perhaps state-by-state abrogation is the practical, next-best solution.

In most of the world, and certainly in almost all of Latin America, countries have legislated for employment stability. Thus, it appears that the United States needs a statute to limit employers' "divine right" to terminate employees.[149] Especially with the increase in precarious work,[150] such protection seems more important than ever.[151]

In the United States, however, labor organizations have tried to promote employment stability through collective bargaining, not by statute.[152] One could argue that the most institutionally meaningful way to promise employment stability in the United States is not through for-cause dismissal federal legislation, which the United States has never experienced, but through collective bargaining. But at 6 percent union membership, collective bargaining has become elusive in the United States. Given partisan stalemates, congressional attempts to amend the NLRA have yielded no results in many decades.[153] Therefore, hanging the hat of employment stability on collective bargaining seems like "pie in the sky."

Another way to provide a stronger ground for employment continuity in the United States may be by increasing employment levels in the public sector. Public sector employees enjoy for-cause termination rules and, as such, are not under the employment-at-will framework. However, the United States has had historically low

---

[148] *See* Arnow-Richman, *supra* note 124, at 1; Summers, *supra* note 8. For a Puerto Rican view of a dismissal statute from within the United States, *see* Farinacci-Fernós, *supra* note 5 (arguing that the Commonwealth of Puerto Rico is the only American jurisdiction with a strong pro-worker "for-cause" dismissal statute and can serve as the basis for other dismissal statutes in the United States).

[149] Clyde W. Summers, *Employment at Will in the United States: The Divine Right of Employers*, 3 U. PA. J. LAB. & EMP. L. 65 (2000); Summers, *supra* note 8, at 484.

[150] *See* Arne L. Kalleberg, *Precarious Work, Insecure Workers: Employment Relations in Transition*, 74 AM. SOC. REV. 1 (2009).

[151] For more recent calls for statutory changes to employment at will in the United States, *see* Arnow-Richman, *supra* note 124 (proposing a notice requirement before termination); Estreicher & Hirsch, *supra* note 10 (arguing that employment at will could be curbed by a statutory requirement that employers justify terminations as business needs); Yamada, *supra* note 97, at 561 (calling for just-cause protections and specific requirements for large-scale layoffs, including a showing of economic necessity). *But see* Estreicher & Hirsch, *supra* note 10 (proposing that, compared to other countries, the United States is not exceptional in failing to protect workers at the point of dismissal once one considers practical matters such as access to justice and remedies available).

[152] *See* Summers, *supra* note 8, at 482–83.

[153] DAU-SCHMIDT ET AL., *supra* note 12, at 115–16 (describing the political near impossibility of reforming labor law given decades-old legislative deadlock on the issue).

levels of public employment—currently only 9 percent of all employed workers in the country.[154] Increasing that rate by any significant amount is anathema to historical precedent. Especially in light of American hostility toward government employment, it is unfathomable that public employment will increase by any significant rate in the short to medium term in the United States to buffer a larger slice of American workers from employment at will.[155]

Another possibility to provide for continuity in employment would be through some form of "flexicurity," a term popularized by the International Labor Organization.[156] Flexicurity refers to the Danish model where employers are generally free to terminate employees, but employees retain strong social security rights through unemployment benefits, training, and reemployment as part of "active labor market" policies.[157] Because of flexicurity, employees in Denmark remain active in the labor market despite episodic dismissals. While in many ways ideal, perhaps even more so for countries with free-dismissal rules, flexicurity is inimical to the U.S. liberal market model. It pervades in Denmark, an economy traditionally associated with Nordic coordinating mechanisms, where labor unions and the state play an important part in commandeering the economy, but is not suited for a liberal, market model such the United States.[158]

Related to flexicurity, some advocates, scholars, policymakers, and even some Silicon Valley CEOs in the United States, have argued for universal basic income as a solution to American employment instability.[159] The increase in so-called "gig" work has made the idea of universal basic income even more attractive for some

---

[154] Compare that rate with Denmark's 29 percent, France's 21 percent, Austria's 16 percent, and the United Kingdom's 16 percent; the United States appears to be below other countries. *See* Organisation for Economic Co-Operation and Development, *Government at a Glance—2017 Edition: Public Employment and Pay*, OECD.Stat (Aug. 14, 2018), https://stats.oecd.org/Index.aspx?QueryId=78408.

[155] Greenstone & Looney, *supra* note 7.

[156] *See, e.g.*, Flexicurity: A Relevant Approach in Central and Eastern Europe (Sandrine Cazes & Alena Nešporová eds., 2007).

[157] Bredgaard, *supra* note 14, at 221–22 (explaining the Danish system of flexicurity).

[158] Netherlands has a system that is similar to Denmark's flexicurity. However, in the Netherlands, as in Denmark, the state has had a historic role in coordinating, if not compelling, national level collective bargaining, and in easing the possibility of an effective transplantation of coordinated market activities, including retraining, job matching, and provision of strong unemployment benefits. Flexicurity in the United States would most likely require significant increases in unemployment benefits and retraining programs, as well as policies actively attempting to promote employment through specific government expenditures and other incentives to promote job creation, in addition to job matching. These policies, while existing in some weak versions in some parts of the United States, are just not strong enough to provide for something such as Danish flexicurity. The political environment to increase social protections and provide for active employment policies that would establish the foundations for flexicurity appear too unfeasible for the United States. *See* Thelen, *supra* note 14, at 141–42.

[159] *See* Philippe Van Parijs & Yannick Vanderborght, Basic Income: A Radical Proposal for a Free Society and a Sane Economy (2017).

of its advocates. Universal basic income would provide workers not with employment stability, but with income stability despite employment precarity. One could even argue that universal basic income may also help workers choose jobs that better match their education, skills, and interests, helping them build better careers, and not just accept whatever job comes their way. Universal basic income thus de-commoditizes workers.[160] It increases their bargaining power and, as such, provides for protection, all in line with the protective principle that we covered in chapter 2.

Of course, universal basic income in the United States seems close to a pipe dream. How will it be funded, given U.S. allergies to more taxes? Will the United States ever muster sufficient political consensus favoring universal basic income? Will universal basic income's benefits be enough to bring its participants out of poverty and, hence, truly de-commodify labor? Will its participants receive sufficient education, training, and other support to find meaningful work? In other words, there are many unknowns in this program as well as missing parts to realistically resolve the problem of employment precarity in the United States.

Which brings us back to a legislative strategy, advocated already by numerous U.S. scholars.[161] In his influential article on the subject, Professor Clyde Summers argued that a fair termination statute should essentially codify the "law of the shop" regarding dismissal, a doctrine which labor arbitrators have been crafting for decades.[162] However, Clyde Summers argued for such a statute forty years ago. No federal just-cause dismissal law has even come close to being legislated in the United States. The less ambitious calls made by others have also fallen on deaf ears.[163] But *state* legislation may actually prove effective, at least in some U.S. states. State and local labor laws, including those for paid sick time and minimum wages that exceed the federal levels, have been on the upswing in the last few years in the United States.[164] In fact, as stated above, at least three American jurisdictions no

---

[160] *See* GØSTA ESPING-ANDERSEN, THREE WORLDS OF WELFARE CAPITALISM 27–28 (1990) (describing how social provision "de-commodifies").

[161] Arnow-Richman, *supra* note 124, at 506; Farinacci-Fernós, *supra* note 5, at 147; Estreicher & Hirsch, *supra* note 10, at 467; Summers, *supra* note 8, at 532.

[162] Summers, *supra* note 8, at 506.

[163] Arnow-Richman, *supra* note 124 (proposing a notice requirement before termination); Estreicher & Hirsch, *supra* note 10 (calling for requirement where businesses justify terminations); Yamada, *supra* note 97 (calling for just-cause protections and specific requirements for large-scale layoffs, including a showing of economic necessity).

[164] *See* UC Berkeley Labor Center, *Inventory of US City and County Minimum Wage Ordinances*, CENTER FOR LABOR RESEARCH AND EDUCATION (Aug. 14, 2018), http://laborcenter.berkeley.edu/minimum-wage-living-wage-resources/inventory-of-us-city-and-county-minimum-wage-ordinances/; Workplace Fairness, *State and Local Paid Sick Leave Laws* (Aug. 14, 2018), https://www.workplacefairness.org/paid-sick-leave (listing state and local paid sick leave ordinances).

longer follow the employment-at-will doctrine: Montana,[165] Puerto Rico,[166] and the U.S. Virgin Islands.[167] Just-cause termination laws, whether codified by the common law of the shop, or those following the Montana, Puerto Rico, or U.S. Virgin Islands models, could thus hold some promise in states and localities where progressive employment legislation has been enacted.[168]

But even if the U.S. needs new positive law to protect workers from unfair dismissal, let's be clear: protections do exist. Despite an uneven and weak presence of continuity in the United States, we cannot overstate the fact that the exceptions to employment at will are real and matter. There are statutory protections against some sorts of dismissals, and there is a law against "wrongful discharge."[169] The cruder form of employment at will, under which "bad" reasons can justify all terminations, is no longer the rule.[170] And while employers may modify employment contracts or extinguish them by selling their companies, courts have recognized some successorship liabilities. Legal scholars and social scientists have even shown how workplace protections against wrongful discharge are so widely recognized that many employers overzealously guard themselves against liability.[171] Labor advocates and adversaries cannot simply disregard the present-day employment stability protections in the United States despite how dim or uneven they may be.

CONCLUSION: STATES OF (DIS)CONTINUITY

This chapter has described the principle of continuity in Latin America, particularly in Argentina, Brazil, Chile, and Uruguay. Continuity is perhaps the most important substantive principle of labor law after protection since it protects the worker at the point where he or she is most vulnerable, the point of dismissal. It also provides workers with continued employment rights despite changes in the terms and parties to an employment contract. Finally, it also provides courts with the authority to reform precarious contracts into more stable ones.

However, because of employment at will, this important principle fails to exist robustly in the United States. In the United States continuity exists as an exception. It

[165] MONT. CODE ANN. §§ 39-2-901–915 (2007).

[166] P.R. LAWS ANN. tit. 29, § 185a–m (2010). *See also* Farinacci-Fernós, *supra* note 5.

[167] V.I. CODE ANN. tit. 24, § 76 (2017).

[168] Other American scholars have called for notice terminations rules that derogate from the employment-at-will rule to a lesser extent. *See* Estreicher & Hirsch, *supra* note 10, Arnow-Richman, *supra* note 124.

[169] Estlund, *supra* note 11, at 1662.

[170] *Id.* at 1656.

[171] Cynthia L. Estlund, *How Wrong Are Employees about Their Rights, and Why Does It Matter?*, 77 N.Y.U. L. REV. 6, 11 (2002).

exists in most of the public sector, which employs about 9 percent of the U.S. labor force. It also exists in collective bargaining agreements, which cover about 6 percent of the private sector workforce. It may also exist in individual contracts, mostly those of workers with strong bargaining positions in relation to employers.

Continuity also pervades in the United States, albeit in a limited fashion, in the various protections against discrimination and doctrines of wrongful dismissal. Once employees make a prima facie case of discrimination, retaliation, or wrongful dismissal, employers have to come forward with evidence showing that they did not dismiss the worker in violation of the law or public policy. If employers fail to rebut the prima facie case, courts can order damages for the workers despite employment at will. They might also reinstate the worker. Employers who acquire other employers, continue to run a similar business as the predecessor, and employ a majority of the predecessor's employees may retain successor liability under some federal statutes.

However, because continuity remains the exception rather than the rule in the United States, workers, not employers, tend to be the ones who have to prove their cases in courts of law, stacking the legal process against those with fewer resources to litigate cases. In this fashion, continuity still remains an elusive goal in U.S. labor law. Therefore, as others before us, we agree that continuity must be legislated in the United States, such as Montana, Puerto Rico, the U.S Virgin Islands, and most other countries of the world have already done. State-by-state abolition of employment at will is more likely to happen than with a federal law. And while a state-by-state abrogation strategy may further underscore the unevenness of employment stability in the United States, it appears to be the better method to extend and strengthen the continuity principle today.

6

THE RETURN OF LABOR PRINCIPLES: CONFLICT OR HARMONY?

INTRODUCTION

In these pages, we have described and explained how principled labor law can reinvigorate U.S. labor law. We started with a hypothetical scenario of striking drivers of an app-based taxi company such as Uber or Lyft who signed judicial litigation and class action waivers. We explained how a principled perspective would deal with the threshold employee or independent contractor question that may surface if these taxi drivers sought labor law protections. Adjudicators would need to answer the question based on facts—whether the putative employee's relationship actually counts as one of "employee"—and not on what the formal contracts state. But given that employment legal tests tend to be vague, and may not help too much to clearly answer the question, *in dubio pro operario* would direct the adjudicator to answer the question in favor of the worker if the worker can at least make a reasonable case for his or her employee status, and grant him or her the rights provided by labor law. Thereafter, the adjudicator would have to deny enforcement of any class action waiver, absent clear rules to the contrary (which do not exist under the Federal Arbitration Act (FAA)), under the principle of nonwaiver. While U.S. law does not generally presume continuity due to the doctrine of employment at will, a mild form of the continuity principle may enter the picture if the workers allege that the employer terminated them because they were members of a protected class, engaged in

Principled Labor Law. Sergio Gamonal C. and César F. Rosado Marzán.

protected activities, or filed a complaint against the employer, among other specific reasons. Even if the worker has the final burden to prove an alleged illegal termination, these claims would force the employer to at least provide evidence showing that legitimate, employment-based reasons triggered the termination. A lighter form of continuity would pervade.

Critics of this book might argue, among many other things—some of them already explored in the preceding chapters—that even if labor law was mostly concerned with worker protection and *in dubio pro operario* would apply, the principled method still needs to resolve conflicts between labor law principles and other laws and their principles. Not all cases dealing with labor issues are concerned narrowly with labor law. What if labor law conflicts with an employer's right to manage his or her own business—with employer property rights? Should *in dubio pro operario* apply? It cannot be the case that labor law and the protective principle will prevail in every case.

We acknowledge that principled labor law does not immediately reconcile conflicts with other law. Principled labor law helps adjudicators deal with gaps and vague *labor* law, but not with conflicts with other laws. Jurisdictions still need to use their own methods of dealing with legal conflicts to resolve disagreements between labor law and other law. However, in this chapter we argue that while principled labor law does not provide mechanical solutions to conflicts of law, principles help us to better comprehend law and, as such, determine whether or not there are conflicts with other laws and, if so, how to reconcile them.

We have already dealt with some conflicts in the preceding pages. Labor law conflicts with employment at will, for example. Therefore, if labor law is to better protect workers, we argued that state legislatures need to rescind employment at will through statute. We also explained in these pages that labor law need not conflict with the FAA if we understood that the exceptions in the FAA were intended to exclude weaker bargaining parties, workers, from its coverage. Given that the U.S. Supreme Court has already held that the FAA and the National Labor Relations Act (NLRA) would conflict if courts excluded workers from the FAA, Congress needs to amend the FAA and the NLRA to expressly cover class actions in the NLRA and exclude workers from FAA coverage. But even if the practical solution to procedural waiver requires statutory reform, as we argued in these pages, *Epic Systems v. NLRB*,[1] where the Supreme Court declared that the NLRA does not protect workers who are engaged in class actions, and *Gilmer v. Interstate/Johnson Lane Corp.*,[2] where the Supreme Court held that the FAA applied to employees, were wrongly decided.

---

[1] 138 S. Ct. 1612 (2018).

[2] 500 U.S. 20 (1991).

In this chapter, we take on two other conflicts between labor law and other U.S. law, the constitutional rights concerning property and free speech, to argue how labor law need not conflict and, hence, can live side to side with those important constitutional rights. Given the importance of free speech and property rights in contemporary, liberal societies, the U.S. case can help illuminate similar questions elsewhere.

LABOR LAW AND PROPERTY RIGHTS

Labor law regulates the employment contract. This means, as we have been describing in these pages, that parties may not agree to whatever terms they might desire in an employment relationship. Matters of public concern, such as guaranteeing a minimum wage that provides workers with sufficient means to sustain themselves with dignity, override individual freedom of contract. In the United States, employers may also not infringe on "the right to self-organization, to form, join, or assist labor organizations, to bargain collectively through representatives of their own choosing, and to engage in other concerted activities for the purpose of collective bargaining or other mutual aid or protection."[3] Therefore, the National Labor Relations Board (NLRB) has held that employers cannot deny employees access to nonworking areas during nonworking time in order to speak to coworkers about union organizing, or about other matters concerning their terms and conditions of employment.[4] These limits on employers' property interests have long been held to be legitimate, as are many others.

However, in order to run their businesses and, hence, use and enjoy their property, the U.S. Supreme Court determined that employers may permanently replace economic strikers.[5] Employers may replace the strikers despite the fact that the NLRA protects the right to strike.[6] The Supreme Court reached its permanent

---

[3] 29 U.S.C. § 157 (2012).

[4] New York–New York, LLC v. NLRB, 676 F.3d 193, 196–200 (D.C. Cir. 2012), *cert. denied*, 568 U.S. 1244 (2013) (enforcing NLRB order where NLRB determined that the employees of contractor working onsite in a hotel and casino had rights to distribute union propaganda in nonworking areas of the hotel, even if hotel was not their employer and the hotel generally could expel trespassers).

[5] NLRB v. Mackay Radio & Tel. Co., 304 U.S. 333, 345 (1938). Employers may not, however, replace noneconomic strikers or strikers protesting an employer unfair labor practice. *See id.* at 345. As the Supreme Court stated, "it does not follow that an employer, guilty of no act denounced by the statute, has lost the right to protect and continue his business by supplying places left vacant by strikers." What the phrase implies is that if the employer is "guilty" of an act, such as is an unfair labor practice, then it cannot replace the strikers. *Id.* at 345. The NLRB has thus established rules to determine unfair labor practice strikes where employees cannot be replaced. *See* Gatliff Business Products, 276 NLRB 543, 563 (1985) (defining economic and unfair labor practice strikes).

[6] 29 U.S.C. § 163 (2012).

strike replacements conclusion in *dictum,* without giving it any thought; it exists as a matter of the Court's "common sense."[7] And yet, not only does that common sense *dictum* go against the words of the statute, but it also goes against the U.S. Constitution's protection of the right of employees to quit their jobs,[8] present in the Thirteenth Amendment, and against international labor standards.[9] The doctrine of permanent strike replacements closely aligns with the infamous case of *Lochner v. New York*, where the U.S. Supreme Court invalidated a New York statute limiting the hours of bakers on the grounds that the law limited freedom of contract.[10] But as Justice Oliver Wendell Holmes famously dissented in *Lochner*, "[The] Constitution is not intended to embody a particular economic theory, whether of paternalism and the organic relation of the citizen to the state or of *laissez faire*."[11] If Congress decided to protect striking workers, the courts, under the Constitution, under the express words of Congress, and under international labor standards, should honor that protection.

Moreover, the idea of permanent strike replacements is pure sophistry: according to the U.S. Supreme Court, employers may not *terminate* employees who strike because, to do so, would violate the NLRA.[12] But employers may *permanently replace* them. Most people who learn about this strange distinction between termination and permanent replacement might scratch their heads. What's the difference? The difference is the following: under the permanent strike replacement doctrine, an employer may offer a strikebreaker a permanent job left by a striker.[13] The employer must give that job back to a striker once the job opens up again (such as when the strikebreaker voluntarily quits).[14] On the other hand, terminated employees have no right to get their jobs back if they become vacant. In the real world, the difference between permanent replacement and termination is purely formal. Workers' mounting bills and empty stomachs will not notice the difference.

Moreover, a law that only favors employers' property interests is extremely one-sided. What of workers' property interests? When unions were strong and the middle class was in a less precarious condition, home ownership was more commonplace

---

[7] James Gray Pope, *How American Workers Lost the Right to Strike, and Other Tales*, 103 MICH. L. REV. 518, 518–19 (2004).

[8] *See* chapter 2.

[9] LANCE COMPA, UNFAIR ADVANTAGE: WORKERS FREEDOM OF ASSOCIATION IN THE UNITED STATES UNDER INTERNATIONAL HUMAN RIGHTS STANDARDS 196 (2nd ed. 2004).

[10] 25 S. Ct. 539 (1905).

[11] Lochner v. New York, 25 S. Ct. 539.

[12] *See* Laidlaw Corp., 171 N.L.R.B. 1366, 1368 (1968).

[13] *Id.*

[14] *Id.*

in the United States.[15] Today, U.S. workers are highly indebted, in fact, more than ever.[16] Low wages force society to subsidize workers' earnings.[17] These subsidies end up being paid by all taxpayers, threatening taxpayers' property interests as well. In this manner, enforceable minimum wages, protection of workers' concerted activities for their mutual aid and protection, among other labor protections, help to defend the earnings of all taxpayers and, therefore, society's property interests. Labor law need not be seen as in conflict with property rights. Labor law might, in fact, help provide a more robust legal system and political economy for everyone's property rights.

LABOR LAW AND FREE SPEECH

The U.S. Supreme Court has recently elevated free speech to such a high standing that it seems to swallow all else whole, including, importantly, economic regulations.[18] In *Janus v. AFCME Council 31*, for example, decided in 2018, the Court held that state governments could no longer legislate public sector labor laws that force workers to pay union agency fees to unions.[19] Such fees, if coerced, threaten the free speech rights of workers who disagree with unions' bargaining positions, even if those unions must fairly represent the dissident workers.[20] Because public sector unions' demands at the bargaining table are necessarily a matter of public concern, e.g., they overlap with government spending and taxing issues, workers who disagree with the public sector unions' demands necessarily disagree with the union on issues of public concern.[21] When workers are forced to pay the union agency fees, workers,

---

[15] In 2016, home ownership rates were lower than in 1965. *See* U.S. Bureau of the Census, Homeownership Rate for the United States [RHORUSQ156N], retrieved from FRED, Federal Reserve Bank of St. Louis; https://fred.stlouisfed.org/series/RHORUSQ156N, Sept. 9, 2018.

[16] *U.S. household debt rises to $13.3 trillion in second quarter*, REUTERS, Aug. 14, 2018, https://www.reuters.com/article/us-usa-fed-debt/u-s-household-debt-rises-to-13-3-trillion-in-second-quarter-idUSKBN1KZ1QZ.

[17] *See Walmart on Tax Day: How Taxpayers Subsidize America's Biggest Employer and Richest Family*, Americans for Tax Fairness, at 3 (2014), https://americansfortaxfairness.org/files/Walmart-on-Tax-Day-Americans-for-Tax-Fairness-1.pdf (nonpartisan policy group reporting that "Walmart and the Walton family receive tax breaks and taxpayer subsidies estimated at more than $7.8 billion a year").

[18] *See* Charlotte Garden, *The Deregulatory First Amendment at Work*, 51 HARV. C.R.-C.L. L. REV. 324 (2016) (explaining how First Amendment jurisprudence is increasingly taking on a deregulatory role in the Supreme Court).

[19] Janus v. AFSCME Council 31, 138 S. Ct. 2448, 2486 (2018). Agency fees, or fair share fees, is the percentage of union dues that go directly to represent workers in collective bargaining and grievance processing. They do not include union expenses in political lobbying, supporting political candidates, and other activities unrelated to representing their members in collective bargaining and grievances.

[20] *Id.* at 2478.

[21] *Id.*, at 2474-76.

in effect, are subsidizing speech they disagree with.[22] Hence, the Supreme Court decided to ban agency fees in the pubic sector. Unions in the public sector can now only charge fees that workers have voluntarily agreed to pay.[23]

American legal scholars and pundits criticized the U.S. Supreme Court's 5–4 *Janus* opinion as being fundamentalist about the First Amendment.[24] As the four-member minority opined through the words of Justice Elena Kagan, the Supreme Court's then-existing forty-one-year old precedent, *Abood v. Detroit Board of Education*,[25] which had found agency fees constitutional, balanced various principles, including states' authority to regulate economic and social matters, manage their workforces, and workers' free speech rights.[26] As Kagan's dissent opined:

> [*Abood*] fit comfortably with this Court's general framework for evaluating claims that a condition of public employment violates the First Amendment. The Court's decisions have long made plain that government entities have substantial latitude to regulate their employees' speech—especially about terms of employment—in the interest of operating their workplaces effectively. *Abood* allowed governments to do just that. While protecting public employees' expression about non-workplace matters, the decision enabled a government to advance important managerial interests—by ensuring the presence of an exclusive employee representative to bargain with. Far from an "anomaly," . . . the *Abood* regime was a paradigmatic example of how the government can regulate speech in its capacity as an employer.[27]

Justice Kagan then went on to declare that the conservative majority "weaponized" the First Amendment, enabling the Court to step into regulatory debates and undo state legislation concerning public sector work forces, and many other forms of economic and social policy altogether.[28] As Kagan dissented:

> And maybe most alarming, the majority has chosen the winners by turning the First Amendment into a sword, and using it against workaday economic and

[22] *Id.*, at 2466.

[23] *Id.*, at 2486.

[24] *See, e.g.*, Benjamin Sachs & Sharon Block, *How Democratic Lawmakers Should Help Unions Reeling from the Janus Decision*, Vox, June 27, 2018, https://www.vox.com/the-big-idea/2018/6/27/17510046/public-unions-janus-reforms-fees-decline-reform-supreme-court-hope; Charlotte Garden, *The Deregulatory First Amendment Strikes Back*, Take Care, July 3, 2018, https://takecareblog.com/blog/the-deregulatory-first-amendment-strikes-back.

[25] 431 U.S. 209 (1977).

[26] Janus v. AFCME Council 31, 138 S. Ct. 2448, 2487 (2018) (Kagan, J., dissenting).

[27] *Id.*

[28] *Id.* at 2501.

> regulatory policy. Today is not the first time the Court has wielded the First Amendment in such an aggressive way . . . And it threatens not to be the last. Speech is everywhere—a part of every human activity (employment, health care, securities trading, you name it). For that reason, almost all economic and regulatory policy affects or touches speech. So the majority's road runs long.[29]

In essence, Kagan argued that the conservative majority was going against democracy itself. Judges can now enter what are otherwise partisan debates on how to regulate economic activity and decide who wins. As she concluded: ". . . at every stop are black-robed rulers overriding citizens' choices. The First Amendment was meant for better things. It was meant not to undermine but to protect democratic governance—including over the role of public-sector unions."[30]

Agency fees, or fair share fees, are binding on workers only after democratically elected legislatures pass laws and workers democratically choose to be represented by a union. Dissidents need only pay the fraction of dues related to their representation by the union at the bargaining table and in grievance processing. The fees protect unions, once chosen democratically by workers, from collective action problems and free riding.[31]

The U.S. Supreme Court, however, opined that resolving worker collective action problems and free riding were not "compelling state interest[s]" that justified agency fees in light of their First Amendment implications.[32] As Justice Alito stated in his opinion, "free-rider arguments . . . are generally insufficient to overcome First Amendment objections."[33] He went on to add: "To hold otherwise across the board would have startling consequences. Many private groups speak out with the objective of obtaining government action that will have the effect of benefiting nonmembers. May all those who are thought to benefit from such efforts be compelled to subsidize this speech?"[34]

The main problem with this reasoning is that we are here dealing with a special problem of social inequality: that of employers over workers. Unions provide workers with the capacity to rebalance power equations at work. Without such protections, social and economic inequality remains unchecked, threatening the very structure

---

[29] *Id.* at 2501–02.

[30] *Id.* at 2502.

[31] *See* Mancur Olson, The Logic of Collective Action: Public Goods and the Theory of Groups (1965).

[32] Janus v. AFSCME Council 31, 138 S. Ct. 2448, 2466 (2018).

[33] *Id.*

[34] *Id.*

of a democratic republic.[35] This is why, as we explain below, workers' freedom of association and effective collective bargaining are considered internationally to be universal human rights. This is also why labor law should be constitutionalized through the Thirteenth Amendment of the U.S. Constitution, as we have argued in these pages.

Janus is now law. Labor unions and ordinary workers will have to find alternate ways to fund labor organizations in the public sector. The reason we bring up *Janus* is to underscore why understanding the principles of labor law matter so much. By killing agency fees and providing little in their stead, the Supreme Court also is killing unions, institutions needed to better equalize social relationships. Public sector unions that charged agency fees already had a number of democratic checks placed on them, starting with lawmaking by a democratically elected legislature, and ending with a labor union selected by a majority of the workers to represent them in collective bargaining. However, the five-member conservative Court majority decided to ignore these democratic processes based on its fundamentalist view of free speech. The conservative majority could not even appropriately balance free speech with democratic principles.

LABOR RIGHTS ARE HUMAN RIGHTS

Workers need special legal protections. Those special protections are contained in labor law. And labor law is not trivial regulation. Labor rights are human rights, hence why we insist they be constitutionalized under the U.S. Thirteenth Amendment.[36] Thus, adjudicators need to grant labor law principles high priority when dealing with conflicts of laws. Labor rights are in the Universal Declaration of

---

[35] *See, e.g.*, JACOB HACKER & PAUL PIERSON, WINNER-TAKE-ALL POLITICS (2011); JOSEPH STIGLITZ, THE PRICE OF INEQUALITY (2012).

[36] For example, the Universal Declaration of Human Rights of 1948 states:

> Article 4
> No one shall be held in slavery or servitude; slavery and the slave trade shall be prohibited in all their forms.

It also states:

> Article 23
> 1. Everyone has the right to work, to free choice of employment, to just and favourable conditions of work and to protection against unemployment.
> 2. Everyone, without any discrimination, has the right to equal pay for equal work.
> 3. Everyone who works has the right to just and favourable remuneration ensuring for himself and his family an existence worthy of human dignity, and supplemented, if necessary, by other means of social protection.
> 4. Everyone has the right to form and to join trade unions for the protection of his interests.

Human Rights and the conventions of the ILO.[37] They are also in the International Covenant on Civil and Political Rights,[38] the International Covenant on Economic, Social and Cultural Rights,[39] the American Convention on Human Rights (Pact of San Jose, Costa Rica),[40] and the European Convention for the Protection of Human Rights and Fundamental Freedoms,[41] among others. Latin America, of course, has been a main actor shaping many of these international human rights treaties and other instruments.[42] Most of them prohibit, inter alia, slavery and involuntary servitude.[43] They enshrine the right to work and fair working conditions.[44] They establish nondiscrimination, the right to a fair remuneration, freedom of association, rights to rest and paid vacations, and the protection of motherhood.[45] Since almost all countries are part of these declarations and treaties, we can conclude that, beyond national differences, workers share basic human rights at work.[46]

Article 24

Everyone has the right to rest and leisure, including reasonable limitation of working hours and periodic holidays with pay.

Article 25

1. Everyone has the right to a standard of living adequate for the health and well-being of himself and of his family, including food, clothing, housing and medical care and necessary social services, and the right to security in the event of unemployment, sickness, disability, widowhood, old age or other lack of livelihood in circumstances beyond his control.
2. Motherhood and childhood are entitled to special care and assistance. All children, whether born in or out of wedlock, shall enjoy the same social protection.

G.A. Res. 217A (III), arts. 4, 23–26, Universal Declaration of Human Rights (*adopted* Dec. 10, 1948) [hereinafter UDHR].

37 *See id.*

38 International Covenant on Civil and Political Rights (Dec. 16, 1966, *entered into force* Mar. 23, 1976), 999 U.N.T.S. 171 [hereinafter ICCPR].

39 International Covenant on Economic, Social and Cultural Rights (Dec. 16, 1966) 993 U.N.T.S. 171 [hereinafter ICESCR].

40 American Convention on Human Rights (Nov. 22, 1969) 1144 U.N.T.S. 123.

41 European Convention for the Protection of Human Rights and Fundamental Freedoms, 213 U.N.T.S. 221 (*entered into force* Jun. 2, 1952, *opened for signature* Nov. 4, 1950).

42 Kathryn Sikkink, Evidence for Hope Making Human Rights Work in the 21st Century 119–20 (2017).

43 UDHR, *supra* note 36, arts. 4, 23–26; ICCPR, *supra* note 38, art. 8; American Convention on Human Rights, *supra* note 40, art. 6.

44 UDHR, *supra* note 36, art. 23(1); ICCPR, *supra* note 38, art. 8(3)(a); ICESCR, *supra* note 39, art. 6.

45 UDHR, *supra* note 36, arts. 23(3–4), 24, 25(2); ICCPR, *supra* note 38, arts. 22, 23; ICESCR, *supra* note 39, arts. 7, 10, 22; American Convention on Human Rights, *supra* note 40, art. 16.

46 Colin Fenwick & Tonia Novitz, *Conclusion: Regulating to Protect Worker's Human Rights*, Human Rights at Work. Perspectives on Law and Regulation 586–89 (Colin Fenwick & Tonia Novitz eds., 2010) [hereinafter Fenwick & Novitz, *Conclusion*].

Now, it is true that not all human rights instruments consecrate labor rights in the same way, and that there are important institutional differences and traditions affecting labor rights.[47] Jurists and policymakers also discuss whether labor rights are "civil and political rights," or "economic, social and cultural rights," hence receiving greater or lesser importance in relationship with other rights and policies.[48] Moreover, Professor Samuel Moyn has shown that global human rights discourse has not been sufficient to advance social and economic rights; human rights doctrine has been inadequate to disseminate egalitarian norms and redistribute resources.[49] Professor Kathryn Sikkink, more optimistic about the power of human rights, recognizes their importance, albeit in conjunction with "government and politics."[50] She argues that addressing issues of economic inequality also require inclusive social and tax policies, such as Uruguay has generally had, or those in the social democracies of Western Europe.[51]

But aside from the doubts about the power of human rights for social and labor rights, the normative influence of human rights has grown since the post–World War II period.[52] For example, today human rights doctrine favors human rights in the hard case, as acknowledged by the principle of *in dubio pro libertate*, or the general freedom right.[53] According to this principle, the jurist must opt for the most favorable interpretation that secures a person's human rights.[54] We should not be surprised with the uncanny similarity of *in dubio pro libertate* with *in dubio pro*

---

[47] *Id.* at 597. In the case of South Africa, for example, there is a divide between the Constitutional Court and the traditional labor courts; the Constitutional Court is more respectful of labor human rights than the labor courts. *Id.* at 598. *See also* Stefan Van Eck, *Constitutionalisation of South Africa Labour Law: An Experiment in the Making*, *in* HUMAN RIGHTS AT WORK: PERSPECTIVES ON LAW AND REGULATION 290–91 (Colin Fenwick & Tonia Novitz eds., 2010).

[48] Tonia Novitz & Colin Fenwick. *The Application of Human Rights Discourse to Labour Relations: Translation of Theory into Practice*, *in* HUMAN RIGHTS AT WORK: PERSPECTIVES ON LAW AND REGULATION 11–12 (Colin Fenwick & Tonia Novitz eds., 2010).

[49] SAMUEL MOYN, NOT ENOUGH: HUMAN RIGHTS IN AN UNEQUAL WORLD (2018). *See also* César F. Rosado Marzán, *The Limits of Human Rights for Labour Rights: A Retrospective Look at the Case of Chile*, *in* THE ILO FROM GENEVA TO THE PACIFIC RIM: WEST MEETS EAST 206–32 (Jill M. Jensen & Nelson Lichtenstein eds., (2016) (arguing that a human rights frame helped to stop state repression of union activists in Chile, but was ineffective and may have even contributed to individualistic, neoliberal *Plan Laboral* (labor laws) of the Pinochet regime, whose main contours continue unabated to this day, almost three decades after democracy was restored).

[50] SIKKINK, *supra* note 42, at 199–200.

[51] *Id.*

[52] *Id.* at 134; Fenwick & Novitz, *Conclusion*, *supra* note 46.

[53] ANTONIO E. PÉREZ LUÑO, DERECHOS HUMANOS, ESTADO DE DERECHO Y CONSTITUCIÓN 315 (1995); GERMÁN J. BIDART CAMPOS, TEORÍA GENERAL DE LOS DERECHOS HUMANOS 398 (1991)

[54] PÉREZ LUÑO, *supra* note 53; BIDART CAMPOS, *supra* note 53.

operario because, as Professor Sikkink has described, human rights, like labor rights, are also concerned with protecting the weak.[55] Legal institutions must thus protect the weak; protecting the weak is a universally recognized legal obligation.

CONCLUSION

Indeed, principled labor law has no immediate answers to cases where labor law principles conflict with other law. However, because principled labor law provides the adjudicator with a fuller understanding of labor law, he or she can better recognize the existence of a conflict and, if there is a conflict, find ways of reconciling labor law with other law without recurring to displace either labor law or the law with which it might conflict.

We have argued that labor law need not be seen as in conflict with property rights if we understand how labor law generally helps to protect the property rights of workers and capitalism, generally. We have also argued that if we understand labor rights to be constitutional, democratic, and part of human rights, then we can justify some encroachments into employer property rights. The adjudicator needs to balance employer and labor rights. To the extent the employer can still run a profitable business, basic labor rights, such as those regarding strikes, should be protected. Employers need not have rights to permanently replace economic strikers, for example, once one understands the relative importance of the right to strike to maintain a power balance in society and to preserve democracy. Democratic deficits can also lead to impoverished workers who will not be able to consume. Businesses might simply go under if workers can no longer afford their goods. Similarly, free speech and mandatory agency fees need not conflict. If a democratically elected legislature grants unions the right to bargain on behalf of all workers, and a majority of workers vote in favor of union representation, then mandatory agency fees paid to the union representing the workers conform to democratic and republican principles. Free speech rights remain protected by the democratic checks. Because labor law is part of the human rights system and is friendly, not antagonistic to democratic principles, it need not lose against property rights or be seen as violating free speech. Labor law could be accommodated and the rights of everyone be equitably respected. To reach these conclusions, however, one must be fully cognizant of labor law principles and how they interrelate with other principles.

---

[55] *See* SIKKINK, *supra* note 42, at 88.

7

CONCLUSION

A Universal Idea

IN THIS BOOK, we have provided a Latin American perspective of U.S. labor law to offer a conceptual scheme of labor protection that can better align U.S. labor law with international labor standards. We showed how two important New Deal–era statutes, the National Labor Relations Act (NLRA) and the Fair Labor Standards Act (FLSA), contain the protective principle sufficiently enough to justify broad interpretation, in the manner of Latin America's *in dubio pro operario*. However, we also described that the courts, including the U.S. Supreme Court, and even administrative agencies such as the National Labor Relations Board and the Department of Labor, have unevenly developed a labor-protective jurisprudence. In fact, the U.S. Supreme Court recently walked back from its decades-old doctrine of broadly interpreting the FLSA.[1] Today's more conservative Court, more than ever aligned with big business, and following a philosophical inclination attached to textualism, further weakens a principled labor law in the United States.

Given the courts' grudging liking for labor law—at best—and some agencies' spotty acknowledgment of labor protection in the New Deal statutes, we also argued that U.S. labor protective legislation should be lifted to a higher constitutional rank through the Thirteenth Amendment of the U.S. Constitution. The Thirteenth Amendment is the product of the post–Civil War Reconstruction period. It calls

[1] Encino Motorcars, LLC v. Navarro et al., 138 S. Ct. 1134 (2018).

Principled Labor Law. Sergio Gamonal C. and César F. Rosado Marzán.

Congress to protect one of the most important rights of all, human freedom, by eradicating involuntary servitude. We have argued here that involuntary servitude can prevail in unregulated capitalism. Labor law constitutionalized through the Thirteenth Amendment would thus send a strong signal to all legal actors that labor protections deserve the highest degree of deference, even if such protections somewhat impinge on other rights, such as employer property interests.

In the book, we also described how primacy of reality pervades in the United States. It could be further strengthened through an invigorated protective principle, especially when dealing with hard cases. Despite facts, sometimes the law still leaves adjudicators with doubts as to which legal conclusion they need to reach. *In dubio pro operario* may supplement primacy of reality to channel adjudicative discretion in favor of the worker. As we argued here, for example, if a putative employee makes at least a reasonable case that he or she is an employee under the applicable employment test, then adjudicators should hold in favor of employee status and cover the worker under the relevant labor laws.

We also detailed that nonwaiver generally also exists in the United States, with the great exception of so-called "procedural" waivers, where employees can waive their rights to litigate their cases in court and, instead, file an individual arbitration claim. The U.S. Supreme Court has legitimized procedural waivers through a coerced reading of the Federal Arbitration Act (FAA) of 1925. Congress needs to change the FAA to more clearly tell the courts that such coerced readings are inapposite to the will of Congress and, hence, of the people. It should also amend the NLRA to clearly protect worker participation in class and collective actions under the more general protections of concerted, protected activities. Congress could outright ban procedural waivers to more fully extend the nonwaiver principle. However, in these pages we have chosen to argue in favor of regulating employment arbitration. By creating standards for arbitration that would protect the due process rights of workers, as Professor Martin Malin has argued,[2] the United States might actually come closer than ever in its history to create labor courts where workers can seek quick, cheap, and simple procedures that are essential for effective labor justice.

Continuity is the least present principle in the United States due to employment at will. Like Professor Clyde Summers argued decades ago, we stated that the United States needs to derogate employment at will through statute.[3] However, given the political realities, employment at will might only be rescinded if done state by state.

---

[2] Martin H. Malin, *The Arbitration Fairness Act: It Need Not and Should Not Be an All or Nothing Proposition*, 87 Ind. L.J. 289, 294 (2012).

[3] Clyde W. Summers, *Individual Protection against Unjust Dismissal: Time for a Statute*, 62 Va. L. Rev. 481 (1976).

Employment stability might be achievable at this time only through state-by-state derogation of employment at will.

In all, labor law principles exist in U.S. positive law and could be strengthened if constitutionalized through the Thirteen Amendment, and by excluding the reach of the FAA into the employment realm, or regulating arbitration, while rescinding employment at will through statute. But even if the principles can be strengthened with further legislation, they are not so absent in current U.S. positive law to justify decades of judicial erosion of workers' rights.

Through this case study of the United States, we also wanted to show how principled labor law can be useful for other jurisdictions. We insist that, despite globalization, neoliberalism, labor law crises, and whatnot, by now many countries have deep traditions, legal and otherwise, that support protecting the weak. If the United States, one of the least labor-protective jurisdictions in the developed world, has the potential of having a labor-protective jurisprudence, other countries might do even better.

In the rest of this conclusion, we underscore some points that we have already developed throughout the book, to wit, the need developed countries have to improve their labor law, how Latin America can help them, and the importance of protecting weak parties as the central concept of labor law. Before concluding, we acknowledge that our account in this book has been partial to state-enforced labor law, discussing little the importance of freedom of association. We assert that freedom of association remains a necessary aspect for workers' rights. We then conclude.

DEVELOPED COUNTRIES NEED LABOR LAW

We have argued that Latin American jurisprudence has solidly lodged labor protection in its legal system despite informality, neoliberalism, and the comings and goings of authoritarian governments and brutal dictatorships. One could even argue that the relative salience of legal principles used by adjudicators to interpret positive law in the region might in some way result from the relative weakness of labor unions and collective bargaining to regulate the workplace. As legislatures and courts have become more salient than collective bargaining in other countries, legal principles to protect basic labor rights also might matter more there. Hence the importance of the Latin American experience for countries similarly relying on legal institutions to protect workers.

Critics might argue that what we are proposing here—that developed countries like the United States need to better protect their workers, and that developing countries such as those in Latin America can contribute to developed countries' legal institutions—seems ludicrous. For example, Nikki Haley, the United States' United Nations Ambassador under the Donald Trump administration, said in 2018 that the United States is beyond the purview of economic human rights because the United States is the richest country in the world.[4] In her rebuke of a U.N. report on poverty in the United States, Ambassador Haley claimed that the United Nations should spend its scarce resources studying poverty in Africa and other Third World regions, but not in the United States, where she claimed poverty is not much of a problem.

Yet, as Philip Alston, the author of the rebuked U.N. report retorted, human rights are universal and therefore apply to rich and poor countries alike.[5] Additionally, poverty is an acute problem in the United States; it is a factual reality. We would respond similarly to our critics. Worker conditions in the United States and in many developed countries are not improving, and without labor law's normative revival, things are apt to get worse. And yes, Latin America may have something to contribute.

LATIN AMERICA CAN HELP

As we detailed in this book, Latin America played a fundamental role during labor law's twentieth-century ascendance. The region can similarly step in today. The region's contribution, principled labor law, conforms to international labor standards. It is also simple and relatively straightforward to apply. While we do not want to ignore complex legal realities, e.g., conflicting norms, legal ambiguity, and related issues in the law, it is also important to keep law cogent, clear, and simple so that those called to implement it can do so consistently.[6] In this sense, we argued that principled labor law differs from its close cousin, the purposivism of Professor Guy Davidov, which looks to match and reconcile rules with a plurality of legal purposes. In line with the Latin American tradition, we kept labor law's principles tied to the

---

[4] Nikki Haley, *The United Nations' Patently Ridiculous Report on American Poverty*, National Review, July 9, 2018, https://www.nationalreview.com/2018/07/united-nations-report-on-american-poverty-distorts-and-misrepresents/.

[5] Mythili Sampathkumar, *UN Official Attacks Nikki Haley over Human Rights Council Withdrawal as He Presents Damning Report on US Poverty*, The Independent, June 22, 2018, https://www.independent.co.uk/news/world/nikki-haley-human-rights-council-us-poverty-un-report-trump-philip-alston-states-a8411871.html. For the U.N. report, *see* Human Rights Council, *Report of the Special Rapporteur on Extreme Poverty and Human Rights on his Mission to the United States of America*, United Nations General Assembly, May 4, 2018, http://undocs.org/A/HRC/38/33/ADD.1.

[6] *See, e.g.*, Adelle Blackett, *Emancipation in the Idea of Labour Law*, *in* The Idea of Labor Law 435 (Guy Davidov & Brian Langille eds., 2011) (on the importance of keeping the idea of labor law simple).

basic notion of worker protection and its derivative principles—primacy of reality, nonwaiver, and continuity—while Davidov's has many others.

We also argued how the Latin American principled method is also different from perspectives seeking to cast aside the need to protect weaker parties. We argued that a "capacities" method aiming to phase out inequality of bargaining power as a central concept for legal protections, and as argued by some scholars, such as Professor Brian Langille, would throw out the labor law baby with the bathwater. Rather than replacing protection of the weak with a capacities approach, we want to include labor law in a larger scheme that might include a capacities strategy, such as universal basic income.[7] But labor law, as its own system of rights, with its own principles, should retain its internal consistency and character, such as Latin America has done in light of its experiments with noncontributory pensions and cash assistance for the poor.

In chapter 6, we also sketched how labor law principles may complement other laws and principles, such as property rights, free speech, and democratic governance. Labor law does not have to conflict with other laws and legal principles. Rather, it can and does fit into the legal mainstream. Essentially, we propose that labor law is an instrument to resolve important social problems; it could be used in conjunction with other tools such as universal basic income, non-contributory pensions, universal healthcare, free public education, and many others. We could toss dirty bathwater, but let's keep the baby. *This* has been the Latin American way.

PROTECTING THE WEAK

Some critics of principled labor law might argue that the concept of worker protection appears too foreign to be transplanted elsewhere. But as we have detailed here, worker protection is a central principle in International Labor Organization (ILO) norms. In fact, world religious traditions uphold the idea of protecting weaker parties. Christian, Jewish, and Islamic faiths, the "Abrahamic" traditions, all teach social justice and fairness, particularly for workers.[8] Buddhists also value work that

---

[7] Professor Adelle Blackett has argued a line similar to ours. While she favors a capacities perspective that helps to emancipate workers, she never claims that state protection of the weak needs to be phased out as obsolete. Blackett, *id.* at 435.

[8] Kenneth Dau-Schmidt et al., Labor Law in the Contemporary Workplace 13–14 (2nd ed. 2014). For example, Pope John Paul II expressed the following in his Centesimus Annus:

> The State, however, has the task of determining the juridical framework within which economic affairs are to be conducted, and thus of safeguarding the prerequisites of a free economy, which presumes a certain equality between the parties, *such that one party would not be so powerful as practically to reduce the other to subservience.*

is meaningful, interesting, and welcoming; working under different conditions may be tantamount to something "criminal" under Buddhist traditions.[9]

Protection of the weak also exists in literature, such as in writing by Cervantes, Dickens, Sinclair, Steinbeck, Zola, and many others.[10] It is also present in legal fields beyond labor law, such as human rights, which has enshrined the principle of *in dubio pro liberate*, as we explained in chapter 6. Protecting the weak is observable in contract law, consumer law, and landlord-tenant law, among many other areas of law. In fact, the equitable tradition in Anglo-American law is centrally worried about injustice.[11]

Other jurisdictions, even those with liberal market economies, also recognize, although perhaps not always consistently, the principles laid out here. Take the United Kingdom. Oxford University Professor Jeremias Prassl reports how in 2016 an employment tribunal in London, applying something akin to the principle of primacy of reality, was more than slightly unimpressed by the way Uber, the platform taxi company, tried to brand itself as a nonemployer.[12] As Professor Prassl reported:

> When faced with Uber's strenuous denial of employer status in the autumn of 2016, an employment tribunal in London ruled that the ride-sharing platform's resorting in its documentations to fictions, twisted language and even brand new terminology merited "a degree of scepticism." The judge could not "help being reminded of Queen's Gertrude's most celebrated line: The lady doth protest too much methinks". And whilst the Shakespearean flourish might be lacking in other jurisdictions, more and more courts around the world are similarly refusing to be fooled by carefully designed contractual euphemisms.[13]

> The State must contribute to the achievement of [dignity at work, a just and secure wage, and humane working conditions] both directly and indirectly. Indirectly, by creating favorable conditions for the free exercise of economic activity, which will lead to abundant opportunities for employment and sources of wealth. *Directly, by defending the weakest, by placing certain limits on the autonomy of the parties who determine working conditions*, and by ensuring in every case the necessary minimum support for the unemployed worker.

CENTESIMUS ANNUS 15 (1991), *cited in* DAU-SCHMIDT ET AL., *id.* (emphasis added).

See also the Bible, *e.g., Psalms* 3–4; *Proverbs* 31:8–9; *Isaiah* 1:17; *Jeremiah* 22:3.

[9] *Id.* at 14.

[10] MIGUEL DE CERVANTES SAAVEDRA, THE INGENIOUS KNIGHT, DON QUIXOTE DE LA MANCHA: VOLUME I 128, 206–08 (1881); CHARLES DICKENS, HARD TIMES (Simon & Schuster, 2007); ÉMILE ZOLA, GERMINAL (Penguin Classics, 2004); UPTON SINCLAIR, THE JUNGLE (Dover Thrift Edition, 2001); and JOHN STEINBECK, THE GRAPES OF WRATH (Penguin Books, 2002).

[11] *See* Hessel E. Yntema, *Equity in the Civil Law and the Common Law*, 60 AM. J. COMP. LAW 60 (1966–1967).

[12] *Id.* at 45, 98.

[13] JEREMIAS PRASSL, HUMANS AS A SERVICE: THE PROMISE AND PERILS OF WORK IN THE GIG ECONOMY 45 (2018).

The court clearly had a keen eye for primacy of reality. And labor law principles do not stop at primacy of reality in the United Kingdom. As Prassl also reported, courts in the United Kingdom, aware of "inequality of bargaining power at work," are evermore willing to look behind contractual language to unearth the reality of working relationships and assign employer liabilities.[14] The United Kingdom, despite its liberal market economy, recognizes the protective principle, at least sometimes. Other countries likely do also. The task at hand, therefore, is to strive for labor-protective consistency through litigation strategies, regulatory actions, and statutory reform—whatever may be most viable. For workers to prevail in those forums, however, a labor-protective jurisprudence must be developed and made more salient. This book contributes to that needed labor-protective law.

A NOTE ON FREEDOM OF ASSOCIATION

Some skeptics of our principled labor law thesis might argue that our method, narrowly focusing on state-enforced law, is insufficient to provide for a robust system of labor rights. Without their own form of power, workers are apt to wage an ultimately losing battle. Workers can make gains and find allies in the state, but only in specific times. At other times, the state might just come out to crush workers' rights. In the words of Professor Adelle Blackett, labor law should include a protective role for the state and "an enabling one for actors."[15] Emancipation requires agency, something that a mere paternalistic state will likely hinder at some politically opportune time.

We agree. Workers need unions, collective bargaining, and other forms of free association to act as true, free agents. In fact, in Latin America, some jurists discuss "labor union autonomy" as another central principle of labor law.[16] Labor union autonomy is used to develop doctrines related to workers' freedom of association—free from employer and state control. However, we did not discuss labor union autonomy in this book because we wanted to focus on justiciable rights, given their relative salience and contemporary importance in relation to collective bargaining. Also, freedom of association in Latin America is fraught with too many limitations to be a model for the world. Additionally, labor lawyers can readily draw from the well-respected, decades-old jurisprudence of the ILO's Freedom of Association Committee to better develop freedom of association doctrine.

---

[14] *Id.* at 99.

[15] Blackett, *supra* note 6, at 435.

[16] Sergio Gamonal C., Introducción al Derecho del Trabajo 60–66 (1998).

Our stress on judicially enforceable rights, however, does not mean that we think those rights are superior to rights attainable through collective bargaining and other forms of worker self-organization and free association. We support attempts to solidify collective bargaining and freedom of association more generally, even if this book focused more narrowly on jurisprudence.[17] We dare not throw the freedom of association baby out with the bathwater.

Overall, our main goal was to develop a juridical narrative in favor of protecting workers as weaker bargaining agents. Without it, working relationships and society at large are on morally tenuous ground. Workers without protections risk being treated like commodities, objects without autonomy, forced to accept terms by compulsion. While that moral concern should be sufficient to induce a robust labor law, we also need to be concerned with worsening income inequality, which affects social stability and the health of our democratic institutions. Certainly, the struggle against commodification and for freedom also requires agency, as argued by Professor Blackett. In this sense, this book only offered a necessary but partial solution to the cause of workers.

LABOR LAW: A VICTIM OF ITS OWN SUCCESS

Not everyone might agree that we need healthy and strong labor law to maintain democracy. But here, labor law might just have hidden its own twentieth-century successes. Many of us might simply have forgotten working conditions, social instability, and political conflict before labor law. We might have forgotten about the threats totalitarianism posed in the 1930s, at the height of World War II, and how labor law was important to construct a postwar order of increased peace, better social stability, and human rights. Labor law might be a victim of its own success. But as amnesia turns labor law opaque and we let labor rights slide, many employers and members of the political right are emboldened and demand more concessions from workers, fueling inequality and eroding democratic control of our institutions. Others demagogically claim to represent workers and "the people" but, rather than building autonomous working class power and labor law, chose to fan the flames of racism, nationalism, and xenophobia, leading us to well-known, dark paths. Therefore, our hope is that this book provides lessons from the past and reconstructs a juridical narrative for the future that reasserts the moral and social imperative of generally protecting the weak and hence, specifically, protecting workers.

---

[17] We should not forget, however, that positive law and jurisprudence can effectively support collective bargaining; in fact, it is essential. *See, e.g.*, RUTH DUKES, THE LABOUR CONSTITUTION: THE ENDURING IDEA OF LABOUR LAW 3–4 (2014) (underscoring the need of a labor constitution, i.e., collective bargaining aided by state law or labor law).

Bibliography

Adelstein, Harvey A. and Harry T. Edwards. "The Resurrection of Hearst v. NLRB: Independent Contractors Under the National Labor Relations Act." *The University of Kansas Law Review* 17, no. 2 (December 1969): 191–205.

Alexy, Robert. *A Theory of Constitutional Rights*. Translated by Julian Rivers. Oxford: Oxford University Press, 2010.

American Law Institute. *Restatement of the Law Second, Contracts.* Philadelphia: The American Law Institute, 1981.

Americans for Tax Fairness. "Walmart on Tax Day: How Taxpayers Subsidize America's Biggest Employer and Richest Family." Last modified April 2014. https://americansfortaxfairness.org/files/Walmart-on-Tax-Day-Americans-for-Tax-Fairness-1.pdf.

Anderson, Elizabeth. *Private Government How Employers Rule Our Lives (and Why We Don't Talk about It)*. Princeton: Princeton University Press, 2017.

Andrias, Kate. "The New Labor Law." *Yale Law Journal* 126, (October 2016): 2–100.

Arese, César. *Derechos humanos laborales. Teoría y práctica de un nuevo derecho del Trabajo.* Buenos Aires: Rubinzal Culzoni, 2014.

Arnow-Richman, Rachel. "Mainstreaming Employment Contract Law: The Common Law Case for Reasonable Notice of Termination." *Florida Law Review* 66, (July 2014): 1513–1597.

Arnow-Richman, Rachel. "Modifying At-Will Employment Contracts." *Boston College Law Review* 57, (March 2016): 428–505.

Aronowitz, Stanley. "The Last Good Job in America." *Social Text* 51, (Summer 1997): 93–108.

Arthurs, Harry W. "Labour Law After Labour." In *The Idea of Labour Law*, edited by Guy Davidov and Brian Langille, 13–29. Oxford: Oxford University Press, 2011.

Asociación Uruguaya de Derecho del Trabajo. *Anuario de Jurisprudencia Laboral.* Montevideo: Fundación de Cultura Universitaria, 2011.

Principled Labor Law. Sergio Gamonal C. and César F. Rosado Marzán.

Atkinson, Joe. "Book Review: A Purposive Approach to Labour Law." *Industrial Law Journal* 46, (July 2017): 303–308.

Atleson, James. *Values and Assumptions in American Labor Law*. Amherst: University of Massachusetts Press, 1983.

Austin, Regina. "Employer Abuse, Worker Resistance, and the Tort of Intentional Infliction of Emotional Distress." *Stanford Law Review* 41, (November 1988): 1–59.

Auzero, Gilles, Dirk Baugard, and Emmanuel Dokés. *Droit du travail*. Paris: Dalloz, 31a ed. 2018.

Barbagelata, Héctor Hugo. "Tendencias de los procesos laborales en Iberoamérica." *Revista Facultad de Derecho de la Universidad de la República* 21, (2002): 27–44.

Barbagelata, Héctor Hugo. *Curso sobre la evolución del pensamiento juslaboralista*. Montevideo: Fundación de Cultura Universitaria, 2009.

Barbagelata, Héctor Hugo. *El particularismo del derecho del trabajo y los derechos humanos laborales*. Montevideo: Fundación de Cultura Universitaria, 2nd ed. 2009.

Barenberg, Mark. "The Political Economy of the Wagner Act: Power, Symbol, and Workplace Cooperation." *Harvard Law Review* 106, (May 1993): 1379–1496.

Barros, Enrique. "Reglas y principios en el derecho." *Anuario de Filosofía Jurídica y Social* 2 (1984): 269–281.

Barry, Ellen, Robert L. Nelson, and Laura Beth Nielsen. *Rights on Trial: How Workplace Discrimination Law Perpetuates Inequality*. Chicago: The University of Chicago Press, 2017.

Baviera, Inmaculada. "Employment Stability in Spanish Labor Law: Between Regulatory Tradition and Social Reality." *Comparative Labor Law and Policy Journal* 34, (Spring 2013): 677–696.

Baylos, Antonio and Joaquín Pérez Rey. *El despido o la violencia del poder privado*. Madrid: Trotta, 2009.

Becker, Craig. "Democracy in the Workplace: Union Representation Elections and Federal Labor Law." *Minnesota Law Review* 77, (February 1993): 495–603.

Belous, Richard S. "The Rise of the Contingent Workforce: The Key Challenges and Opportunities." *Washington and Lee Law Review* 52, (1995): 863–878.

Bensusán, Gaciela. "Legislation and Labor Policy in Latin America: Crisis, Renovation, or Restoration?" *Comparative Labor Law and Policy Journal* 34, (Spring 2013): 655–676.

Bensusán, Gaciela. "Organizing Workers in Argentina, Brazil, Chile and Mexico: The Authoritarian-Corporatist Legacy and Old Institutional Designs in a New Context." *Theoretical Inquiries in Law* 17, (January 2016): 131–161.

Bernstein, Irving. *The Turbulent Years: The History of the American Worker 1933–1941*. Boston: Houghton Mifflin, 1969.

Bidart Campos, Germán José. *Teoría general de los derechos humanos*. Buenos Aires: Astrea, 1991.

Blackett, Adelle. "Emancipation in the Idea of Labour Law." In *The Idea of Labour Law*, edited by Guy Davidov and Brian Langille, 420–36. Oxford: Oxford University Press, 2011.

Blackstone, William. *Commentaries on the Laws of England, Volume 1*. Chicago: The University of Chicago Press, 1979.

Blanpain, Richard, Susan Bisom-Rapp, William R. Corbett, Hilary J. Josephs, and Michael J. Zimmer. *The Global Workplace: International and Comparative Employment Law Cases and Materials*. New York: Aspen Publishers, 2nd ed. 2012.

Bredgaard, Thomas. "Flexibility and Security in Employment Regulation: Learning from Denmark." In *Rethinking Workplace Regulation: Beyond the Standard Contract of*

Employment, edited by Katherine V.W. Stone and Harry Arthurs, 213–233. New York: Russell Sage Foundation, 2013.

Bronfman Vargas, Alan, José Ignacio Martínez Estay, and Manuel Núñez Poblete. *Constitución política comentada*. Santiago: AbeledoPerrot, 2012.

Brudney, James J. "Neutrality Agreements and Card Check Recognition: Prospects for Changing Paradigms." *Iowa Law Review* 90, (March 2005): 819–886.

Burton, Steven J. "Breach of Contract and the Common Law Duty to Perform in Good Faith." *Harvard Law Review* 94, (December 1980): 369–404.

Burton, Steven J. *Principles of Contract Law*. St. Paul: West Academic Publishing, 2012.

Cabrelli, David. *Employment Law in Context: Text and Materials*. Oxford: Oxford University Press, 2016.

Carroll, Lewis. *Alice's Adventures in Wonderland*. Mineola: Dover Publications, 2012.

Castello, Alejandro. *Grupo de Empresa y Derecho del Trabajo*. Montevideo: Fundación de Cultura Universitaria, 2006.

Castillejo de Arias, Olga. "Teoría General del derecho del Trabajo." In *Derecho del Trabajo*, edited by Carlos A. Livellara and Olga Castillejo de Arias, 107–127. Buenos Aires: La Ley, 2004.

Cazes, Sandrine. *Flexicurity: A Relevant Approach in Central and Eastern Europe*, edited by Sandrine Cazes and Alena Nešporová. Geneva: International Labour Organization, 2007.

Collins, Hugh. "Is There a Third Way in Labour Law?" In *Labour Law in an Era of Globalization: Transformative Practices and Possibilities*, edited by Joanne Conaghan, Richard Michael Fischl, and Karl Klare, 449–469. Oxford: Oxford University Press, 2002.

Collins, Hugh. *Employment Law*. Oxford: Oxford University Press, 2010.

Colvin, Alexander J.S. "Empirical Research on Employment Arbitration: Clarity Amidst the Sound and Fury?" *Employee Rights and Employment Policy Journal* 11, no. 2 (2007): 405–447.

Colvin, Alexander J.S. "An Empirical Study of Employment Arbitration: Case Outcomes and Processes." *Journal of Empirical Legal Studies* 8, no. 1 (March 2011): 1–23.

Colvin, Alexander and Mark D. Gough. "Comparing Mandatory Arbitration and Litigation: Access, Process and Outcomes, Research Report to the Robert L. Habush Endowment of the American Association for Justice." *Research Studies and Reports* (2014).

Colvin, Alexander J.S. and Kelly Pike. *Saturns and Rickshaws Revisited: What Kind of Employment Arbitration System Has Developed? 29 Ohio State Journal on Dispute Resolution* 59 (2014).

Compa, Lance. *Unfair Advantage: Workers' Freedom of Association in the United States under International Human Rights Standards*. New York: Human Rights Watch Books, 2000.

Cook, Maria Lorena. *The Politics of Labor Reform in Latin America: Between Flexibility and Rights*. University Park: The Pennsylvania State University Press, 2007.

Coutu, Michel. "With Hugo Sinzheimer and Max Weber in Mind: The Current Crisis and the Future of Labor Law." *Comparative Labor Law and Policy Journal* 34, (Spring 2013): 605–626.

Coutu, Michel, Martine Le Friant, and Gregor Murray. "Broken Paradigms: Labor Law in the Wake of Globalization and the Economic Crisis." *Comparative Labor Law and Policy Journal* 34, (Spring 2013): 565–583.

Dannin, Ellen. *Taking Back the Workers' Law: How to Fight the Assault on Labor Rights*. Ithaca: Cornell University Press, 2006.

Dau-Schmidt, Kenneth, Martin Malin, Roberto Corrada, Christopher Cameron, and Catherine Fisk. *Labor Law in the Contemporary Workplace*. St. Paul: West Academic Publishing, 2014.

Davidov, Guy. *A Purposive Approach to Labour Law*. Oxford: Oxford University Press, 2016.

Davidov, Guy. "The Status of Uber Drivers: A Purposive Approach. *Spanish Labour Law and Employment Relations Journal* 6, (2016): 6, 10–13.

Davidov, Guy and Brian Langille, eds. *The Idea of Labour Law*. Oxford: Oxford University Press, 2011.

Davies, Paul and Mark Friedland. *Towards a Flexible Labour Market: Labour Legislation and Regulation Since the 1990s*. Oxford: Oxford University Press, 2007.

de Cervantes Saavedra, Miguel. *The Ingenious Knight, Don Quixote de la Mancha: Volume 1*. London: C.K. Paul & Co., 1881.

De la Villa Gil, Luis Enrique and Lourdes López Cumbre, eds. *Los Principios del Derecho del Trabajo*. Madrid: Centro de Estudios Financieros, 2003.

De Luca Tamajo, Raffaele and Adalberto Perulli. "Labor Law (individual and collective dimensions) and Decentralization of Production." *General Report, Theme 2, XVIII World Congress on Labour Law* (2006).

de Oliveira, Jean Marcel Mariano. *Direito Constitucional do Trabalho e a Reforma Trabalhista de 2017*. Brasil 2018.

de Soto, Hernando. *The Other Path: The Economic Answer to Terrorism*. New York: Basic Books, 2002.

Deakin, Simon. "Capacitas: Contract Law, Capabilities and the Legal Foundations of the Market." In *Capacitas: Contract Law and the Institutional Preconditions of a Market Economy*, edited by Simon Deakin and Alain Supiot, 1–29. Oxford: Hart Publishing, 2009.

Deakin, Simon and Frank Wilkinson. *The Law of the Labour Market: Industrialization, Employment, and Legal Evolution*. Oxford: Oxford University Press, 2005.

Delong, Sidney W. "An Agnostic's Bible." *Seattle University Law Review* 20, (Winter 1997): 295–317.

Desdentado Bonete, Aurelio. "El Principio Pro Operario." In *Los Principios Del Derecho Del Trabajo*, edited by Luis Enrique de la Villa Gil and Lourdes López, 73–105. Madrid: Centro de Estudios Financieros, 2003.

Dickens, Charles. *Hard Times*. New York: Simon & Schuster, 2007.

Dobbin, Frank. *Inventing Equal Opportunity*. Princeton: Princeton University Press, 2009.

Dubal, V.B. "Wage Slave or Entrepreneur?: Contesting the Dualism of Legal Worker Identities." *California Law Review* 105, (February 2017): 65–123.

Dukes, Ruth. *The Labour Constitution: The Enduring Idea of Labour Law*. Oxford: Oxford University Press, 2014.

Dworkin, Ronald. *Taking Rights Seriously*. Cambridge: Harvard University Press, 1977.

Edelman, Lauren B. *Working Law: Courts, Corporations, and Symbolic Civil Rights*. Chicago: The University of Chicago Press, 2016.

Edelman, Lauren B., Linda H. Krieger, Scott R. Eliason, Catherine R. Albiston, and Virginia Mellema. "When Organizations Rule: Judicial Deference to Institutionalized Employment Structures." *American Journal of Sociology* 117 (2011): 888–954.

Editorial Board. "The Supreme Court Sticks It to Workers, Again." *The New York Times*. Last modified May 24, 2018. https://www.nytimes.com/2018/05/24/opinion/supreme-court-workers-payment.html.

Edwards, Sebastian. *Left Behind: Latin America and the False Promise of Populism*. Chicago: The University of Chicago Press, 2010.

Eisenberg, Melvin Aron. "The Principles of Consideration." *Cornell Law Review* 67, (April 1982): 640–665.

Ely, John Hart. "The Wages of Crying Wolf: A Comment on Roe v. Wade." 82 *Yale Law Journal* 82, 920 (1973): 920–949.

Epstein, Richard A. "In Defense of the Contract at Will." *University of Chicago Law Review* 51, (Fall 1984): 947–982.

Epstein, Richard A. "A Common Law for Labor Relations: A Critique of the New Deal Labor Legislation." *Yale Law Journal* 92, (July 1983): 1357–1408.

Ermida Uriarte, Óscar. "Crítica de la Libertad Sindical." *Revista de la Facultad de Derecho* no. 68 (2012): 33–61.

Ermida Uriarte, Óscar. "Protección, Igualdad, Dignidad, Libertad y No Discriminación." *Cadernos de Amatra IV* 15, (2011): 9–23.

Esping-Andersen, Gosta. *The Three Worlds of Welfare Capitalism*. Princeton: Princeton University Press, 1990.

Estlund, Cynthia L. "Wrongful Discharge Protections in an At-Will World." *Texas Law Review* 74, (June 1996): 1655–1692.

Estlund, Cynthia L. "The Ossification of American Labor Law." *Columbia Law Review* 102, (October 2002): 1527–1612.

Estlund, Cynthia L. "How Wrong Are Employees About their Rights, and Why Does it Matter?" *New York University Law Review* 77, (April 2002): 6–35.

Estlund, Cynthia L. "The Death of Labor Law." *Annual Review of Law and Social Science* 2, (2006): 105–123.

Estreicher, Samuel and Miriam M. Cherry. *Global Issues in Employment Law*. St. Paul: Thomson/West, 2008.

Estreicher, Samuel and Jeffrey M. Hirsch. "Comparative Wrongful Dismissal Law: Reassessing American Exceptionalism." *North Carolina Law Review* 92, (January 2014): 343–468.

Etala, Carlos Alberto. *Interpretación y aplicación de las normas laborales*. Buenos Aires: Editorial Astrea, 2004.

Evans, Peter. "Collective Capabilities, Culture, and Amartya Sen's Development as Freedom." *Studies in Comparative International Development* 37, no. 2 (June 2002): 54–60.

Farinacci-Férnós, Jorge M. "The Search for a Wrongful Dismissal Statute: A Look at Puerto Rico's Act No. 80 as a Potential Starting Point." *Employee Rights and Employment Policy Journal* 17, no. 1 (2013): 125–156.

Feinman, Jay M. "The Development of the Employment at Will Rule." *American Journal of Legal History* 20 (1976): 118–135.

Fenwick, Colin and Tonia Novitz. "Conclusion: Regulating to Protect Worker's Human Rights." In *Human Rights at Work: Perspectives on Law and Regulation*, edited by Colin Fenwick and Tonia Novitz, 585–615. Oxford: Hart Publishing, 2010.

Fineman, Jonathan. "The Inevitable Demise of the Implied Employment Contract." *Berkeley Journal of Employment and Labor Law* 29, (2008): 345–404.

Fink, Leon and Juan Manuel Palacio, eds. *Labor Justice across the Americas*. Champaign: University of Illinois Press, 2018.

Finkin, Matthew W. "'Workers' Contracts' Under the United States Arbitration Act: An Essay in Historical Clarification." *Berkeley Journal of Employment and Labor Law* 17, (1996): 282–303.

Finkin, Matthew W. "NAFTA/NAALC Member Countries, United States." In *International Labor and Employment Laws*, edited by William L. Keller and Timothy J. Darby. Arlington: Bloomberg BNA, 2008.

Fishkin, Joseph R. and William Forbath. *The Anti-Oligarchy Constitution*. Cambridge: Harvard University Press, forthcoming.

Fiss, Owen M. "Against Settlement." *Yale Law Journal* 93, (May 1984): 1073–1090.

Forbath, William E. "The Ambiguities of Free Labor: Labor and the Law in the Gilded Age." *Wisconsin Law Review* 1985, (1985): 767–817.

Forbath, William E. *Law and the Shaping of the American Labor Movement*. Cambridge: Harvard University Press, 1991.

Forbath, William E. "The New Deal Constitution in Exile." *Duke Law Journal* 51, (October 2001): 165–222.

Fram, Nicholas and T. Ward Frampton. "A Union of Amateurs: A Legal Blueprint to Reshape Big-Time College Athletics." *Buffalo Law Review* 60, (August 2012): 1003–1078.

Fried, Charles. *Contract as Promise: A Theory of Contractual Obligation*. Cambridge: Harvard University Press, 1981.

Fudge, Judy. "Labour as a 'Fictive Commodity': Radically Reconceptualizing Labour Law." In *The Idea of Labour Law*, edited by Guy Davidov and Brian Langille, 120–136. Oxford: Oxford University Press, 2011.

Gaete Berríos, Alfredo. *Principales modificaciones que ha introducido el derecho social al derecho civil en materia de contratos y obligaciones*. Santiago: Talleres Gráficos Gutenberg, 1936.

Galanes, Phillip. "Catharine MacKinnon and Gretchen Carlson Have a Few Things to Say." *The New York Times*. Last modified March 17, 2018. https://www.nytimes.com/2018/03/17/business/catharine-mackinnon-gretchen-carlson.html.

Gamonal C., Sergio. *Introducción al derecho del trabajo*. Santiago: Editorial Jurídica ConoSur, 1998.

Gamonal C., Sergio. "Comentario de la jurisprudencia laboral del año 2003." *Revista de Derecho de la Universidad Adolfo Ibáñez* 1, (2004): 754.

Gamonal C., Sergio. "Comentario de la jurisprudencia laboral del año 2004." *Revista de Derecho de la Universidad Adolfo Ibáñez* no. 2 (2005): 1234.

Gamonal C., Sergio. *Fundamentos de derecho laboral*. Santiago: LexisNexis, 2008.

Gamonal C., Sergio. *Derecho colectivo del trabajo*. Santiago: Editorial Legal Publishing, 2011.

Gamonal C., Sergio and César F. Rosado Marzán. "Protecting Workers as a Matter of Principle: A Latin American View of U.S. Work Law." *Washington University Global Studies Law Review* 13, (2014): 605–665.

Garden, Charlotte. "Disrupting Work Law: Arbitration in the Gig Economy." *The University of Chicago Legal Forum* 2017 (2018): 205–234.

Garden, Charlotte. "The Deregulatory First Amendment at Work." *Harvard Civil Rights-Civil Liberties Law Review* 51, (Summer 2016): 323–362.

Garden, Charlotte. "The Deregulatory First Amendment Strikes Back". *Take Care* (July 3, 2018). https://takecareblog.com/blog/the-deregulatory-first-amendment-strikes-back.

Garmendia Arigón, Mario. *Orden público y derecho del trabajo*. Montevideo: La Ley Uruguay, 2001.

Getman, Julius G. *The Betrayal of Local 14: Paperworkers, Politics, and Permanent Replacements*. Ithaca: Cornell University Press, 1998.

Ghezzi, Giorgio and Umberto Romagnoli. *Il rapporto di lavoro*. Bologna: Zanichelli, 1987.

Giugni, Gino. *Lavoro legge contratti*. Bologna: Il Mulino, 1989.

Godinho Delgado, Mauricio. *Princípios de Direito Individual e Coletivo do Trabalho*. São Paulo: LTr, 2004.

Goetz, Charles and Robert E. Scott. "Principles of Relational Contracts." *Virginia Law Review* 67, (September 1981): 1089–1150.

Goetz, Charles and Robert E. Scott. "The Mitigation Principle: Toward a General Theory of Contractual Obligation." *Virginia Law Review* 69, (September 1983): 967–1024.

Goldin, Adrián. *Contrato de trabajo y renuncia de derechos*. Buenos Aires: Hammurabi, 1987.

Goldin, Adrián. "Global Conceptualizations and Local Constructions of the Idea of Labour Law." In *The Idea of Labour Law*, edited by Guy Davidov and Brian Langille, 69–87. Oxford: Oxford University Press, 2011.

Goldin, Adrián and Jorgelina F. Alimenti. *Curso de derecho del trabajo y la seguridad Social*. Buenos Aires: La Ley, 2009.

Goldstein, Bruce, Marc Linder, Laurence E. Norton, II, and Catherine K. Ruckelshaus. "Enforcing Fair Labor Standards in the Modern American Sweatshop: Rediscovering the Statutory Definition of Employment." *UCLA Law Review* 46, (April 1999): 983–1163.

Goluboff, Risa L. "The Thirteenth Amendment and the Lost Origins of Civil Rights." *Duke Law Journal* 50, (April 2001): 1609–1685.

González, Joanisabel. "La junta fiscal accede a los pedidos de Ricardo Rosselló: el ente fiscal no tocará el presupuesto de la legislatura a cambio de la Ley 80." *El Nuevo Día*. Last modified May 22, 2018. https://www.elnuevodia.com/negocios/economia/nota/lajuntafiscalaccedealospedidosdericardorossello-2423632/#cxrecs_s.

Grassi, Davide. "Democracy and Social Welfare in Uruguay and Paraguay." *Latin American Politics and Society* 56, no. 1 (February 2014): 120–143.

Greenstone, Michael and Adam Looney. "A Record Decline in Government Jobs: Implications for the Economy and America's Workforce." *Brookings*. Last modified August 3, 2012. http://www.brookings.edu/blogs/jobs/posts/2012/08/03-jobs-greenstone-looney.

Gross, James A. *A Shameful Business: The Case for Human Rights in the American Workplace*. Ithaca: Cornell University Press, 2010.

Gross, James A. *Rights, Not Interests: Resolving Value Clashes under the National Labor Relations Act*. Ithaca: Cornell University Press, 2017.

Guastini, Ricardo. *Distinguiendo: Estudios de teoría y metateoría del derecho*. Barcelona: Gedisa Editorial, 1999.

Gurrieri, Vin. "Uber's Move Away from Arbitration Falls Short, Attys Say." *Law360*. Last modified May 15, 2018. https://www.law360.com/articles/1043804/uber-s-move-away-from-arbitration-falls-short-attys-say.

Hacker, Jacob S. and Paul Pierson. *Winner-Take-All Politics: How Washington Made the Rich Richer—and Turned Its back on the Middle Class*. New York: Simon & Schuster, 2011.

Haley, Nikki. "The United Nations' Patently Ridiculous Report on American Poverty." *National Review*. Last modified July 9, 2018. https://www.nationalreview.com/2018/07/united-nations-report-on-american-poverty-distorts-and-misrepresents/.

Hartley, Roger C. "Non-Legislative Labor Law Reform and Pre-Recognition Labor Neutrality Agreements: The Newest Civil Rights Movement." *Berkeley Journal of Employment and Labor Law* 22, (2001): 369–408.

Harvey, David. *A Brief History of Neoliberalism*. Oxford: Oxford University Press, 2007.

Hayek, Friedrich A. "El paro y los sindicatos en los años ochenta (El falseamiento de los precios relativos por el monopolio del mercado de trabajo)." In *Sindicatos, ¿Para Qué?* 95 (2009), 41–103.

Human Rights Council. "Report of the Special Rapporteur on Extreme Poverty and Human Rights on his Mission to the United States of America." United Nations General Assembly. Last modified May 4, 2018. http://undocs.org/A/HRC/38/33/ADD.1.

Informe Relasur. Colección informes de Organización Internacional del Trabajo, las relaciones laborales en Uruguay. Madrid: Ministerio de Trabajo y Seguridad Social, Centro de Publicaciones, 1995.

International Finance Corporation and World Bank. "Ease of Doing Business in Uruguay." The World Bank. Last modified July 2, 2013. http://www.doingbusiness.org/data/exploreeconomies/uruguay/.

International Labour Office. "Report VI, Labour protection in a transforming world of work: A recurrent discussion on the strategic objective of social protection (labour protection)." International Labour Conference. 104th Session, 2015. http://www.ilo.org/wcmsp5/groups/public/---ed_norm/---relconf/documents/meetingdocument/wcms_358295.pdf.

Irureta Uriarte, Pedro. *Constitución y orden público laboral: un análisis del art. 19 no. 16 de la constitución chilena*. Santiago: Facultad de Derecho Universidad Alberto Hurtado, 2006.

Izquierdo y de la Cueva, Ana Luisa. *El humanismo jurídico de Mario de la Cueva (Antología)*. Mexico City: Fondo de Cultura Económica, 1994.

Javillier, Jean-Claude. *Derecho del trabajo*. Madrid: Instituto de Estudios Laborales y de Seguridad Social, 1982.

Javillier, Jean-Claude. *Droit du Travail*. Paris: LGDJ, 1996.

Kahn-Freund, Otto. *Trabajo y derecho*. Madrid: Ministerio de Trabajo y Seguridad Social, Centro de Publicaciones, 1987.

Kalleberg, Arne L. "Precarious Work, Insecure Workers: Employment Relations in Transition." *American Sociological Review* 74, (February 2009): 1–22.

Kalleberg, Arne L., Barbara F. Reskin, and Ken Hudson. "Bad Jobs in America: Standard and Nonstandard Employment Relations and Job Quality in the United States." *American Sociological Review* 65, no. 2 (April 2000): 256–278.

Kearns, Ellen C., Aaron D. Kaufmann, and Dennis M. McClelland, eds. *The Fair Labor Standards Act*. Arlington: Bloomberg BNA, 2010.

Keller, William L. and Timothy Darby, eds. *International Labor and Employment Laws, Third Edition*. Washington, D.C.: Bureau of National Affairs, 2008.

Klare, Karl. "Judicial Deradicalization of the Wagner Act and the Origins of Modern Legal Consciousness, 1937–1941." *Minnesota Law Review* 62, no. 3 (1978): 265–340.

Krotoschin, Ernesto. *Manual de derecho del trabajo*. Buenos Aires: Ediciones Depalma, 1993.

Langille, Brian. "Labor Law's Theory of Justice." In *The Idea of Labour Law*, edited by Guy Davidov and Brian Langille, 101–119. Oxford: Oxford University Press, 2011.

Langille, Brian. "'Take These Chains from My Heart and Set Me Free': How Labor Law Theory Drives Segmentation of Workers' Rights." *Comparative Labor Law and Policy Journal* 36, (Winter 2015): 257–279.

Linder, Marc. "Towards Universal Worker Coverage Under the National Labor Relations Act: Making Room for Uncontrolled Employees, Dependent Contractors, and Employee-Like Persons." *University of Detroit Law Review* 66, no. 4 (Summer 1989): 555–602.

Linder, Marc. "Dependent and Independent Contractors in Recent U.S. Labor Law: An Ambiguous Dichotomy Rooted in Simulated Statutory Purposelessness." *Comparative Labor Law and Policy Journal* 21, (Fall 1999): 187–230.

Linder, Marc and Ingrid Nygaard. "Rest in the Rest of the World." *Comparative Labor Law and Policy Journal* 20, (Fall 1998): 105–124.

Lobel, Orly. "The Law of the Platform." *Minnesota Law Review* 101, (November 2016): 87–166.

Lofaso, Anne Marie. "Toward a Foundational Theory of Workers' Rights: The Autonomous Dignified Worker." *UMKC Law Review* 76, (Fall 2007): 1–65.

López-Medina, Diego Eduardo. "La teoria impura del diritto: La trasformazione della cultura giuridica latino americana." *Rivista di Diritto Privato* 29, no. 2 (2011): 195–222.

López-Medina, Diego Eduardo. "El nacimiento del derecho comparado moderno como espacio geográfico y como disciplina: instrucciones básicas para su comprensión y uso desde América Latina." *International Law: Revista Colombiana de Derecho Internacional* no. 26 (June 2015): 117–159.

Macchiavello Contreras, Guido. *Derecho del trabajo: teoría jurídica y análisis de las actuales normas chilenas*. Santiago: Fondo de Cultura Económica,1986.

Macchiavello Contreras, Guido. *Manual de Derecho Procesal del Trabajo*. Santiago: Jurídica de Chile, 1997.

Malin, Martin H. "The Arbitration Fairness Act: It Need Not and Should Not Be an All or Nothing Proposition." *Indiana Law Journal* 87, (Winter 2012): 289–315.

Marques de Lima, Francisco Meton. *Os Princípios De Direito Do Trabalho Na Lei E Na* Jurisprudencia. Sao Paulo: LTR 4th ed. 2015.

Marshall, Shelley and Colin Fenwick. "Labour Law and Development: Characteristics and Challenges." In *Labour Regulation and Development: Socio-Legal Perspectives*, edited by Shelley Marshal and Colin Fenwick, 1–32. Cheltenham: Edward Elgar Publishing, 2016.

Martins Catharino, José. *Direito do trabalho*. Porto Alegre: Juridica Universitária. 1978.

Marvit, Moshe Z. "The Way Forward for Labor Is Through the States." *The American Prospect*. Last updated September 1, 2017. http://prospect.org/article/way-forward-labor-through-states.

Mascaro Nascimento, Amauri. *Iniciação ao direito do trabalho*. São Paulo: LTr. 1997.

Mascaro Nascimento, Amauri. "History of Labor Law in Brazil." In *Panorama of Brazilian Law*, edited by Jacob Dolinger and Keith Rosenn, 233–265. Miami: University of Miami North-South Center Press, 1992.

Mazzotta, Oronzo. *Manuale di Diritto del Lavoro*. Milan: CEDAM, 2017.

McCann, Michael W. *Rights at Work: Pay Equity Reform and the Politics of Legal Mobilization*. Chicago: The University of Chicago Press, 1994.

McCormick, Robert A. and Amy Christian McCormick. "The Myth of the Student-Athlete: The College Athlete as Employee." *Washington Law Review* 81, (February 2006): 71–157.

Meyer, Nadège. *L'ordre public en droit du travail: Contribution à l'étude de l'ordre public en droit privé*. Paris: LGDJ, 2006.

Monsalvo, Manuel. "Los principios del derecho del trabajo." In *Curso de derecho del trabajo y de la seguridad social*, edited by Adrián Goldin and Jorgelina F. Alimenti, 109–137. Buenos Aires: La Ley, 2009.

Monteiro Fernandes, António Lemos. *Direito do Trabalho*. Coimbra: Almedina, 1999.

Morris, Charles. "How the National Labor Relations Act Was Stolen and How It Can Be Recovered: Taft-Hartley Revisionism and the National Labor Relations Board's Appointment Process." *Berkeley Journal of Employment and Labor Law* 33, (2012): 1–72.

Moyn, Samuel. *Not Enough: Human Rights in an Unequal World*. Cambridge: Harvard University Press, 2018.

Nogueira Alcalá, Humberto, Emilio Pfeffer Urquiaga, and Mario Verdugo Marinkovic. *Derecho constitucional, Tomo I*. Santiago: Editorial Jurídica de Chile, 1994.

Novitz, Tonia and Colin Fenwick. "The Application of Human Rights Discourse to Labour Relations: Translation of Theory into Practice." In *Human Rights at Work: Perspectives on Law and Regulation*, edited by Colin Fenwick and Tonia Novitz, 1–38. Oxford: Hart Publishing, 2010.

OECD Organisation for Economic Co-Operation and Development. "Government at a Glance—2017 Edition: Public Employment and Pay." OECD.Stat. Last accessed September 10, 2018. https://stats.oecd.org/Index.aspx?QueryId=78408.

Olson, Mancur, Jr. *The Logic of Collective Action: Public Goods and the Theory of Groups*. Cambridge: Harvard University Press, 1965.

Ontiveros, Maria L. "Noncitizen Immigrant Labor and the Thirteenth Amendment: Challenging Guest Worker Programs." *University of Toledo Law Review* 38, (Spring 2007): 923–939.

Paixâo, Gicelli. *Comentários sobre à Reforma Trabalhista*, Sao Paulo (2018).

Palacio, Juan Manuel. "From Social Legislation to Labor Justice." In *Labor Justice across the Americas*, edited by Leon Fink and Juan Manuel Palacio, 16–43. Champaign: University of Illinois Press, 2018.

Palomeque López, Manuel Carlos. *El derecho del trabajo e ideología*. Madrid: Ediciones Akal, 1985.

Paul, Sanjukta M. "The Enduring Ambiguities of Antitrust Liability for Worker Collective Action." *Loyola University Chicago Law Journal* 47, (Spring 2018): 969–1048.

Pérez Luño, Antonio Enrique. *Derechos humanos, estado de derecho y constitución*. Madrid: Editorial Tecnos, 1995.

Perillo, John. *Calamari and Perillo on Contracts*. St. Paul: West Academic Publishing, 2009.

Persiani, Mattia and Giampiero Proia. *Diritto del Lavoro*. Milan: CEDAM, 2008.

Pierce, Richard J., Jr. "Valuing Bureaucracy Is a Quixotic Project." *The Regulatory Review*. Last modified December 13, 2017. https://www.theregreview.org/2017/12/13/pierce-valuing-bureaucracy-quixotic-project/.

Piña, Maria del Carmen. *La condición laboral y el principio protectorio*. Córdoba: Lerner Editora (2007).

Piore, Michael J. and Andrew Schrank. "Toward Managed Flexibility: The Revival of Labour Inspection in the Latin World." *International Labour Review* 147, no. 1 (2008): 1–23.

Plá Rodríguez, Américo. *Los principios del derecho del trabajo*. Buenos Aires: Ediciones Depalma, 1998.

Poblete Troncoso, Moisés. *Evolución del derecho social en América*. Santiago: Editorial Nascimento, 1942.

Polanyi, Karl. *The Great Transformation: The Political and Economic Origins of Our Time*. Boston: Beacon Press, 1957.

Pope, James Gray. "Labor's Constitution of Freedom." *Yale Law Journal* 106, (January 1997): 941–1031.

Pope, James Gray. "Contract, Race, and Freedom of Labor in the Constitutional Law of 'Involuntary Servitude.'" *Yale Law Journal* 119, (May 2010): 1474–1567.

Pope, James Gray. "How American Workers Lost the Right to Strike, and Other Tales." *Michigan Law Review* 103, (December 2004): 518–553.

Portes, Alejandro and Richard Schauffler. "Competing Perspectives on the Latin American Informal Sector." *Population and Development Review* 19, no. 1 (1993): 33–60.

Posner, Eric A. "ProCD v Zeidenberg and Cognitive Overload in Contractual Bargaining." *University of Chicago Law Review* 77, (2010): 1181–1194.

Prassl, Jeremias. *Humans as a Service: The Promise and Perils of Work in the Gig Economy*. Oxford: Oxford University Press, 2018.

Prebisch, Raúl. *The Economic Development of Latin America and Its Principal Problems*. Lake Success: United Nations Department of Economic Affairs, 1950.

Quintard-Morénas, François. "The Presumption of Innocence in the French and Anglo-American Legal Traditions." *American Journal of Comparative Law* 58, (Winter 2010): 107–149.

Radin, Margaret Jane. *Boilerplate: The Fine Print, Vanishing Rights, and the Rule of Law*. Princeton: Princeton University Press, 2013.

Raso Delgue, Juan. *La contratación atípica del trabajo*. Montevideo: Ediciones Amalio Fernández, 2009.

Riva Sanseverino, Luisa. *Elementi di Diritto Sindacale e del Lavoro*. Milan: CEDAM, 1980.

Roa, Luis. "Irrenunciabilidad de derechos: itinerarios de un principio general." In *Estudios de teoría crítica de derecho del trabajo*, edited by Guillermo Gianibelli and Oscar Zas, 239–259. Buenos Aires: Bomarzo Latinoamericana, 2006.

Rogers, Brishen. "Employment Rights in the Platform Economy: Getting Back to Basics." *Harvard Law & Policy Review* 10, (Summer 2016): 479–520.

Rosado Marzán, César F. "No More Solitude? Workers' Conditions and Rights in Latin America During the Great Recession." *Employee Rights and Employment Policy Journal* 17, no. 2 (2013): 291–307.

Rosado Marzán, César F. "The Limits of Human Rights for Labour Rights: A Retrospective Look at the Case of Chile." In *The ILO from Geneva to the Pacific Rim: West Meets East*, edited by Jill M. Jensen and Nelson Lichtenstein, 206–232. London: Palgrave Macmillan, 2016.

Rubin, Edward L. "Toward a General Theory of Waiver." *UCLA Law Review* 28, no. 3 (February 1981): 478–563.

Ruprecht, Alfredo J. *Los principios normativos laborales y su proyección en la Legislación*. Buenos Aires: Zavalía, 1994.

Russell Gao Hodges, Graham. *Taxi! A Social History of the New York City Cabdriver*. New York: NYU Press, 2007.

Sachs, Benjamin and Sharon Block. "How Democratic Lawmakers Should Help Unions Reeling from the Janus Decision." *Vox*. Last modified June 27, 2018. https://www.vox.com/the-big-idea/2018/6/27/17510046/public-unions-janus-reforms-fees-decline-reform-supreme-court-hope.

Sampathkumar, Mythili. "UN Official Attacks Nikki Haley over Human Rights Council Withdrawal as He Presents Damning Report on US Poverty." *The Independent*. Last modified

June 22, 2018. https://www.independent.co.uk/news/world/nikki-haley-human-rights-council-us-poverty-un-report-trump-philip-alston-states-a8411871.html.

Santos, Ozéias J. *Reforma Trabalhista Ponto a Ponto: Prática trabalhista*. Campinas: Editora Vale do Mogi, 2018.

Scalia, Antonin and Bryan A. Garner. *Reading Law: The Interpretation of Legal Texts*. St. Paul: Thomson/West, 2012.

Schwartz, David S. "Enforcing Small Print to Protect Big Business: Employee and Consumer Rights Claims in an Age of Compelled Arbitration." *Wisconsin Law Review* 1997, (1997): 33–132.

Scott, Robert E. and Jody S. Kraus. *Contract Law and Theory*. Durham: Carolina Academic Press, 2013.

Sen, Amartya. *Development as Freedom*. Oxford: Oxford University Press, 2000.

Sikkink, Kathryn. *Evidence for Hope: Making Human Rights Work in the 21st Century*. Princeton: Princeton University Press, 2017.

Silva Bascuñán, Alejandro and María Pía Silva Gallinato. *Tratado de derecho constitucional Tomo XIII*. Santiago: Editorial Jurídica, 2010.

Sinclair, Upton. *The Jungle*. New York: Dover Thrift Edition, 2001.

Slawson, W. David. "Unilateral Contracts of Employment: Does Contract Law Conflict with Public Policy?" *Texas Wesleyan Law Review* 10, (Fall 2003): 9–32.

Smith, Peggie, Ann Hodges, Susan Stabile, and Rafael Gely. *Principles of Employment Law*. St. Paul: West Academic Publishing, 2009.

Standing, Guy. *The Precariat: The New Dangerous Class*. London: Bloomsbury Academic, 2011.

Steinbeck, John. *The Grapes of Wrath*, New York: Penguin Books, 2002.

Stempel, Jeffrey W. "Reconsidering the Employment Contract Exclusion in Section 1 of the Federal Arbitration Act: Correcting the Judiciary's Failure of Statutory Vision." *Journal of Dispute Resolution* 1991, (1991): 259–305.

Sternlight, Jean R. "Disarming Employees How American Employers Are Using Mandatory Arbitration to Deprive Workers of Legal Protection." *Brooklyn Law Review* 80, (Summer 2015): 1309–1356.

Stiglitz, Joseph. *The Price of Inequality: How Today's Divided Society Endangers Our Future*. New York: W.W. Norton & Company, 2012.

Stone, Katherine Van Wezel. "Mandatory Arbitration of Individual Employment Rights: The Yellow Dog Contract of the 1990s." *Denver University Law Review* 73, (1996): 1017–1050.

Stone, Katherine V.W. and Harry Arthurs, eds. *Rethinking Workplace Regulation: Beyond the Standard Contract of Employment*. New York: Russell Sage Foundation, 2013.

Stone, Katherine V.W. and Harry Arthurs, eds. "The Transformation of Employment Regimes: A Worldwide Challenge." In *Rethinking Workplace Regulation: Beyond the Standard Contract of Employment*, edited by Katherine V.W. Stone and Harry Arthurs, 1–20. New York: Russell Sage Foundation, 2013.

Suarez-Potts, William J. *The Making of Law: The Supreme Court and Labor Legislation in Mexico, 1875–1931*. Redwood City: Stanford University Press, 2012.

Sullivan, Charles A. and Timothy P. Glynn. "The FAA Triumphal: A Modest Opinion." *Employee Rights and Employment Policy Journal* 19, no. 1 (2015): 103–124.

Summers, Clyde W. "Employment at Will in the United States: The Divine Right of Employers." *University of Pennsylvania Journal of Labor and Employment Law* 3, no. 1 (2000): 65–86.

Summers, Clyde W. "Individual Protection against Unjust Dismissal: Time for a Statute." *Virginia Law Review* 62, (1976): 481–530.

Summers, Clyde W. "The Rights of Individual Workers: The Contract of Employment and the Rights of Individual Employees: Fair Representation and Employment at Will." *Fordham Law Review* 52, (May 1984): 1082–1109.

Summers, Clyde W., Kenneth G. Dau-Schmidt, and Alan Hyde. *Legal Rights and Interests in the Workplace: Statutory Supplement and Materials*. Durham: Carolina Academic Press, 2007.

Supiot, Alain. *Crítica del derecho del trabajo*. Madrid: Ministerio de Trabajo y Seguridad Social, Centro de Publicaciones, 1996.

Swidler, Ann. "Culture in Action: Symbols and Strategies." *American Sociological Review* 51, no. 2 (April 1986): 273–286.

Thelen, Kathleen. *Varieties of Liberalization and the New Politics of Social Solidarity*. Cambridge: Cambridge University Press, 2014.

Tilly, Charles. "Globalization Threatens Labor's Rights." *International Labor and Working-Class History* 47, (Spring 1995): 1–6.

Tomassetti, Julia. "Who Is a Worker? Partisanship, the National Labor Relations Board, and the Social Content of Employment." *Law and Social Inquiry* 37, (Fall 2012): 815–847.

Tosca, Diego. "Aplicación del principio 'pro operario' en la valoración de la prueba en caso de duda." In *La relación de trabajo*, edited by Mario E. Ackerman and Alejandro Sudera, 209–216. Buenos Aires: Rubinzal-Culzoni Editores, 2009.

Tosca, Diego. "La regla de la irrenunciabilidad." In *Tratado de Derecho del Trabajo*, edited by Mario E. Ackerman and Diego M. Tosca, 351–381. Buenos Aires: Astrea, 2005.

Turczanski, Laura A. "Closing the Door on the Public Policy Exception to At-Will Employment: How the Washington State Supreme Court Erroneously Foreclosed Wrongful Discharge Claims for Whistleblowers in Cudney v. ALSCO, Inc." *Seattle University Law Review* 36, (Summer 2013): 2025–2056.

UC Berkeley Labor Center. "Inventory of US City and County Minimum Wage Ordinances." Center for Labor Research and Education. Last modified August 14, 2018. http://laborcenter.berkeley.edu/minimum-wage-living-wage-resources/inventory-of-us-city-and-county-minimum-wage-ordinances/.

Ugarte, José Luis. *La subordinación en el derecho laboral chileno*. Santiago: LexisNexis, 2008.

U.N. Human Rights Council. "Report of the Special Rapporteur on Extreme Poverty and Human Rights on His Mission to the United States of America." United Nations General Assembly. Delivered on May 4, 2018. https://digitallibrary.un.org/record/1629536/files/A_HRC_38_33_Add-1-EN.pdf.

United States Department of Labor. "Fact Sheet 13: Am I an Employee?: Employment Relationship Under the Fair Labor Standards Act (FLSA)." Wage and Hour Division. Last modified July 2008. https://www.dol.gov/whd/regs/compliance/whdfs13.pdf.

United States Department of Labor. "Interpretation No. 2015-1, The Application of the Fair Labor Standards Act's "Suffer or Permit" Standard in the Identification of Employees Who Are Misclassified as Independent Contractors." Wage and Hour Division. Last modified July 15, 2015. https://www.blr.com/html_email/AI2015-1.pdf.

United States Department of Labor. "Administrator's Interpretation No. 2016-1, Joint employment under the Fair Labor Standards Act and Migrant and Seasonal Agricultural Worker Protection Act." Wage and Hour Division. Issued on January 20, 2016.

Vachet, Gérard. "Le principe de faveur dans les rapports entre sources de droit." In *Les Principes dans la Jurisprudence de la Chambre Sociale de la Cour de Cassation*, edited by Bernard Teyssié, 79–93. Paris: Dalloz, 2008.

Vallebona, Antonio. *Lavoro e Spirito*. Turin: Giappichelli, 2011.

Van Eck, Stefan. "Constitutionalisation of South Africa Labour Law: An Experiment in the Making." In *Human Rights at Work: Perspectives on Law and Regulation*, edited by Colin Fenwick and Tonia Novitz, 259–291. Oxford: Hart Publishing, 2010.

Van Parijs, Philippe and Yannick Vanderborght. *Basic Income: A Radical Proposal for a Free Society and a Sane Economy*. Cambridge: Harvard University Press, 2017.

VanderVelde, Lea S. "The Labor Vision of the Thirteenth Amendment." *University of Pennsylvania Law Review* 138, (December 1989): 437–504.

VanderVelde, Lea S. "Where Is the Concept of Good Faith in the Restatement of Employment." *Employee Rights and Employment Policy Journal* 21, no. 2 (2017): 335–375.

VanderVelde, Lea S. "The At-Will Doctrine in a Laborers' Republic: From Reconstruction's Anti-Subordination to the Gilded Age's Precarity" (unpublished manuscript on file with author. 2018).

Veneziani, Bruno. "Tre Commenti alla Critique du Droit du Travail de Supiot." *Giornale di Diritto del Lavoro e di Relazioni Industriali* 67, Anno XVII, (1995): 477–484.

Verdugo Marinkovic, Mario, Emilio Pfeffer, and Humberto Nogueira. *Derecho Constitucional*. Santiago: Editorial Jurídica de Chile, 2nd ed. 1999.

Verkuil, Paul R. *Valuing Bureaucracy: The Case for Professional Government*. Cambridge: Cambridge University Press, 2017.

Weil, David. *The Fissured Workplace: Why Work Became So Bad for So Many and What Can Be Done to Improve It*. Cambridge: Harvard University Press, 2014.

Weiss, Manfred and Marlene Schmidt. *Labour Law and Industrial Relations in Germany*. Alphen aan den Rijn: Kluwer Law International, 2008.

Wellington, Harry H. "Freedom of Contract and the Collective Bargaining Agreement." *University of Pennsylvania Law Review* 112, (February 1964): 467–498.

Winfield, Percy H. "Public Policy in the English Common Law." *Harvard Law Review* 42, (November 1928): 76–102.

Winn, Peter, ed. *Victims of the Chilean Miracle: Workers and Neoliberalism in the Pinochet Era, 1973–2002*. Durham: Duke University Press, 2004.

Workplace Fairness. "State and Local Paid Sick Leave Laws." Last modified August 14, 2018. https://www.workplacefairness.org/paid-sick-leave.

Wyman, Katrina. "Problematic Private Property: The Case of New York Taxicab Medallions." *Yale Journal on Regulation* 30, (Winter 2013): 125–187.

Yamada, David C. "Workplace Bullying and American Employment Law: A Ten-Year Progress Report and Assessment." *Comparative Labor Law and Policy Journal* 32, (Fall 2010): 251–284.

Yntema, Hessel E. "Equity in the Civil Law and the Common Law." *The American Journal of Comparative Law* 15, no. 1/2 (1966–1967): 60–86.

Zietlow, Rebecca E. "The Ideological Origins of the Thirteenth Amendment." *Houston Law Review* 49, (Spring 2012): 393–458.

Zietlow, Rebecca E. *The Forgotten Emancipator: James Mitchell Ashley and the Ideological Origins of Reconstruction*. Cambridge: Cambridge University Press, 2017.
Zola, Émile. *Germinal*. London: Penguin Classics, 2004.
Zuretti, Mario E. "Principios." In *Curso de derecho del trabajo y de la seguridad social*, edited by Jorge Rodriguez Mancini, 49–63. Buenos Aires: Astrea, 2000.

Index